Goldwin Smith

The United States

an outline of political history, 1492-1871

Goldwin Smith

The United States
an outline of political history, 1492-1871

ISBN/EAN: 9783337078553

Printed in Europe, USA, Canada, Australia, Japan

Cover: Foto ©Suzi / pixelio.de

More available books at **www.hansebooks.com**

THE UNITED STATES

AN OUTLINE OF POLITICAL HISTORY

1492–1871

BY

GOLDWIN SMITH, D.C.L.

*" This will sometime hence be a vast Empire, the seat of power and
learning. Nature has refused it nothing, and there will grow a people out
of our little spot, England, that will fil' this vast space and divide this portion of the globe with the Spaniards, who are possessed of the other half."* —
General Wolfe

*" I am not wanting in affection and love for America. I am rather
wanting in distrust and ingratitude towards Europe."* — Dr. Roque Saenz
Pena, Speech at the Pan-American Conference at Washington, 1890

New York

THE MACMILLAN COMPANY

LONDON: MACMILLAN & CO., LTD.

1907

Norwood Press:
J. S. Cushing & Co. — Berwick & Smith.
Boston, Mass., U.S.A.

PREFACE.

To an Englishman, particularly if he is visiting America, an outline of the political history of the United States may not be unwelcome. An American, being familiar with the main facts and the general relations of parties, would look for details. It is, therefore, for English rather than American readers that this sketch is intended. If it comes into the hands of an American, his liberality will make allowance for the position of an Englishman who regards the American Commonwealth as the great achievement of his race, and looks forward to the voluntary reunion of the American branches of the race within its pale, yet desires to do justice to the mother country, and to render to her the meed of gratitude which will always be her due.

Should this volume find acceptance it may be followed by a companion volume on the same scale, and treating, necessarily with the same succinctness, the recent history of parties, and the questions of the present day.

A complete list of all the authorities consulted would be out of proportion to the book itself, but special obligations should be acknowledged to Gordon's "History of the American Revolution," Bancroft's "History of the United States," Hildreth's "History of the United States,"

Palfrey's "History of New England," Henry Adams's
"History of the United States," Schouler's "History of
the United States," McMaster's "History of the People
of the United States," Bryant's "Popular History of
the United States," Justin Winsor's "Narrative and
Critical History of America," Charles K. Adams's "Columbus," Draper's "The Civil War in America," the
"Epochs of American History" series, the "History of
the Civil War in America" by the Comte de Paris, the
"Cyclopædia of Political Science, Political Economy, and
United States History," the "American Statesmen" series,
the works of Professor Fiske, Swinton's "Decisive Battles
of the War," Sabine's "Loyalists of the American Revolution," Blaine's "Twenty Years of Congress," Thomas
Jones's "History of New York during the Revolutionary
War," published by the New York Historical Society,
and the "American Commonwealths" series, also Bancroft's "History of the Constitution of the United States."
The writer would be glad to think that his work had been
instrumental in exciting the curiosity of English readers
and leading them to resort to the sources of ample information mentioned in this list.

The writer cannot send this fourth edition of his work to press,
without specially acknowledging the kindness of his American readers
and reviewers, whose reception of a book which in some things con-
travenes cherished traditions is a proof of American candour and
liberality. Perhaps they have discerned, beneath the British critic of
American History, the Anglo-Saxon who, to the Republic which he
regards as the grand achievement of his race, desires to offer no homage less pure or noble than the truth.

CONTENTS.

CHAPTER I.

THE COLONIES.

Discovery of a western continent by Columbus — Early adventurers — The landing of the *Mayflower* — The Plymouth pilgrims — Their allegiance to the old land — The founding of Massachusetts — The Puritan commonwealth — Early religious strifes — Political aspect of Puritanism — Puritan democracy — A federation formed — Puritan legislation — Social life — Slavery — Relations with the Indians — The new colonies and the Crown — Massachusetts reduced to a dependency — William III and Massachusetts — Decay of Puritanism — Witchcraft — Increase of wealth — Virginia — Virginian life and society — Slavery and slave laws — Politics, the church, and education — The founding of Maryland — Religious strifes and political changes — Georgia — The founding of Pennsylvania — New York and New Jersey — Characteristics of the Middle States — Restrictions on colonial trade — Political embroilments — Benjamin Franklin . . . . Pages 1–63

CHAPTER II.

REVOLUTION, INDEPENDENCE, AND UNION.

French hostilities in the new world — The quarrel with England — The colonial relationship — Cause of the revolt — Separation and the separators — Samuel Adams — Patrick Henry — Irritation of Massachusetts — Fomenting influences — Trade restrictions — The Stamp Act and the tea duty — Ebullition at Boston — Repression — The King's difficulties — Federation for defence — The Declaration of Independence — Opening of the war — Lexington — Bunker's Hill — Evacuation of Boston — The loyalists — Canada attacked — New York

taken — Washington at Valley Forge — Character of Washington —
Burgoyne's expedition — State of the country — Character of the troops
— Financial disturbance — French aid — Arnold and André — British
successes in the South — Capitulation of Cornwallis at Yorktown —
Treatment of the loyalists — England and the separation — The colonies after the revolt — Constitutional and other changes — Impotency
of Congress — Discontent rife — The federal convention — The constitution — Provisions of the constitution .   .   . Pages 64–129

CHAPTER III.

REPUBLIC.

Washington president — Presidential etiquette and state — Success of
the constitution — Birth of parties — Alexander Hamilton — His abil-
ity, character, and principles — His Secretaryship of the Treasury —
Thomas Jefferson — His character, theories, and political principles
— Growth of the Republic — England and the new republic — George
III's reception of John Adams — Washington's second term — The
French Revolution and American parties — The question of belliger
ent rights — Jay's treaty — Retirement of Washington — The city of
Washington — John Adams President — His appearance and character — Resentment against France — The feeling quelled — Bitterness
of party spirit — Jefferson President — His inaugural address — Acquisition of Louisiana — Jefferson's first term — His second term —
International complications: neutral trade, belligerent rights, impressment of seamen — Action of the *Leopard* and *Chesapeake* — Jefferson
places an embargo on trade — Madison President — Diplomatic embroilments — Influence of Kentucky — Henry Clay — Motives leading
to war — The war of 1812 — The treaty of Ghent — Battle of New
Orleans — Results of the war — Boundaries in Maine and Oregon —
Monroe President — The Monroe doctrine   .   . Pages 130–176

CHAPTER IV.

DEMOCRACY AND SLAVERY.

Monroe's Presidency — The era of good feeling — Geographical division
between freedom and slavery — The Presidential fever and its effects
— Reign of the " Machine " — Henry Clay — His character and principles — Daniel Webster — His character — His oratory — John C.
Calhoun — His character and principles — Slavery and the Senate

debates — Benton — Randolph — The tariff question — Free trade vs. protection — Webster ; Clay ; McDuffie — Public land and improvements — John Quincy Adams — His character and principles — Military renown as a political influence — Andrew Jackson's Presidential campaign — Jackson's inauguration — The spoils go to the victor — A court quarrel — Jackson's despotism — The National Bank question — South Carolina rises against the tariff — The Force Bill — Effects of Jackson's policy — Demagogism — Van Buren — Party lines — The anti-Masons — William Harrison's Presidential campaign — Tyler President — Texas and Mexico — Clay's candidature — Polk President — War with Mexico — Texas annexed — Taylor President — Fillmore President — Close of Webster's career — Texas and slavery — End of the Whig party — Pierce President — The Knownothings — The Irish vote — Growth of the Republic — Progress westward — Development and expansion — Political and social democracy . . . . Pages 177–220

CHAPTER V.

RUPTURE AND RECONSTRUCTION.

Slavery forced to the front — The question a thing of the past — Its source — Ancient compared with American slavery — Fusion of races impossible — Emancipation discouraged — Slavery not elevating — Condition of the negro — Sinister aspects and influences of slavery — Slave industry — Aggressive character of slavery — Apologies for the system — Possibilities of a peaceful solution — Dominance of slavery — Its adherents — Protests, political, philosophical, literary — William Lloyd Garrison — Wendell Phillips — Strong feeling in the South — Case of Anthony Burns — Stephen Douglas in politics — Squatter sovereignty — The Kansas-Nebraska Act — Case of Dred Scott — Free Soilers — Disorder in Kansas — Violent debates in Congress — The two parties, Republican and Democratic — John Brown — Abraham Lincoln — His early life — His appearance, capability, and character — His political principles — His powers of debate — Elected President — South Carolina secedes — Other States follow — A Southern Confederacy formed — Slavery the cause of secession — The Confederate government — Buchanan's vacillation — Concessions offered by Congress — The crisis unexpected — Possibilities of peaceful separation — State sovereignty — The struggle a regular war — Lincoln as President — His object the preservation of the Union — War breaks out by the capture of Fort Sumter — The military strength of North and South compared — Means adopted to obtain men and

money — England and the South — Neutrality of the British government — Capture of Messrs. Mason and Slidell — Foreign nations
and the war — Strategy of the North — Chief scene of war — Bull
Run — Northern military organization — General McClellan placed
in command — McClellan and Lincoln — Generals Lee and Jackson
— Pope replaces McClellan — The equipment of the respective armies
— Antietam — Lincoln proclaims emancipation — Enlistment of negroes — Fort Pillow — Burnside put in command — Battle of Fred-
ericksburg — Hooker replaces Burnside — Is defeated — General Grant
— Fort Donelson taken — General Sherman — Battle of Shiloh —
Vicksburg — Farragut — New Orleans taken — Benjamin Butler's
proclamation — Murfreesborough — Character of the battles — The
Merrimack and the *Monitor* — Blockade running — Lee enters Pennsylvania — Irish riot in New York — Battle of Gettysburg — Fall of
Vicksburg — The South in straits — The army of the Potomac —
Battle of the Wilderness — Cold Harbour — Early attacks Washington — Sheridan desolates the Shenandoah Valley — Mechanical skill
displayed in Sheridan's campaign — Hood replaces Johnston — Atlanta falls — Savannah and Charleston surrender — Nashville — Richmond evacuated — Lee surrenders at Appomattox — Lincoln re-elected
— And murdered — His statesmanship — Humanity on the two
sides — The Sanitary Commission — Democracy and war — The
war and the constitution — Little or no disturbance of life at
the North — No military usurpation — Finances — Effects on the
South — Economical evils — War literature — Cost of the war —
— Foreign questions — The *Alabama* question — Reconstruction
— Lincoln's views — Amnesty — Andrew Johnson — The status of
the negro   .   .   .   .   Pages 221–301

THE UNITED STATES

AN OUTLINE OF POLITICAL HISTORY

CHAPTER I.

THE COLONIES.

FOUR centuries ago, Christopher Columbus, one of the 1492. Italian mariners whom the decline of their own republics had put at the service of the world and of adventure, seeking for Spain a westward passage to the Indies as a set-off against the achievements of Portuguese discoverers eastwards, lighted on America. The new continent was thus discovered by the man who had staked most on the belief that no such continent existed, and that the way to the Indies was open by sea. That the daring barques of the Northmen had long before found their way from Greenland to the coast of North America is likely, though not certain. What is certain is that nothing more came, or in that age could come, of their visit than of the visit of a flock of sea-gulls. The basement of an old mill at Newport, which fancy turned into a Norse fortress, the Dighton rock, on which fancy traced Norse runes, the dykes at Watertown, in Massachusetts, in which fancy still sees the defences of the Norse city of Norumbega, only attest the yearnings of a new nation for antiquity.

Columbus sailed in the age of enterprise and discovery, of re-awakened intellect and revived learning, of universal curiosity and romantic aspiration. He was in every way a typical man of his generation. He displayed in the high-

est degree that daring spirit of adventure which could put
forth in a tiny caravel without chart, quadrant, or even a
full acquaintance with the compass, over the wide and wild
Atlantic to an unknown shore; and a shore which, when
found, might teem with perils and be the abode of mon-
sters or of demons. Humanity, since that time, has advanced in many ways; but it has hardly advanced in
fortitude. Columbus was also a devotee of a religion with
more in it of Rome and of the Crusades than of the Gospel, and with more of the forms of devotion than of the
spirit. Morally he was a type of the age which came
between the fall of the Catholic and the rise of the Protestant faith, and had for its head Alexander VI, the moral
monster of the Papacy, whose hand signed the Bull which
divided the new world between two Catholic powers. In
his youth it seems he served on board a pirate fleet. He
began his intercourse with the natives of America by kid-
napping, and he gave the word for the opening of the
slave trade. His dealings with his own companions were
equivocal. He was always in greedy quest of gold, though
he professed, and perhaps believed, that he meant to use
the gold in a crusade. He became the father of a line of
adventurers who, like himself, were gold-seekers or seekers
of lucre, gilding their rapacity with the same profession
of zeal for the extension of religion, who sacked Mexico
and Peru, trampled to pieces there, under the hoofs of
conquest, the highest development of Indian civilization,
worked to death the soft inhabitants of the American
islands, and replaced them by the importation of African
slaves. None of these adventurers looked upon America
as a new home, or thought of founding a nation. The
Huguenots might have founded a nation in Florida had

they not been massacred by the Spaniards. Missionary
enterprise, to some extent, accompanied and redeemed
the gold-seeking. It founded the Jesuit utopia in Para- 1527
guay, and in the establishment of French Canada went 1550.
hand in hand with that kingly thirst of dominion which,
rather than colonization in the proper and beneficent
sense, was the dominant motive of French enterprise in
North America. But the aim of the Jesuit was not to
found a nation. In the settlement of Virginia by Sir 1585
Walter Raleigh, and, when Raleigh's romantic enterprise 1587.
had failed, by a company of commercial adventurers, lucre,
if not gold-seeking, was still the predominant motive.
Of a hundred and forty-three settlers sent out, a large
proportion were broken-down gentlemen seeking to repair
their fortunes; a few only were labourers or mechanics;
the rest were servants. To show how faint was their purpose of settlement, they brought no women. The subsequent reinforcements were of the same kind, with some
goldsmiths and refiners to help in seeking for gold where
no gold was. A ship went home laden with shining mica,
which was mistaken for gold. Food these colonists had to
beg or steal from the Indians. To the crew of vagabonds
were afterwards added jail-birds. Convicts were offered
their choice between the gallows and Virginia, and some,
we are told, chose the gallows. Only by the personal force 1607.
and genius of John Smith, the one true captain, who compelled gentlemen to wield the axe, telling them that if
they would not work they should not eat, was the colony
saved from dissolution. It had been started on the false
principle of joint stock industry, which deprives labour of
its mainspring. Its place, Jamestown, has long been desolate, and only fragments of ruin mark the site. In these

days steam carries all the implements of husbandry, now brought to marvellous perfection, and all needful stores, with the emigrant into his field of settlement. In those days colonization was a death-struggle with nature. Some sustaining motive higher than gain was necessary to give man the victory and enable him to make for himself a new home in the wilderness, and to found a nation.

Such a motive, together with the necessary habits of labour and powers of endurance, was present in the little train of emigrants who, after beating up and down for some days upon a bleak and wintry coast and receiving as their welcome to it a volley of Indian arrows, disembarked from the *Mayflower* on the 22nd of December, 1620. Their landing was on the shore to which John Smith, its first explorer, had given the name of New England, at a spot which they named Plymouth, after the English port of that name from which they had sailed. Setting rhetorical exaggeration aside, we need not doubt that in watching that sad yet hopeful procession of men, women, and children, we are witnessing one of the great events and one of the heroic scenes of history. The story of these emigrants is well known. They were dissenters from the Established Church of England, with simple hearts full of the intense faith and zeal inspired in those days by the new revelation of the pure Gospel. They had fled from the emissaries of church law, first to Holland. There they had found themselves surrounded by a community highly commercial, whose manners their austere simplicity deemed corrupting, which did not strictly keep the Sabbath, and into whose worldliness their children were in danger of being drawn. They feared also the loss of their

1608.

nationality, to which, though persecuted in England,
they clung. They had then determined to seek a home
beyond the Atlantic where they might enjoy their religion
uncontaminated and in peace. A chartered company, the
usual organ of commercial venture in those days, formed
the English basis of their enterprise and the source of
needful supplies.

The Plymouth pilgrims, landing in mid-winter on a
grim coast, underwent the severest sufferings. They
were ill sheltered; they had no bread, and were reduced
to shellfish for food. More than half their number died.
At one time only seven of them were left strong enough
to tend the sick. It seems that they were saved from
the Indian tomahawk only by a distemper which happened
to prevail among the Indians. To use their own words,
"all great and honourable actions are accompanied with
great difficulties, and must be both undertaken and confirmed with answerable courages." "It is not," they had
said, "with us as with other men, whom small things can
discourage or small discontents cause to wish themselves
home again." Their language is instinct with the simple
heroism of their enterprise. "Let it not be grievous to
you," said their friends in England, "that you have been
instruments to break the ice for others: the honour shall
be yours to the world's end." To the world's end the
honour is theirs. If Columbus discovered the new continent, they discovered the new world.

Before landing, the pilgrims, "seeing that some among
them were not well affected to concord," had drawn up
this voluntary compact: —

"In the name of God, amen; we, whose names are
underwritten, the loyal subjects of our dread sovereign

King James, . . . having undertaken, for the glory of God and advancement of the Christian faith, and honour of our King and country, a voyage to plant the first colony in the northern parts of Virginia, do by these presents, solemnly and mutually, in the presence of God, and one of another, covenant and combine ourselves together into a civil body politic, for our better ordering and preservation and furtherance of the ends aforesaid ; and by virtue hereof to enact, constitute, and frame such just and equal laws, ordinances, acts, constitutions, and offices, from time to time, as shall be thought most meet and convenient for the general good of the colony. Unto which we promise all due submission and obedience."

It is true that this covenant was not a political manifesto. It is not less true that it heralded a polity of self-government, and may thus rank among the great documents of history. It breathes good-will to the land which the pilgrims had left, though the rulers of that land had cast them out. The Puritan exile did not say " Farewell, Babylon," but " Farewell, dear England." Unhappily these, in common with other colonists of the period, retained not only their love of the old land, but their political tie to it. They deemed themselves still liegemen of a sovereign on the other side of the Atlantic. This created a relation false from the beginning. Herein lay the fatal seeds of misunderstanding, of encroachment on the side of the home government, of revolt on that of the growing colony, and ultimately of revolution. The Hellenic colonist had gone forth to make his home in a new land, taking with him the sacred fire from the altar-hearth of his native city, but free from any political tie. His only bond to his native city was that of filial affection, gracefully expressed in honours paid to her representatives. The Hellenic colony was a colony in the true sense of the word, not a dependency. The English colony unhappily was a dependency, and when it grew strong enough to spurn dependence there was a bond to be broken which was not likely to be broken without violence and a breach of affection. Dependence was the result of two notions combined, that of the territorial right of discovery, and that of personal and indefeasible allegiance. Let a mariner land and set up a flag on a strange shore, let him even sight that shore from his vessel, the whole region thenceforth, according to the European law of nations, belonged to his sovereign, and was that sovereign's to grant to whom he pleased. His Majesty of 1606 England by his charter granted North America, so far as it was then known, between certain degrees of latitude, in full property, with exclusive rights of jurisdiction, settlement, and traffic, to certain persons incorporated respectively as the London and Plymouth Companies. The Pope's pretension to divide the new world between Catholic powers was hardly more baseless. From the feudal system came down the idea of personal and indefeasible allegiance, with the lingering traces of which international law and diplomacy in our own day have had to deal. This was the beginning of woes, the full measure of which came in 1765.

The foundation of New Plymouth was followed by that of Massachusetts, the great Puritan colony of all, and the leading shoot of American civilization, which presently drew to it New Plymouth, while it threw out from it, in different ways and partly by repulsion, the off-shoots which became Connecticut, Rhode Island, New Hampshire, and

Vermont. The founders of Massachusetts were not, when they came out, Independents, like the company of the *Mayflower*, but Puritans in the proper sense of the term, that is, members of the Church of England who desired to remain within her pale, but to purify her from the vestiges of Rome, and at the same time to uplift her to a higher standard of Christian life. They even anxiously disclaimed any intention of separation. "They esteemed it their honour," they said, "to call the Church of England their dear mother, and could not part from their native country, where she specially resided, without much sadness of heart and many tears in their eyes; ever acknowledging that such hope and part as they had attained in the common salvation they had received in her bosom and sucked from her breasts." But practical divorce from the Anglican hierarchy and ordinances, together with the liberating air of the new world, soon made them, like the Plymouth 1629. emigrants, Independents. From Charles I, who was no doubt glad to see the Puritan spirit carried off by emigration, the Massachusetts Company received a liberal charter, which became the palladium of advancing independence. The colony was an object of fervent interest to the Puritans at home, and was recruited with some of their best 1633. blood. Hither the excellent Cotton led from Boston in Lincolnshire, and the fair church that rises over it, a part of his flock to a Boston which soon became, and has remained, the centre of New England and the focus of 1633. New England civilization. Hither came Hugh Peters, the chaplain that was to be of the regicide republic. 1633. Hither for a time came Henry Vane, as has been said, "young in years, but not yet in sage counsel old," for he brought with him a disquieting ambition. The first governor was Winthrop, a wealthy Sussex gentleman, who left his manor house at the age of forty-two to help in planting a Gospel kingdom in the new world. He was a noble specimen of the Puritan character, uniting with its force the gentle grace which Mrs. Hutchinson has portrayed in her picture of Colonel Hutchinson; a wise counsellor, skilful as Hampden in the management of men, and in all distractions piously serene. Endicott and Dudley were Puritans of the sterner type.

Besides Cotton, other clergymen came, highly educated at Oxford or Cambridge; more from Cambridge than from Oxford, because Cambridge lay in the eastern counties, the home of Cromwell and the Ironsides. The inflow of Puritan life did not cease till the rising of the English nation against Charles and Laud gave the party hope and work at home.

In Massachusetts also the first settlers had their sufferings to undergo on that bleak coast, though not such sufferings as were undergone by the founders of Plymouth, the Massachusetts colony being better provided with funds and more assisted from home. Whatever was to be borne they bore. Like their precursors at Plymouth, they were bent on "laying some good foundation, or at least making some way thereto, for the propagating and advancing the Gospel and the kingdom of Christ in those remote parts of the world; yea, even though they should be but as stepping stones unto others for the performing of so great a work."

The Puritan commonwealth was a theocracy. It was mainly for the purpose of founding a Christian state that these men had given up all and gone forth into the wilderness. No one could be a citizen of Massachusetts

who was not in close communion with one of the
churches.   The churches were organized on the Congregational principle, forming a group, each member of
which was independent of the rest and chose its own
pastor.   But they were bound together by complete sym
pathy, identity of doctrine and of system was preserved,
and discipline was practically enforced by them in concert.   Baptism was limited to the children of those who
were in close communion, and only to those who were
in close communion was the sacrament of the Lord's
Supper administered.   Every citizen was required to
contribute to the maintenance of a church.   Thus, not
only was there a union of church and state, but church
✓ and state were one.   This was still the religious ideal of
the time, however far men might desire to carry church
reform.   It has been the ideal in our own day of such
a liberal as Dr. Arnold.   Puritan theocracy, though strict,
and sure to melt away when the sun of freedom had
mounted higher in the heaven, was not reactionary or
obscurantist.   It had for its rule the Bible, but the Bible
interpreted by reason.   It owed paramount allegiance
not to authority but to truth.   Robinson, the adored
pastor of the Plymouth exiles, had charged them at parting, before God and all the angels, to "follow him no
further than he followed Christ; and if God should reveal
anything to them by any other instrument of his, to be
as ready to receive it as ever they were to receive any
truth by his ministry; for he was very confident the
Lord had more truth and light yet to break forth out of
His holy Word."   Of light and truth to break forth from
nature read by science beyond God's word the Puritan
pastor in those days could have no thought.

Reformers may wish to arrest reform at their own line, but they set in action the forces which will carry it further. The clergy were the leaders, to a considerable extent they were the masters, of the Puritan society and commonwealth. But they were not mere priests. They were well educated; some of them were very learned, and could not fail to have their share of the liberality of learning. Their ascendancy was moral and intellectual; it was not that of caste or of thaumaturgy. Very early Massachusetts founded, out of her poverty 1636. and in troublous times, the University of Harvard, which is now the glory of the literary republic. Harvard's 1700. present rival, Yale, was founded in New Haven later, yet at a date early as compared with the material progress of the colony. Massachusetts led the world in the institution of common schools, to which all citizens were required to contribute, and which all citizens were required to use. Common schools they were in the true sense of the term in that realm of equality, used as well as maintained by all. They would also be in the highest degree religious. The reason given for instituting them was that the children might be able to read the Scriptures aright, notwithstanding the wiles of Satan, whose favourite device was misinterpretation. But the effects of general education would not be limited by the ostensible purpose. Congregations were intelligent, and pastors could maintain their influence only by addressing themselves to intelligence. A printing press, the first on the North American continent, was set up at Cambridge in 1640. Its first fruit was a metrical version of the Psalms by some New England pastors which, if it was not tuneful, was new and showed literary activity, at least in the religious line.

When the more advanced or wilder sectaries, to whom an age of religious fermentation gave birth in swarms, intruded themselves into the theocracy of Massachusetts, they were driven out. In this there could hardly be said to be injustice so long as there was no cruelty. The Puritans had gone out into the wilderness to found a religious commonwealth after their own hearts; in founding it they had undergone great sufferings, and many of them had perished. It was their homestead, and they had a right to keep it, as they had a right to keep their places of worship, to themselves. This they did; at the worst they never were guilty of forcible conversion, nor did they rack conscience like the Inquisition.

1631.   Of the intruders the most memorable was Roger Williams, a quick-witted, warm-hearted, and somewhat flighty Welshman, who came preaching absolute freedom of conscience, and denouncing theocratic government. A political as well as a religious innovator, he denied the right of the King to grant the land and thus impugned the titles of the colonists. In his zeal against idolatry he compromised the loyalty of the colony by persuading the governor to cut the cross, as a Popish emblem, out of 1636. the flag. He was expelled after much tribulation, and went to found Rhode Island on the principle of perfect religious freedom and complete separation of church from state of which, partly perhaps schooled by persecution, he had become the memorable champion. His colony may boast itself the first of all commonwealths in which liberty of conscience was the law. Its political disorders, the consequence of the motley enthusiasm which it drew to it, for a time furnished the theocracy against which its founder had revolted with a theme for warning against religious anarchy. But the principle had been proclaimed and Rhode Island was not long in showing the world that civil society could subsist and political order could be maintained without imposing shackles on spiritual life.

Mrs. Ann Hutchinson also presented herself in Massachusetts. Her opinions appear to have been antinomian, certainly they were anti-clerical and anti-theocratic. From the active part which she took and the leadership to which she aspired, notwithstanding her sex, in theological agitation, she may be regarded as a harbinger of the "revolt of woman." She had evidently great power of winning disciples. Vane, who was in New England at the time, was drawn to her; and it seems to have been partly in this way that he was led into an antagonism to the ruling party in Massachusetts which, combined probably with the attractions of the larger field, sent him back to the old country. Mrs. Hutchinson also was banished. Samuel Gorton was another eccentric spirit who could not brook theocratic rule. He held among other heresies that there was no such place as heaven or hell, a doctrine for which the time was not ripe. Disturbing the existing order and defying the rulers, he, with his followers, was convicted of blasphemy and with more cruelty expelled. He carried his complaint to England, as afterwards did other sufferers by the rigour of theocracy, compromising thereby the cherished independence of Massachusetts. Baptists also when they found their way into the colony were regarded and suffered as disturbers of religious order. They carried with them, however undeservedly, the taint of the social anarchy and war produced by the wild uprisings of the Anabaptists in Europe.

1634.

1637.

1634.

The worst case, and the shame of the theocracy, is
that of the Quakers. Quakers were not at first harmless
people of the inner light with a prim dress and a precise
language of their own. They were sectaries of the
wildest kind, and were sometimes guilty in their religious
ecstasy of indecency and even of outrage. They railed
against church authority; they forced themselves into
places of worship and disturbed the service; they went
about naked to testify against sin. A Quakeress in
Massachusetts thrust herself upon a meeting house clad
in sack cloth and with her face painted black to represent the coming of the small-pox. Quakers were sternly
bidden to depart; laws making them liable to flogging
and imprisonment, to the cropping of their ears, and the
piercing of their tongues with hot irons, were passed
and in some cases cruelly carried into execution. In
defiance of these penalties they still came, till at last a
law was passed banishing them on pain of death. They
returned, eager for martyrdom, and four of them were
hanged. But the touching demeanour of the sufferers
moved the hearts of the people. Public sentiment revolted. Public sentiment in Spain did not revolt against
the *autos-da-fé*. The treatment of the Quakers by the
Puritans is without defence or excuse, except such as
the fallacies of the age, the fear that religion would
perish in an anarchy of sects, and Quaker extravagance,
which seemed to menace social as well as religious order,
might afford. But it is wrong to say that the Puritans
of Massachusetts left the mother country to assert the
principle of liberty of conscience and then shamefully
violated that principle by their own practice. They came
out, not to assert liberty of conscience, a principle which

1656
to
1660.

had not dawned on their minds, but to found a religious
commonwealth on their own model and in it live the
spiritual life to which they aspired. Rhode Island, however, had now an opportunity of showing her loyalty to
her new born principle of religious freedom. To the
appeal of Massachusetts for co-operation in putting down
the Quakers the people of Rhode Island replied " that
they had no law among them whereby to punish any for
only declaring by words their minds and understandings
concerning the things and ways of God as to salvation and
an eternal condition." They admitted that the doctrines
of the Quakers tended "to very absolute cutting down
and overturning relations and civil government among
men," but said that experience taught them that " in those
places where these people aforesaid, in this Colony, are
most of all suffered to declare themselves freely, and are
only opposed by arguments and discourse, there they
the least of all desire to come," inasmuch as they delight
"to be persecuted by civil powers, and when they are
so they are like to gain more adherence by the conceit
of their patient sufferings than by consent to their per-
nicious sayings." In one respect the Rhode Islanders
were mistaken ; the Quakers remained among them and
added to the disturbance of their settlement. Perhaps
Massachusetts as the school of political and social order,
and Rhode Island as the school of freedom of opinion,
were unconsciously supplements of each other till the
fulness of time in which the harmony of the two principles should be revealed.

On its political side Puritanism was everywhere in
spirit republican, the tendency to political liberty going
hand in hand with religious independence. The mon-

archy, moreover, the court, and the aristocracy had been
left on the other side of the Atlantic. Unlike the dependencies of Spain or France, Massachusetts was from the
outset practically a republic, albeit retaining her allegiance to the King of England, founding her rights upon
his charter, included in his declarations of war and his
treaties of peace, regarding his law as the basis of her
own, and recognizing his privy council as her ultimate
court of appeal.   Her polity was based on the township, that elementary cell and school of public life about
which much has been said by De Tocqueville and other
political philosophers.   The townships were afterwards
gathered into counties, forming another step in the
ascending scale of self-government.   At the centre was
an elective and representative assembly.   The executive was an elective Governor.   Representation went
with taxation.   But the republic was not at first democratic.   Its chiefs in fact repudiated democracy as not a
fit government either for church or state.   They asked,
if the people were to govern, who was to be governed?
Some of them would fain have had all offices held for
life.   Winthrop and Dudley did actually enjoy almost
a life term.   There was no idle aristocracy; all alike
were workers, but social distinctions were kept up.   The
order of gentlemen was recognized, it was exempted from
corporal punishment, the title of Mr. was confined to
it, "Goodman" being the title of a commoner.   The
principal families had the chief seats in church; their
sons ranked first among the students at Harvard. "Concerning liberty," said Governor Winthrop in a homily
against democratic turbulence, " I observe a great mistake
in the country.   There is a twofold liberty, natural (I

mean as our nature is now corrupt) and civil, or federal. The first is common to man with beasts and other creatures. By this, man, as he stands in relation to man, simply hath liberty to do what he lists; it is a liberty to evil as well as to good. This liberty is incompatible and inconsistent with authority, and cannot endure the least restraint of the most just authority. The exercise and maintaining of this liberty makes men to grow more evil, and, in time, to be worse than brute beasts: *omnes sumus licentia deteriores* — we all become worse by licence. That is the great enemy of truth and peace, that wild beast, which all the laws of God are bent against, to restrain and subdue it. The other kind of liberty I call civil or federal; it may also be called moral in reference to the covenant between God and man in the moral law, and the political covenants and constitutions among men themselves. This liberty is the proper end and object of authority, and cannot subsist without it, and it is a liberty to that only which is just, good, and honest. This liberty you are to stand for at the hazard not only of your goods, but of your lives, if need be. Whatsoever crosseth this is not authority, but a distemper thereof. This liberty is maintained and exercised in a way of subjection to authority; it is of the same kind of liberty wherewith Christ hath made us free." Such, expressed by the highest Puritan authority, was the principle of the Puritan commonwealth. Authority was surrounded with as much state as the infant colony could afford. The Governor, it seems, was preceded by four halberdiers. When Lord Say-and-Sele, Lord Brooke, and other Puritan noblemen thought of coming out from England, they proposed that Massachusetts should institute an

hereditary order of nobility forming an Upper House.
But this the commonwealth respectfully declined. She
answered by the hand of Cotton, " When God blesseth
any branch of any noble or generous family with a spirit
and gifts fit for government, it would be a taking of
God's name in vain to put such a talent under a bushel,
and a sin against the honour of magistracy to neglect such
in our public elections. But if God should not delight
to furnish some of their posterity with gifts fit for magistracy, we should expose them rather to reproach and
prejudice, and the commonwealth with them, than exalt
them to honour, if we should call them forth, when God
doth not, to public authority." Thus gently but decisively did the new world break with hereditary government, and commit itself to the principle of election. But
aristocracy, had it been planted in New England, could
never have taken root. In the colony there were no great
estates to support peerages. Of the equal comradeship
of Saxon rovers English self-government was born; in
the equal partnership of religious colonists after a thousand years of monarchy and aristocracy it was renewed.

1627.   The Company having been transferred from England to
Massachusetts, no tie to England was left but that of allegiance to the king. Though the Puritan republic was
not in its birth democratic, democracy was not long in
raising its head and foreshadowing its destined empire.
Town meetings were pretty certain to breed village politicians, while the common schools would foster equality.
Elections were by the democratic mode of ballot. We see
the rudiment of a democratic caucus. Self-taxation is the
political lever of democracy, and New Englanders jeal-
ously refused to pay any taxes without representation. It

was a democratic spirit that demanded a written code of
laws instead of Mosaic principles administered at the discretion of the general court. It was a democratic spirit
that successfully protested against life-tenure of office. A
change in the constitution dividing the general court,
which had been a single council, into two branches, one
of which was popular, had its origin in a democratic
agitation caused by what the people resented as an oligarchical decision of the council in the great case of Mrs.
Sherman's sow. We have here a glimmering of the
conflict to come in after times between the "classes" and
the "masses." "He," Mrs. Sherman's antagonist in the
suit, "being accounted a rich man and she a poor woman,
this so wrought with the people, as being blinded with
unreasonable compassion, they could not see or would not
allow justice her reasonable course." These are the words
of a governor opposed to democracy, yet they are likely to
have been true. A feeling of the deputies of the townships against the central power, likewise premonitory in
its way, seems also to have played its part. To the
learned and revered Cotton, who held that democracy
was not a fit government for church or state, was opposed
the learned and revered Thomas Hooker, who maintained
that "the foundation of authority is laid in the free consent of the people, that the choice of the public magistrates
belongs to the people of God's own allowance, and that
they who have the power to appoint officers and magistrates have the right also to set the bounds and limitations
of the power and place unto which they call them."
These sentiments Hooker and his friends embodied in the
constitution of Connecticut, a settlement which was in
some measure a democratic secession from Massachusetts,

and may thus claim to be the cradle of American democracy as Rhode Island may claim to be the cradle of liberty
of conscience. The constitution of Connecticut has been
pronounced the first written constitution known to history
which created a government. This assertion may be a
little hazardous with regard to ancient Greece and Rome,
possibly with regard to the Italian republics; it is certainly
true with regard to America. It is true, and it is highly
important. We have passed from the world of unwritten
to that of written constitutions, from a world of government by usage, tradition, and chartered privileges wrested
from kings, to a world of government by public reason
embodied in codes of political law.

In 1642 the federal principle appears on the scene where
it was destined in the fulness of time to receive its grand-
est application. A federation was formed of the four
colonies then in existence; Massachusetts, Plymouth,
Connecticut, and New Haven. The motive was the same
which has given birth to confederations in general, mutual
defence against hostile force; the hostile force in this case
being that of the Dutch who pressed from the south, and
that of the French Canadians who pressed from the north,
while there was always danger from the Indians. In the
instrument of federation the language used implied the
possession by the contracting parties of independent and
sovereign power, such as would enable them to make
peace and war. The difficulties of the system were
illustrated by the jealousies and disputes which arose
notwithstanding the simple nature in this case of the
federal functions and the strong inducement to unanimity
afforded by common peril. Light was thrown, too, on the
conditions requisite for federation, which seems to be ap-
plicable only to a group of states, nearly equal or so

balanced as to preclude the domination of any one state
and the jealousies which such domination or the apprehension of it excites. Massachusetts, being much larger
and stronger than her three sisters, and naturally claiming
influence in proportion to her contribution, domineered,
or was believed by her partners to domineer, and instead
of harmonious action there was strife.

The belief that the scriptures contained the rule of civil
as well as that of spiritual life, coupled with the belief
that the Old Testament was of equal authority with the
New, could not fail to sit heavy on the Puritans of New
England, as well as those of the mother country. Their
legislation was tainted with Mosaism. Blasphemy, witchcraft, adultery, smiting or cursing parents, were treated
as capital crimes, though we have no record of an inflic-
tion of the death penalty for blasphemy, adultery, or
filial rebellion. For death as the punishment in the
case of adultery was afterwards substituted a milder
penalty, a part of which was the wearing of the scarlet
letter A as a mark of infamy. Sabbath-breaking was
punished with extreme severity. It is the inherent
tendency of theocracy to deal with sins as crimes. But
in the framing of the code, with the spirit of Mosaism
incarnate in Cotton and the ministers, a part was taken
by the spirit of law-reform, embodied in Ward, a clergyman who in England had been bred to the law. The
code of Massachusetts and those of other New England
colonies are on the whole a great improvement on those
of the mother country in humanity and civilization.
Their use of the death penalty is sparing indeed compared with the use of it in the code of the mother country,
where at last there were a hundred and sixty capital

offences. Cruelty to animals was forbidden. Though
equality did not yet fully reign, there was enough of it
to prevent aristocratic prodigality of the blood of the
poor. Imprisonment for debt was discarded. The en-
snaring technicalities of the pleading system were relaxed.
1641. A written code was framed, which being rational and
intelligible, was an improvement upon the chaotic pedantry of English jurisprudence, while the great under-
lying principles of English justice, and with them the
English right of trial by jury, were retained. The aristocratic right of primogeniture in succession to estates
was reduced to a double share. Women were protected
against the violence of their husbands, and a share of
the husband's goods was secured to the widow. Such
reforms Cromwell would probably have made in England
had he been able to overcome the interested prejudices
of his lawyers. The celebration of marriage, which the
Puritan deemed no sacrament, was transferred from
the clergyman to the magistrate. Barbarous punishments,
such as flogging, setting in the stocks, tongue-boring,
and ear-cropping, were still in vogue. Civilization had
nowhere advanced beyond them. New Haven was some-
1638. what more Mosaic and sterner than Boston. It had been
founded by men for whom Boston was too little Puritan,
and who were called the Brahmins of the sect. Its chief
rulers were styled "The Seven Pillars," and it rejected
jury trial as unsanctioned by the scriptures. "Never
elsewhere, I believe," says Dr. Bacon, "has the world seen
magistrates who felt more deeply that they were God's
ministers executing God's justice." God's justice must
have been inquisitorial if it extended to misbehaviour on
the part of servants, to keeping suspicious company on

the Lord's day, and to kissing. But it is not to be supposed that the scriptural ideal which these pious people
embodied in their enactments could be literally carried
into effect. The Blue Laws of Connecticut are at all
events a fable. When no government was free from
fallacy the fruits must be judged by comparison. Under
the discipline of Puritan theocracy, combined with the
training of industry and of bold seafaring, the foundations
of a strong character were laid.

The Puritan colonists had begun with the common
ownership of land. They soon found that common ownership meant common neglect and hunger, as had the colonists of Virginia till a leader by sheer force compelled
them to work. They then divided the land into lots,
after which industry became strenuous, and there was
food enough. Some common land, however, was retained,
and the lovely public gardens of Boston are a monument
of the primitive system. An attempt was made to regulate the rate of wages, and when the wage-earners complained of their reduced power of purchasing, an attempt
was made to regulate prices also. Even under a theocracy both experiments failed. Thus these pioneers of
trade and industry in their day "relegated political
economy to Saturn," and found that it returned. A
better measure was the enactment that no house should
be built at more than a certain distance from a place of
worship. If the primary object of this law was ecclesiastical it brought with it the economical and moral advantages of close settlement, it favoured the growth of
towns, and, therefore, of social and political life.

Life was of course austere. Much in which Merry
England delighted and might well delight was forbidden.

There were no May-poles nor Christmas pies. There was
no theatre; the acting even of "Comus" would not have
been endured. There were no drinkings of healths, and
of course no cards nor dice. On the other hand there was
no bear-baiting, no cock-fighting, no cocking on Shrove
Tuesday, no beastly drinking bout, no beating of watch-
men, no outrage of aristocratic Mohocks. There were
social meetings for the young, such as raising bees and
sewing bees. There seems even to have been dancing.
Neither in respect of food nor in respect of drink was
Puritanism ascetic. Its preachers had their casks of rum
or brandy. Thanksgiving Day, its chief festival in the
new world, was probably kept with as good cheer as the
prelatical Christmas. Frugality as well as religious principle would check excess of all kinds even when riches
had increased, else denial of amusement is apt to lead to
greater indulgence in the pleasures of the table. Gaiety
of apparel was discouraged, but on the Sabbath all appeared in their best clothes. Military drill and muster,
which the neighbourhood of the Indians and the hostile
Dutch and French always enforced and to which all citizens were bound, besides keeping up manly vigour, would
be a thread of variety and picturesqueness in the sad-
coloured web of existence. Still, New England life must
have been austere. Nor can the danger of moral reaction
against over-strictness and formality have been absent.
The religious exercises were such as would far surpass our
powers of pious endurance. Could any but the liveliest
faith have drunk in with delight the interminable sermon
of a Calvinistic pastor in an unwarmed meeting house,
with temperature below zero? However, the faith of
these men was the liveliest, and they did fully believe

that the world in which they practised this self-denial and patiently listened to these discourses was the threshold of a home prepared for the saints in heaven.

New England was not free from the stain of slavery. The law of Massachusetts said, "There shall be no bond-slavery, villainage, or captivity amongst us unless it be lawful captives taken in just wars and such strangers as willingly sell themselves or are sold to us." This licences slavery and the slave trade, though the provision which grants to the slave "all the liberties and Christian usages which the law of God established in Israel," the Hebrew code having been merciful for its day, would render slavery in New England comparatively mild. Slavery was sanctioned by the Bible; that was enough for the Puritan, who knew nothing about evolution or the education of the human race, and whose Christianity had not recognized the equal humanity of the heathen. Ships from New England took part in the slave trade, though the members of the religious commonwealth who made a murderous raid upon an African village on the Sabbath were brought to justice for their double crime. Fortunately for New England, she had no industry like that of cotton, tobacco, or rice, in which slave labour could be profitably employed. Slaves do not make good husbandmen or seamen.

Relations with the aborigines are a sad page in the history of colonies. At the time of American secession the charge was revived against the New England Puritans of exterminating the natives on a hideous scale. The number of savages who wandered over those expanses seems to have been really small, nor were they exterminated, though they were decimated by war and, perhaps still more, by the contraction of their hunting-grounds and their adoption of white vices. Indian tribes were always carrying on wars of extermination against each other. In their conduct towards the savages with whom they came into contact, the Puritans may at least challenge comparison with the conduct of the Spanish Catholics towards the far more civilized people of the same race who were found in Mexico and South America. In their first advances the new-comers showed a wish for peace and justice. For the seed corn which they had taken from an Indian store they tendered fair compensation. Compensation of some sort was made for the lands taken from the natives, though while on the one hand mere roaming over a vast region could hardly make the Indian hunter its proprietor, on the other nothing could compensate the wandering hunter for the loss of the wilderness and the game. Nor did the settlers ever cease to recognize the Indian as a man having a right to justice against the Englishman. The missionary efforts of Eliot were fully as noble as those of Las Casas or the Jesuits, while they were not, like those of the Jesuits, tainted with an equivocal ambition. He could number several thousand Indian converts, some hundreds of whom had learned to read a language reduced by him to writing. His Indian Bible was an almost super-

1661. human monument of philanthropic labour. He strove to combine civilization with conversion, and aimed at making his converts men, not sheep. But the Red Indian in reality, though not in the romance of Fenimore Cooper, was of all savages the most irreclaimable. Wild virtues, notably fortitude, he had, as well as keenness of sense and power of endurance, but his life was full of slaughter and rapine, his cruelty was fiendish. In the Iroquois

the devilish lust of blood and torture was so ingrained,
and was combined with so much cunning and perfidy,
that it was scarcely possible to deal with him otherwise
than as with the most dangerous and untameable of
wild beasts.   On the border no one could sleep secure
against the sudden onslaught of the savage with the
tomahawk and the firebrand.   While the congregation
was in church, armed men stood guard at the door.
The Puritan also had his cruel moods, and his notions
about smiting the Canaanite in New England as well as
in Ireland.   He was in one of those moods when, in the 1637.
Pequod war, he destroyed, in one holocaust, four hundred
Indians, men, women, and children.   Yet more terrible 1674–6.
was the war in later days against the Indian chief called
King Philip, who, as the colonists believed, had been
forming a league to drive them out of the land.   This
war lasted for two years, during which nearly two-thirds
of the eighty or ninety towns of Massachusetts were
raided by the savages, ten or twelve were totally destroyed, and ten per cent of the men of military age
were killed in fight or carried off to be tortured to death.
Piteous is the tale of a matron who was led into captivity
with her wounded child.   A desperate heroism was bred
by these struggles in the women as well as in the men.
Hannah Dustin, being carried off with her nurse and
a white boy, got the white boy to join her, rose in the
night, killed the Indians with their own tomahawks,
scalped them, and made her way back a hundred miles
to her home.   No wonder if disturbed fancy added its
terrors to those of reality, if Indian bows were seen in
the sky and scalps in the moon, if the aurora borealis
was taken for a blood-red portent of coming war.   No

wonder if the Puritan conscience was alarmed and looked
for causes of divine wrath in curled hair and ribbons,
naked breasts and arms, swearing and tippling, suspicious
ridings of youths and maidens to town under pretence of
attending lectures, hurrying away from meeting before
blessing asked, and toleration of Quakers. It is marvellous, and creditable to the Puritan religion that the
humanity of the colonists did not altogether give way.
A solution of the fatal problem by a mixture of the
races was out of the question. The marriage of Pocahontas with the Virginian Rolfe, hailed as auspicious
at the time, had no sequel. Few were the inter-marriages
between the whites and the Indians, though Indian blood,
instead of being deemed, like negro blood, a disgrace, has
been rather a subject of pride among Americans, and
one of the most eminent of Virginian politicians was fond
of reminding his hearers that it ran in his veins. The
higher the race is, the less does it mingle with lower
races. The Anglo-Saxon is to lower races a ruler, and in
dealing with them his exclusiveness is at once his strength
and his weakness.

Massachusetts always professed allegiance to the British
Crown, which, and not Parliament, it must be remembered, in those days was, or was taken to be, the real
government; in other respects she always bore herself as
an independent and almost sovereign commonwealth.
She made war and peace; she formed a confederation;
she taxed herself, paying no tribute of any kind; she
coined her own money, the pine-tree shilling; she dealt
freely with her own constitution; she framed her own
code of laws, including the law of capital punishment,
though as a general basis the English common law pre-

vailed. She framed her own treason law, enacting that
if any man should rebel or conspire against the commonwealth, or should attempt the alteration or subversion of
her fundamental government, he should suffer death.
This practically puts the commonwealth in the place of
the king; had such been the treason law of England
there would have been no difficulty in framing the indictment of Strafford. When there was any attempt on
the part of the home government actually to enforce the
obedience of the colony, the colonists met it with sage
diplomacy, fortified by fasting and prayer. The distance
from the imperial country favoured the tactics of delay.
It furnished also a conclusive plea for military independence. "If we in America," said Winthrop, "should
forbear to unite for offence and defence against a common enemy till we have leave from England, our throats
might be all cut before the messenger could be half seas
through." The smaller Puritan colonies in Rhode
Island, Connecticut, and New Hampshire, pervaded by
the same spirit as Massachusetts, like her were bent on
enjoying practical independence. They, especially Rhode
Island, had less difficulty in obtaining a large measure of
it, since the Crown was inclined to make them its allies
against Massachusetts, whose ambitious aspirations and
hostility to Episcopalianism, the royal religion, combined
with its power, gave special umbrage to the Crown.
There is always the same strain upon the bond, false
from the beginning, between the dependent colony and
the mother country; and the stronger and more self
reliant is the colony, the greater is the strain.

As Protestants militant the New Englanders were bound
up with the fortunes of their cause in Europe. With

eager eyes they had watched the victorious career of Gustavus Adolphus. With eyes still more eager would they watch the struggle in their mother country between high church despotism and protestant liberty. They triumphed in the victory of the Parliament. Yet they were careful in their relations with the Parliament not to compromise their own independence. Presbyterianism, dominant for the time in England, and believing as firmly as did Popery or Anglicanism in its divine origin, would fain have extended its dominion to the colonies. A synod of the Massachusetts churches was held and the Westminster Confession was approved, but the Congregational theocracy of New England underwent no change. The policy of the Protector towards the colonists was large-minded and liberal. He offered them, instead of their niggard soil and chilly climate, the rich and sunny Jamaica. At another time he proposed to transplant them to Ireland. Happily they declined both offers. In Jamaica they would have sunk into slave-owners; in Ireland they would have had to make room for themselves by smiting the Canaanites of that land with the edge of the sword. New England accepted the Restoration, but did not welcome it.

1661. After more than a year's delay Charles II was proclaimed at Boston, but to drink his health was not allowed; his Majesty himself having strictly forbidden it, as the rulers, by a pious fiction, declared. The colony gave an asylum to the regicides Whalley, Goffe, and Dixwell, who, hunted by royal emissaries, were sheltered by popular sympathy. A cave near New Haven is still shown as the refuge of Goffe and Whalley. Tradition makes Goffe suddenly appear on the scene to rally a party of colonists who were hard pressed in fight by Indians, and who took the mys-

terious stranger for an angel sent to their rescue. Connecticut and Rhode Island were, as usual, more prompt in
their submission than Massachusetts, and the royal countenance beamed on them accordingly.

By this time, however, a change had come over the
spirit of Massachusetts herself. Trade had grown active,
wealth had increased, and there had arisen a class more
commercial than religious, which lusted after the flesh-
pots, material and social, of the Royal and Anglican
Egypt. Against austerity, often tainted with conceit and
sometimes with hypocrisy, a reaction was sure to take
place like that of the Restoration against the reign of the
saints in England. The root of colonial Puritanism in the
mother country was dead, for Puritanism of the genuine
kind ended there with the Restoration, and nothing
remained but the far less lofty and energetic spirit of
political non-conformity. Trade had brought a mixed
population. The theocratic burghers were a minority,
according to the excluded a mere fraction of the community, and their political privileges had become an object
of just jealousy and hatred to those who were excluded
from the pale. Among the new-comers were members of
the Anglican Church who demanded liberty for their religion. It must not be left out of sight that in some sort
religious liberty in Massachusetts looked to the English
monarchy for protection and thus justified the interference
of the home government. Ungodly wealth looked wist-
fully at the pomp and trappings of British monarchy
and aristocracy. Political and religious malcontents alike,
Royalists, Episcopalians, Baptists, and Quakers, turned
their eyes to Westminster and there urged their complaints and carried on their intrigues. The germs of

the Tory and Whig parties of the Revolution had been formed. This invited the despotic aggression of the later Stuarts. The colonial government seems to have felt its weakness, since upon the arrival of the news of the Restoration and of the complaints lodged against it in England it sent to Charles II an apologetical address in which the colony was designated as "the King's poor Mephibosheth, by reason of lameness in respect of distance not until now appearing in his presence, kneeling with the rest of his subjects before His Majesty as her restored King." The pine-tree shilling being an offensive token of monetary independence, the pine was ingenuously passed off as the royal oak. But the storm was not averted by loyal language or by a condemnation of Eliot's republican treatise on the "Commonwealth," which, in some degree, reminds us of the tributes paid to monarchy in the condemnation of republican writings by loyal universities in England. The agents of Massachusetts brought back with them a royal missive demanding the repeal of all laws inconsistent with the King's authority; the administration of justice in his name, the renewal of the oath of allegiance, the substitution of property qualifications for church membership as the title to the franchise and to office, and the admission of all people of honest views to baptism and the Lord's Supper: the two last articles importing nothing less than the abolition of theocracy. Thus in the colony, as in the mother country, the Romanizing Stuart figured in a sinister way as the patron of toleration. The Quakers, however, though the King at first gave ear to their complaints, obtained little relief in the end. They filled the Stuarts' own prisons. Permission was given to make a sharp law against them,

and the sharp law was executed on two young married
Quakeresses, who walked naked through the streets in
imitation of the prophet Ezekiel, as a sign of the naked-
ness of the land. Royalty had in the colony its party
arrayed against the zealous defenders of the theocracy,
and headed by Joseph Dudley, son of the stern Puritan
Governor, but himself a shifty politician, the counterpart
of the Lauderdales and Shaftesburys of the mother country. Besides the threatened change in her constitution,
Massachusetts was menaced with a blow to her territorial ambition by a decision adverse to her aggrandizement in Maine, the proprietary colony of Sir Ferdinando
Gorges which she had been striving to appropriate. Relief
from pressure was probably afforded to the colony by the
reaction against the court in England consequent on the
Popish Plot, which gave birth to the Exclusion Bill.
But when the court had triumphed over the opposition,
and was sending the Whig leaders to the scaffold, prayers,
money — the effect of which upon the courtiers seems
now to have been tried — and partial submission proved
alike unavailing any longer to avert the impending blow.
A *quo warranto* went forth; the charter of Massachusetts,
like the charters of the English municipalities, was annulled; and, by a colourable process of law, for the later
Stuarts did everything in form of law, the commonwealth
was reduced to a dependency under the arbitrary power of
the Crown, which by the same act became again lord of all
the land, and had the title of every freeholder legally at its
mercy. Under James II the colony narrowly escaped
having the sanguinary Kirke as its Governor. Sir Edmund Andros came out in that capacity instinct with
the spirit of his master. He appeared as Governor of the

whole of New England, and apparently as destined Gov-
ernor-General of all the colonies. Under him as president of
the council was Joseph Dudley, playing Sunderland to the
viceroy of James II. Andros, like his master, assumed
the despot. He levied arbitrary taxes, he compelled
freeholders to purchase new patents for their lands, and
if they complained he told them, with the insolence of
another Jeffreys, by the mouth of his deputy, that they
had nothing left them except the privilege of not being
sold as slaves. He killed liberty in its source by putting
an end to the freedom of the press and making the obse-
quious Dudley censor. He forcibly introduced the Church
of England, seized a meeting house for its prelatical
services, and caused the Anglican surplice to be displayed before the eyes of the scandalized Puritans. He
took away the celebration of marriages from the magistrates and confined it to Episcopal clergymen, of whom
there was only one in the colony. To bring Connecticut
under his despotism he went to Hartford and demanded
the surrender of the charter, but the discussion lasting
into the night the lights were suddenly put out and in
the darkness the precious document disappeared and was
hidden in an oak which became sacred as the Charter
Oak. It seems wonderful that there was no serious
resistance except in New Hampshire, where the people
rose against arbitrary taxation, that capital grievance
which, even under the Tudors, English blood would not
endure. But the party of liberty in England was pros-
trate: the trade of the colony and its seaboard towns
lay at the mercy of the royal fleet: nor was the king
without partisans where, as at home, he could play, pend-
ing the re-installation of his own persecuting religion,

the part of a protector against persecution. He could look also for some support to Connecticut and Rhode Island, always jealous of their too powerful sister; while Rhode Island was mortally opposed to a theocracy such as still struggled for life in Massachusetts. One day, however, there sailed into Boston harbour an English ship bringing the glad tidings of the Revolution and the order to proclaim William and Mary. That order was joyfully obeyed. Andros fell like Jeffreys, and like Jeffreys had a narrow escape from popular vengeance.

William III had saved the liberties of Europe from Louis XIV. But his own trade was to be a king, and he soon had a Tory Parliament. After some deliberation he **1692.** restored the charter of Massachusetts, not, however, without serious changes. The governor was thenceforth to be appointed by the king, not elected by the people. Toleration was secured to all religions except the Roman Catholic. The qualification for the franchise was to be property, not church membership. This was the legal end of the theocracy, though practically the theocratic influence still held its ground in the government, and moulded laws as well as manners, while the Congregational ministry remained on something like the footing of an established clergy supported by general contributions. The press, without formal emancipation, slipped its neck out of the yoke of the censorship much as it did in England. That the counter revolution was not violent in the colony any more than in the mother country is shown by the retention of Dudley, the friend of prerogative, in office.

Other foes of theocracy, however, more powerful than the legal enactments of the English king and parliament, were now at work. The system had served as the mould

of New England character and institutions. The Puritanism which was its informing spirit was now rapidly dying
in the colony, as after the fall of the Commonwealth it
had died in the mother country. Surviving forms of
enthusiasm had become hollow; people could no longer
be brought to recount their spiritual experiences to their
fellows. To meet the wants of citizens whose parents had
contrived, against the strict rule, to have them baptized,
but who did not inherit the zeal essential to a full participation in church ordinances and life, "half-way communion" was, to the dismay of the saints, introduced.
Of the saints themselves the more politic, including Cotton Mather, had at last to consent to the compromise.
Trade brought immigrants of different religions who could
not, like Roger Williams and the Quakers, be cast out.
Wealth inclined to the doctrinal laxity and practical indulgence as well as to the liturgical pomp and aristocratic
associations of the Episcopal church. The Baptists set up
an altar against God's altar and would not allow it to be
pulled down. Close at hand was Rhode Island, always
proclaiming liberty of conscience; and if her principle
was somewhat discredited by political disorder, its enunciation could not fail to tell on free spirits. In Boston at
this time, according to Dunton, a roving bookseller, there
were thirteen bookstores, a formidable mine under the
foundations of the theocratic edifice. The ministers were
not field preachers: they received a learned education at
Harvard, and with learning the spirit of inquiry found its
way. Latitudinarianism began to creep in. Presently
Unitarianism raised its head, and in time possessed itself
of the government of the University. Even Rationalism,
or a tendency which the Calvinist would deem rational-

istic, to limit the domain of the supernatural, was gaining
ground. Perception of the invisible world grew faint as
interest in the visible world grew strong. Not that Cal-
vinism died out; many years afterwards it shot up with
almost terrific force and under its grimmest aspect in the
predestinarian writings of Jonathan Edwards and in the
revival of which he was the chief.

It was, perhaps, fear that the belief in the supernatural,
and notably in the supernatural agency of the Evil One,
was dying out which led Cotton Mather, a minister of
prodigious though ill-digested learning and at the same
time full of spiritual self-conceit, to countenance the horrible delusion of Salem witchcraft which has left a dark
stain on New England history, as readers of Hawthorne's
" House of the Seven Gables " know. Belief in witchcraft
was an hallucination common to all the churches, and in
all of them it had led to judicial murder. In the Church
of Rome it had led to judicial murder on the largest scale.
No one, not even Blackstone, who believed that the Pen-
tateuch was literally inspired, could deny the reality of
the crime. Salem, the chief scene of these horrors, was 1692.
the original seat of the Massachusetts Bay colony, and
over its quiet streets the spirit of primitive Puritanism
still broods. An epidemic of disease had predisposed the
minds of the people to an epidemic of superstition. Nineteen persons were put to death on charges as fantastic as
a lunatic's visions, and chiefly on the evidence of wicked
or perverted children whose cunning and persistency in
their fabrications are not the least remarkable part of the
episode. One man who was eighty years of age refusing
to plead, that he might save the inheritance of his children, suffered the penalty of the *peine forte et dure*, being

pressed to death with heavy weights. Even to Harvard
College the tide of delusion seems to have extended.
Then came a revulsion of public feeling. The demeanour
of some of the victims touched the feelings and shook the
convictions of the people. Of the authors of the persecution, some repented. Judge Sewall stood up in church
while his declaration of contrition was read. Cotton
Mather remained impenitent and probably was only confirmed in his obduracy by the arguments of Calef, an
unlearned but vigorous theologian who attacked the
whole belief. Cotton Mather afterwards partly redeemed
himself by countenancing, at a great sacrifice of his popularity and at some risk of his life, the introduction of
inoculation, which excited the ignorant fury of the mob.
Even in him learning begot something of liberality.
Judge Sewall also redeemed himself by taking up his
parable against slavery.

Godliness, even the strictest Puritan godliness, had
not interfered with material progress. Through the tem-
perance, industry, and frugality which it bred, the other
things were added to it. The Canaan of the Puritan
exiles was not a land flowing with milk and honey.
Though the Virginian exaggerated who said that in New
England you had to put in a herring head with every
stalk of corn to make it grow, much of the soil was
niggard. The American farmer is now deserting it for
the fertile expanses of the West. The climate, too, was
rigorous. That land may almost rank with the marshes
of Holland and the lagoons of Venice as a stern nurse
of the industrial virtues. Yet New England raised
enough to supply with farm products not only herself
but the West Indies. There was ship timber of the best,

such as furnished the finest masts for the "tall amirals" of the royal fleet. There were abundant fisheries both of cod and whale. All these advantages the New Englanders improved to the utmost. They supplied England with timber and marine stores, grew rich and, at the same time, became hardy and adventurous seamen. Population increased. Signs of opulence appeared. Houses with seven gables were built. An austere richness marked furniture and apparel. Highways were improved. Snug little inns were opened. The printing press was active, though chiefly in the theological line. There was as yet hardly a legal profession. The people had hitherto been judged not by men learned in the laws, but by the magistrate, as they had been in Israel. That there were physicians we know from an ordinance against quackery, though regular medicine was little better than regular quackery in those days.

Meantime, far to the South and for some time separated from New England by a Dutch plantation, in a land and an air physically more genial, morally less happy, another group of communities had been growing up. These were colonies of the same mother country as New England, but widely different from her in religious, social, and political character, destined presently to be joined to her in an ill-starred union, then to come to an inevitable rupture with the confederation of which she was the soul, and after a desperate struggle to be subjugated and re-annexed. New England was the leading shoot, the moulding force, the prevailing spirit; but Virginia, the queen of the southern group, was the elder colony.

1585-7. Virginia, as we have seen, had been saved when on the point of extinction by John Smith, a true Elizabethan hero and not the least bright star of the constellation, though, like Raleigh and the rest, he was probably not of the regular type of virtue, nor free from a boastfulness which scorned the limits of fact. This man knew what a colony was and how it differed from a gold-hunt. "Who," he asked, "can desire more content that hath small means, or but only his merits to advance his fortunes, than to tread and plant that ground he hath purchased by the hazard of his life? If he have but the taste of virtue and magnanimity, what to such a mind can be more pleasant than planting and building a foundation for his posterity, got from the rude earth by God's blessing and his own industry without prejudice to any?" Smith departed under a cloud of sorrow, but he had triumphed. The Virginia Company sent out supplies and re-inforcements, above all a cargo of maids as wives for the settlers, and the colony struggled into permanent

1610. existence. Then came Lord Delaware as governor with a state rather beyond the needs and means of the colony, whereat rough settlers grumbled, but with power and will to put down misrule. He struck the key note for Virginian society by repairing the dilapidated church at Jamestown, giving it pews and a chancel of cedar, a communion table of black walnut, a lofty pulpit, and bells. Himself regularly attended in full dress with his officers and council, and a guard of fifty halberdiers in red cloaks, and sat in the choir in a green velvet chair with a velvet cushion to kneel on.

Though no longer gold-seekers but real colonists, the men of Virginia were not such colonists as the Puritans.

They were more akin in character to the Spaniard on the
south of them, who made the Indian work for him, than
to the New Englander, who worked for himself.   To
work for them they had from the first a number of indentured servants, or bondsmen, jail-birds, many of them;
some kidnapped by press gangs in the streets of London,
all of depraved character.   Afterwards came in ever-in-
creasing volume African slavery, the destined bane of
Virginia and her ultimate ruin.   Thus were formed the
three main orders of Virginian society: the planter oligarchy: the "poor whites," or as the negro dubbed them,
"mean white trash": and the negro slaves.   Middle class,
in the proper sense of the term, there could hardly be.
The poor whites were destined, after two centuries of a
barbarous and debased existence, to end in a blaze of
glory as the heroic infantry of the South.

Virginia was not like New England, cooped between
mountains and the sea; nor was the soil niggard, though
it was rapidly exhausted by slave labour.   The planters
were far apart, taking each of them instead of the small
lots of the New Englander, large tracts of land.   Population instead of being condensed as in New England was
scattered, and life was isolated instead of being intensely
social.   There was nothing worthy of the name of a town,
much less of a city; though Jamestown, and afterwards
Williamsburg, was the capital of politics, pleasure, and
sport.   There were no townships nor township politics.
The divisions were shires or colossal parishes.   The parish,
as a designation at once ecclesiastical and administrative,
was adopted from England.   The country being inter-
sected by rivers, each plantation could have, and prided
itself on having a wharf of its own, at which, as a port

of entry, ships could load and unload. As each planter
dealt directly with the old country, there were no great
seaports nor centres of distribution. Virginia's staple was
tobacco, which could be well grown by slave labour, and
required large estates because it was exhausting to the
soil. This narcotic, the demand for which increased fast
in Europe, was, as King James I thought, " the diabolical
source " of Virginia's wealth and grandeur. An official
personage, practically-minded, to whom a Virginian de-
legation had commended a measure for the good of souls,
replied, " Damn your souls, grow tobacco." An attempt
was made to introduce silk-growing but it came to nothing. Industry of the higher kinds is shut out by slavery;
the population to which it gives birth would be socially
and politically fatal, as well as economically alien, to a
slave-owning community. It shows the crudity of Virginian commerce that tobacco was not only the staple but
the currency of the province, long after New England had
discarded the use of wampum or bullets as money.

Such was the birth of that famous planter-aristocracy
which made so desperate a fight against democracy, first
in the political arena, then on many a field of battle. It
dwelt, save when it was debating, dancing, or racing at
the capital, in lonely grandeur beside its broad rivers and
private wharves, in mansions styled baronial, and in what
it deemed manorial state, fed by the labour of slaves, and
surrounded by the servility of poor whites. It rode in its
coaches-and-six, the six horses being probably not more than
enough to drag the family chariot over colonial roads. It
had its trains of black lacqueys in brilliant liveries, which
they hustled on when a stranger approached. But in its
life and abodes there were less of comfort and of real

elegance than of grandeur. It spent its time a little in
politics, more in fox-hunting, racing, gambling, cock-fighting, and general dissipation. It had plenty on its board,
and commonly drank too much wine. It was hospitable,
as rich men without neighbours and craving for company
always are. It had something, and fancied that it had
much of the grand manner, the social grace, the chivalrous
sentiment, which marked the territorial aristocracies of
Europe. It was no doubt brave and mettlesome, rode well,
was good at field sports, had a quick sense of conventional
honour, and was ready to fight duels. Of course, living
by the sweat of other men's brows, it was free from anything that is sordid in the industrial or commercial character. Not parsimony but prodigality was its fault, and
while it was master of many slaves it was apt itself to be
the slave of debt. Some of the planters had, among their
English equipment, English books, and prided themselves
on their acquaintance with the British classics; but the
average amount of culture among them was probably low,
and their College of William and Mary was no mate for
Harvard.

The appearance of slavery on the scene when other
slavery had almost disappeared from the face of the civilized world opened a new chapter of evil. It was the
slavery of colour, indelible, without hope of fusion, utterly debased and debasing, and of all slaveries the most
degraded. Its character was impressed on the slave law.
" The black," to use a phrase afterwards made memorable,
" had no rights which the white man was bound to respect." A master was not answerable for the murder of
his slave, the law assuming that he would not wantonly
destroy his own property. A code of terror guarded the

master class. Fugitive slaves were hunted down like wild
beasts and the fugitive might lawfully be shot by anyone
on sight. To quiet all doubt it was expressly enacted
that conversion to Christianity was no bar to slavery. Intermarriage between whites and blacks was forbidden as
incest, so that the gulf between the races was impassable.
If a woman bore children to a white man, she carried them
with her into slavery, and an American historian tells us
that the offspring of men of station might be seen in the
slave mart. Emancipation was not encouraged, and the
emancipated negro was treated as a suspected pariah.
The edge of the law seems to have been sharpened in
Virginia after a negro insurrection. It is not to be supposed that the picture which such legislation presents was
that of a Virginian planter's household. In the household
the relation between master and slave no doubt was often
patriarchal and kind, though even there the slave can
hardly have risen morally or intellectually to a higher
condition than that of a well treated horse or dog. But
on large plantations, such as were multiplied in after
times, more in other slave States than in Virginia, there
being no personal tie between master and slave, the slave
was a beast of labour to be used up without mercy. No
community which had such a code could be healthy, or
fail at last to be brought into conflict with the advance of
moral civilization. Even with regard to the indentured
servants the law was harsh and degrading. They were
liable to the penalty of branding, and their terms of service might for delinquencies real or pretended be prolonged to perpetual servitude. Such social conditions
might, like those under which the Roman aristocracy was
formed, give birth to regicides, but they could scarcely
give birth to republicans of the true stamp.

The political development of the southern colonies, like their industrial and social development, presented a strong contrast to that of New England commonwealths. The industrial and social character of a community is sure, in spite of constitutional forms, to draw the political character with it. The New England colonies were practical republics, owing a nominal allegiance and paying occasional homage to a monarchy on the other side of the Atlantic. Virginia, after some fluctuations between chartered self-government and vice-regal rule, became a colonial monarchy after the English pattern, with a governor who was the delegate of the king and a little image of royal majesty, a council, nominated by the governor, which faintly represented the House of Lords, and a representative assembly which stood in the place of the House of Commons. A governor wielded more personal power than was left to the king at home, and exercised his veto freely when that of the king had been virtually resigned. He also exercised freely his military powers and his powers of appointment. The assembly, however, retained the power of the purse. The suffrage was at one time general; afterwards it was limited to property. But nominal freedom or limitation mattered little, since power was really in the hands of the planters on whom most of the poor whites were dependent. The planters of each shire administered local government and justice in conclaves like the English quarter sessions, and with more than the authority of the English squire. In oligarchical Virginia, taxation took the form of a poll-tax, whereas in republican New England people were taxed according to their means. The oligarchs were not the more inclined to submit to political slavery because they owned slaves. They were tenacious of their own constitutional rights as Englishmen. These they maintained proudly against the governor, as the Barons had maintained them against the English king, and so far they were in political training for the revolution.

The Church of England was established, though in a loose and rather ragged way, without a hierarchy, as well as devoid of the cathedrals and the ancient churches which are the pillars of her ascendancy in her own land. Dispersion of the population must have been much against church going, and in Virginia there was probably little of religious life. Such notices as we have of clerical habits lead us to think that there was at least one Parson Trulliber to every Parson Adams, perhaps to every Dr. Primrose. The parson, like everybody else in the primitive state of commerce, was paid not in money but in tobacco. There were laws against papists as in England, and there was the same contumelious toleration of dissenters. In Western Virginia was a settlement of Presbyterians, driven by persecuting bishops from Ireland with hearts full of bitter feeling against the English church and government, as they were afterwards to show. Here there was religion, and the settlement was one day to give birth to a singular mixture of Old Testament piety with slavery militant, in the person of "Stonewall" Jackson.

Saving the tinge of culture boasted by some of the planters, there was no education or literature. A good royal governor could say in 1670, "I thank God there are no free schools nor printing and I hope we shall not have these hundred years. For learning has brought disobedience into the world and printing has divulged them and libels against the best of Governments: God keep us from both." In a slave state a system of free schools or general education on

any footing would not only have been uncongenial, it
would have been dynamite. Schools even for the rich
there were few, if any. Young planters were brought up
at home under tutors who usually had not much to teach,
and whose pupils were not likely to be docile. Of the
wealthiest some went to the universities of the old land.
Law and medicine must have been weak.

Virginia had of all the colonies the best reputation at the
English court. It was royalist to the core and thoroughly
loyal. Of this its title " The Old Dominion " is a monument. It denounced as impious the execution of Charles I
and afforded an asylum to many of the defeated cavaliers,
whose traditions could not fail to import a fresh strain of
loyalty into the Virginian character. It bowed to the
Commonwealth and the Protectorate, but exulted in the
Restoration. There was, however, a Puritan section, which
having raised its head under the Commonwealth, resisted
the Absolutist and Anglican reaction and could only be
put down by force. That was the time of Governor Berke-   1642.
ley, who so frankly uttered his sentiments on the subject
of free schools and printing. He was the model of a
royalist governor, able and apparently beneficent in his
way, but a devout believer in prerogative and an extermi-
nator of Puritans and Republicans. His vigour brought on
a rebellion which seems to have had its origin among the
freemen of the poorer class and was headed by a Virginian
Gracchus named Bacon. This for a moment convulsed the
colony. Jamestown was razed to the ground by the insurgents. But Bacon died suddenly in mid-career. His fol-   1676.
lowing, drawn from a small and feeble section, at once
broke up, and the governor held a Bloody Assize which is
said to have brought on him a contemptuous ejaculation

from Charles II, who was not a man of blood except when mercy would give more trouble.

Bacon's rebellion seems to have been brought on partly by a suspicion that the governor had an underhand connection for commercial purposes with the Indians, and was disposed to protect them against the whites. The relations of the two races in the land of Pocahontas were pretty murderous, and could hardly fail to affect the character of the dominant race, but the Indians of the South were less ferocious and formidable than those whom the Puritan encountered in the North.

1633.   Maryland, in its origin, was in two respects peculiar; it was founded not by a chartered company but by a proprietor, and its projector was a Roman Catholic. Lord Baltimore, a statesman who had taken great interest in colonization and had convinced himself that companies failed through mismanagement and greed, obtained a grant of the territory from the crown. He was a convert to Roman Catholicism, and endowed the colony with toleration for the special benefit of a church which, elsewhere dominant and persecuting, was depressed and persecuted in England. Lord Baltimore dying, his son Cecil founded Maryland. Jesuits came out with the first colonists and began their missionary work among the Indians. Neither of the peculiar features, however, proved lasting. The proprietor, whose authority was by his patent that of a prince palatine, found it necessary to compound with the English tendencies of the free settlers and allow himself to be reduced to the position of a constitutional ruler, with an assembly of the usual kind, in which was vested the all-important power of taxation.

By the victory of Puritanism over Charles I in England, Puritanism in Maryland, where it formed an element of the motley population, was incited to strike for power, and it defeated the party of the Pope and the Proprietary in a little pitched battle at Providence. In that fight, as at Naseby and Worcester, according to the Puritan writer of "Babylon's Fall in England," "God did appear wonderful in the field and in the hearts of the people: all confessed Him to be the only worker of this victory and deliverance." With the Restoration returned the government of the Proprietary, well administered by Charles Calvert, the third Lord Baltimore, under whom religious quarrels were hushed, toleration reigned, tobacco was grown, and the province prospered. But the Revolution in England brought another rising of Protestants against toleration of the Catholics, and in the end Maryland was made a royal province, received a royal governor, and was settled politically on the regular model with a council and representative assembly. The ecclesiastical settlement was finally the same, in form at least, as that of England, the Church of England being established, though probably in little force, and Protestant dissenters being tolerated, while toleration was, at least legally, withheld from Catholics in the colony of their own foundation. The culture of tobacco led to the employment of slave labour. Maryland was drawn within the fatal circle of the slave States, and became the domain of a planter class like that of Virginia, but less oligarchical. Nothing in political physiology is more marked than the influence of tobacco, cotton, and rice on the social and political character of the Southern States.

1671 to 1700.   The Carolinas, like Maryland, were a proprietary colony founded by a group of leading men in England, to whom Charles II made a rather blind grant of a territory already in part occupied by settlers, and who appear not only to have been desirous of gain but ambitious of founding a model community. Among them was Shaftesbury, whose hand we seem to trace in a special clause peculiar to this charter, which in consideration of the distance from home authorized the proprietaries to establish any religion they chose, a curious indication of the political character of the English State religion. For an ideal constitution the proprietaries applied to the wisdom of Locke, and the wisdom of Locke gave them a Grand Model which, especially considering that it was intended for the rough population of a new settlement, may be regarded as the most awful of warnings to political castle builders. It is an ineffable structure of the feudal type, with a hierarchy of hereditary land owners under the names of Landgraves and Caciques — the latter name being probably intended as a compliment to native sentiment — a division of the land into seignories, and, what seems incredible as a proposal of Locke, a race of hereditary tenants attached like villeins-regardant to the soil. To keep government in the hands of intelligence and property seems to have been the philosopher's aim. This scheme the proprietaries actually tried to put in force. It could produce nothing but disgust, revolt, and confusion. The only thing in it worthy of Locke is complete religious toleration. In the course of the political squabbles which inevitably ensued, South Carolina was severed from North Carolina and transferred from the proprietaries to a royal governor. Into North Carolina, attracted by toleration,

came Huguenots from France, persecuted Covenanters
from Scotland and other religious refugees, whose character, together with the climate and husbandry of an
upland country, was the saving of North Carolina, so that
though in the slave group she was scarcely of it. But of
South Carolina the staple became partly the fatal tobacco,
largely the yet more fatal staple of rice, grown on
swampy tracts where white men could not work. The
consequence was a large importation of negro slaves.
South Carolina had also a sinister connection with the
slave-owning and buccaneering West Indies. Corsairs
such as Captain Kidd and Black Beard found shelter
in her ports. In the upshot she became the typical
slave state, the heart of slavery and the focus of all
the ideas and all the ambitions connected with the system; while Charleston, her social capital and seaport,
became the paradise of planter society with its luxury,
state, and pride. Her slave code transcended even that
of Virginia in cruelty, and expressed still more vividly
the terrors of a dominant race. Everyone who found
a slave abroad without a pass was to flog him on the
spot. All negro houses were to be searched once a fort-
night for arms and for stolen goods. For the fourth lar-
ceny a slave was to suffer death, and the kind of death was
left to the discretion of the judge. For running away
a fourth time the slave was to undergo mutilation. For
punishing a slave so that he died, no one was to suffer any
penalty. For the wilful murder of a slave the penalty
was a fine of forty pounds. It need not be supposed
that the most revolting articles of the code were often
put in force or that they represent the general relations
between master and slave.

1733.   Georgia was founded by the philanthropic General
Oglethorpe, whose heart had been wrung with pity for
the sufferings of debtors imprisoned under the barbarous
law of those days.   It was to be the refuge of the pauper
and the bankrupt, and was to empty the workhouses of
England.   Another object was the erection of a bulwark
against the Spaniards of Florida.   Unluckily the settlers
chosen, instead of being labourers, were men who had
failed in trade and were good for nothing as husbandmen.

1734.   Better elements of population came in, Highlanders,
Moravians, Protestants of Salzburg expelled by their
persecuting Prince Bishop.   But the shiftless and lazy
immigrants called at once for rum, which had been prohibited, and for slaves to do the work.   By the workers
the entrance of slavery was opposed, but the climate and
the contagion of the neighbouring colonies prevailed.
Slavery forced its entrance, and Georgia was numbered
with the slave states.   It is not on the government of the
mother country that in this case the blame can be cast.

1736.   In its earlier days the colony was the scene of an unfortunate episode in the life of Wesley, who there, after a
strange love affair, encountered an evil-speaking generation ; and of the preaching of Whitefield, who kindled a
flame of religion by his preaching, but pleaded for slavery, seeing in it an instrument of conversion.   Whatever
the special fancy of a founder might be, climate, soil,
and natural circumstances generally, together with human
nature, soon prevailed over his will.   Model colonies are
apt to come to nothing except as they may enlist settlers
of high character, and thus lay a good social foundation.

The group of Middle States was formed round the Delaware, New York, and Chesapeake bays. Pennsylvania, as 1681. all know, was the philanthropic utopia of the renowned and somewhat enigmatic character whose name it bears. Quakerism was by this time clothed and in its right mind. It had passed from George Fox to Barclay. It was becoming commercial, even eminently commercial, and its political quietism, which in Penn assumed the form of an equivocal connection with the court, distinguished it favourably from the political sects in the eyes of the Stuarts. Partly in satisfaction of a debt due from the crown to his estate, Penn was made lord of Pennsylvania with almost kingly powers, including those of peace and war, which he of course intended to exercise only in the interests of peace. His scheme of government was popular. He renounced for himself and his successors any power of doing mischief, "that the will of one man might not hinder the good of the whole country." The other characteristics which he impressed upon his settlement were religious toleration, a mild criminal law with the reformation of the criminal in view, and good treatment of the Indians. Toleration was extended to all who believed in God and would be good citizens, though Christianity was recognized as the religion of the community by the enforced observance of Sunday. Murder was the only capital offence. There was a moral and social code of the Puritan type, but there was little of theocratic power to enforce it. To Penn's good treatment of the Indians his colony owed peace in that quarter and uninterrupted progress. Slavery was not excluded. That Penn himself once held slaves a will, though not his last, remains to show: but he strove, though in vain, to secure for the slaves the right of legal marriage. The soil and climate, however, combined with the general character of the settlers, shut out the pest. To Pennsylvania presently came a large exodus of Germans, driven from their homes by war. They gave the province a body of laborious husbandmen, but rather bucolic citizens. Their descendants, who are called the Pennsylvania Dutch, have preserved the two-fold character as well as the traces of their ancestral language. Penn, in spite of his philanthropy and liberalism, became embroiled like other governors and proprietaries with his lieges. His son, whom evil associations had made a libertine, renounced Quakerism in wrath at the treatment of his father by the sect. Toleration made Pennsylvania a religious museum. In it, besides the Quakers, were Anglicans, Lutherans, Scotch Presbyterians, Palatines, Ridge Hermits, Dunkers, and Pietists. Roman Catholics alone were here, as elsewhere, under a ban of suspicion which the persecuting violence of Louis XIV and the Prince Bishop of Salzburg might partly excuse. Power, with a large share of the commerce and wealth of which Philadelphia became the seat, was in the hands of the Quakers, who as rulers were prudent, thrifty, and always averse from war. To war, however necessary, they would contribute only under the form which satisfied their own consciences, of a gift to the government, for the use of which the conscience of the government was to answer, or, as on one occasion they did, as a supply for the purchase of bread, flour, wheat, or other grain, the other grain being understood to be gunpowder. Their institutions sustained their reputation for philanthropy, and by them the first lunatic asylum in America was founded.

1614.   New York, which its ample territory and the possession

of the most magnificent of harbours have now made the
Empire State and the seat of the commercial capital of the
Union, was originally New Netherland, a Dutch colony
founded in the golden age of Holland's naval greatness.
Delaware, the neighbouring state, was a colony of Sweden   1627.
founded in the glorious days of Gustavus Adolphus.   The
Dutchman by his superior power mastered the Swede;
the Englishman mastered the Dutchman.   Hardly could   1664.
the two groups of English colonies north and south have
suffered a wedge of alien dominion to be thrust between
them.   Dutch colonization seems to have been barely
on a par with Dutch commerce and seamanship.   New
Netherland was dominated by the patroons, magnates
invested with vast grants of land, who exercised seignorial
sway and lived in seignorial state.   The ancient title is
still cherished, and about half a century ago the claim
of a patroon for services to be rendered by the tenants
upon what had once been his domain gave birth to a petty
civil war.   At Albany are still Dutch houses, Dutch faces,
and families rejoicing in Dutch pedigrees.   There is still
a Dutch Reformed Church, and an old lady being told
that " Dutch " was to be dropped in order that the character of the church might be universal, replied that she
did not want the church to be universal, it was the church
of the old Dutch families of that state.   After going
through the usual political struggles and sufferings — a
temporary suspension of her liberties under James II and
his satrap Andros followed by a tragi-comic revolution in
which Leisler, a patriot leader, mounted the scaffold of
Russell and Algernon Sidney — New York settled down
politically into the regular form of the English constitution
adapted to the colonies, and with the usual constitutional

bickerings betwe●● the governor and the assembly, the quarrel being chiefly here as elsewhere about money.

1664. New Jersey was created by dismemberment from New York. It had a motley population and hardly any history distinct from that of the larger state. It became a country of gentlemen farmers with a peasantry. It received, however, a colony of persecuted Covenanters which made it one of the chief seats of Presbyterianism and of which Princeton University may be regarded as a noble memorial.

The population of the New England colonies was almost purely English, and reflected the virtues and faults of English character as seen in the Englishman of the middle class, though with Puritan and colonial modifications. The population of the Middle States was very mixed. It comprised, besides Englishmen, detachments or waifs of almost every protestant nation and church in Europe: Scotch Highlanders and Lowlanders, Scotch-Irish, French Huguenots, Germans from different parts of Germany, Moravians, Dutch, Swedes, Finns, and a few Jews. But almost everywhere the English language prevailed. Everywhere there was a constitution after the British model, with a governor representing the king or proprietary, and a representative assembly with two houses answering to the two Houses of Parliament. Local self-government in the Middle States was a mean between the intense local life of the New England townships and the political languor of the Virginian shire. There were not generally any common schools or any regular provision for education, but there was education, there was learning, printing was free. Practical toleration prevailed, saving an occasional outbreak of intolerance against Roman Catholics, whose

church, it must be borne in mind, was always giving provocation by persecuting wherever she had the power. The
social code was far less strict than in Puritan New England. The keeping of the Sabbath was probably about
the only Puritan law that was really enforced. Theatri-
cals, sternly banished from New England, found reception
in the Middle States. Slavery everywhere existed by
law, but it was kept down by the ascendancy of free
labour and by the nature of the products. That the negro
in New York was a slave appeared with dire distinctness
when, in consequence of a vague alarm of incendiarism
in New York city, upon evidence utterly disreputable and 1741.
without fair trial, thirteen negroes were burnt at the stake
and eighteen were hanged. A Catholic priest, accused
of instigating the negroes, was with them judicially
murdered.

With James II royal tyranny ceased, but parliamentary 1688.
tyranny began. Parliament, now the supreme power,
made itself the legislative organ of a commercial interest,
animated by that blind and unscrupulous greed which has
been the bane and disgrace of commerce and continues
to animate the monopolist at the present day. By the
Trade and Navigation Acts England sought to engross
not only the carrying trade but the general trade of her
colonies, and shut them out from the markets of the world.
In doing this she only followed the practice of the time,
and gave effect to the belief universally accepted, and
endorsed even by Montesquieu, that colonies were planted
for the commercial benefit of the imperial country. No
one had yet learned to think of them as the germs of independent nations. The real interests even of the imperial

country were sacrificed, as Adam Smith showed, to those
of the merchants, who were the principal instigators of the
policy. So far, however, from being the chiefest, Great
Britain was the least of sinners in this respect, and Adam
Smith might say with truth that her policy was less illib-
eral and oppressive than that of any other nation. France
strangled by monopoly the fur trade of Canada. Spain
allowed her colonists to trade only with the single port of
Cadiz. England, while she trammelled the trade of her
colonies afforded them the best of markets; especially did
she afford the best of markets for the timber and marine
stores of New England. More odious even than the restraints upon colonial trade were the restraints upon
colonial manufactures. The colonists were not allowed
to make woollens, steel, hats, or any other articles by the
manufacture of which they would compete with the mother
country. This seemed no injustice to Chatham, who proclaimed the right of the imperial country to restrain the
colonies from manufacturing even a horseshoe or a
hobnail. Royal claims to trees of a certain size, as the
perquisite of the royal navy, had been at one time a just
cause of discontent. If England crippled colonial trade
with her restrictions she tried to foster it with bounties,
while of the articles most important to colonial trade some
were exempt from restrictions. The Navigation Act seems
to have stimulated colonial ship-building which was very
prosperous. Yet the system might have been intolerable
had not the pressure of the commercial fetters been relieved by salutary smuggling. In fact the commercial
restrictions seem to have been systematically disregarded.

1695. The Board of Trade, which had been called into existence
by the growth of British commerce, acted as the guardian

power of British monopoly, having its sentinels in the colonial governors, on whose information it was always complaining of violations of the Trade and Navigation Acts. It had even the assurance to propose the abrogation of such colonial charters as remained, in order that the sweep of its action might be unconfined. After all, the gains of the imperial country itself from this wretched policy cannot have anything like equalled the expense of defending the colonies. Certainly they did not countervail the indirect losses from the depression of the colonial trade, the benefit of which, had it been allowed free development, England more than any other nation would have enjoyed.

Wrangling between the governor as the organ of prerogative and the assembly as the trustee of liberty went on in almost all the colonies; Virginia and Maryland almost alone enjoying, in their later days at least, something like political peace. The executive, fitfully supported by the home government, strove to make itself independent by means of fixed revenues and salaries, while the assembly strove to keep the executive dependent on it by a system of annual grants. Supplies for the colonial wars were another subject of contention, especially when the colony lay remote from the seat of war. Nor was there less of niggardliness and fractiousness on the side of the assemblies than there was of a disposition to encroach on the side of the representatives of the crown. These embroilments are recounted with glee by historians who deem them the training school of patriotism and preparatory to the struggle for independence. But such a view would seem to identify patriotism with resistance to government and to glorify revolution. The revolution in

which these bickerings ended in fact did not a little
to foster such sentiments. Anglo-Saxon love of liberty in
the colonies, strong from the beginning, needed no such
contentious training, and right reason will only deplore
the retention of a tie of which strife was the inevitable
consequence, which was at last broken by civil war, and
has left a heritage of malignant memories behind. Revolution is the medicine not the bread of nations, and genuine patriotism in ordinary times is loyal co-operation with
authority.

Of the governors sent out from England, some were
bad, being men appointed from corrupt motives in an era
of political corruption, ruined retainers of a party who
came to retrieve their fortunes, sometimes by illicit means,
or Englishmen ignorant of colonial character and unsuited
in temper for their work. But some, as Bellomont in
New York, Spotswood in Virginia, Calvert in Maryland,
Archdale and Blake in Carolina, were good; and when
the governor was good, it is not unlikely that for quiet
citizens, for all to whom politics were not a trade or a
game, his rule may have been as beneficent and as moral
as any which this continent has seen or is likely soon to
see. One good service the governors, and the home government by which they were supported, certainly did, they
repressed the general tendency of the colonies to raise the
wind by the issue of paper money. Appointments to sub-
ordinate offices in the colonies seem to have been abused
and the evil probably extended to the judiciary. Such
was sure, especially in bad times, to be the consequence
of attempting to govern across an ocean a country greatly
differing from the imperial country in circumstances and
in the character of its people. Mutual ignorance was and
always will be in itself fatal to transatlantic tutelage.

Another source of friction was the endeavour of the Church of England to establish itself in the colonies on the necks of those upon whom high churchmen looked down as dissenters. The Society for the Propagation of the Gospel did good work in improving the character of the colonial clergy, but it was a society for the propagation of episcopacy at the same time. Episcopacy was backed by the court and the Tory party, ever faithful to the policy of the monarch who said "no Bishop, no King." The Rev. Mr. Miller, an episcopal clergyman, writing from New York to the Bishop of London, gives a deplorable picture of colonial society in which he says: "God's grace having been withdrawn, the Evil One has it all his own way." Of this the cause in Mr. Miller's opinion is that there are no churches but only meeting houses with none but "pretended ministers," who, if they have any orders at all, are Presbyterians or Independents and are slaves to the pleasure of their congregations. His specific is the importation of a bishop as suffragan to the Bishop of London with a salary of £1,500 a year and the King's Farm for his palace. The "pretended ministers" would be sure to concur with the Evil One in objecting to the application of this remedy. To the Puritan of New England above all episcopacy was most hateful. Dread of its introduction disposed the puritan clergy to revolution.

Added to all was the general tendency of the imperial people to bear themselves haughtily towards those of the dependencies and of the people of the dependencies to resent imperial haughtiness. This was an inevitable incident of the relation. Every citizen of the imperial country felt himself, as Franklin said, part of a sovereign; and while the colonist acknowledged a superior his vanity smarted. In some measure it is so still.

By this time the political press was born, the New England *Courant* having appeared in 1722 and a political journal at New York having been brought out not long afterwards; and, though the giant was yet in the cradle, journalism was not long in becoming an organ of democratic agitation. It appears that in 1765, when the fatal era was approaching, there were over forty newspapers in America.

Unwillingness to submit to imperial control and nascent tendencies towards independence were already visible. and formed the burden of complaints transmitted by colonial governors or officers to the home government. Admiral Warren, who had been acting with New Englanders, describes them to the ministry as having "the highest notions of the rights and liberties of Englishmen and indeed as almost Levellers." A suspicion that the plantations were "not without thoughts of throwing off their dependence" prevailed in England, and the lieutenant governor of New York exhorted his lieges to allay it by a grant of a fixed revenue. It is true that in reply the members of the assembly took it upon themselves to vouch that not one person in the province had any such thought or desire, "for under what government could they be better protected or their liberties so well secured?" The colonists of England did enjoy of political liberty a large, of personal liberty a full, measure. In spite of all the commercial restrictions the colonies greatly prospered, their population rapidly increased, and most favourable pictures of their condition and progress were drawn by observers at the time.

1706 to 1790. A characteristic as well as a memorable product of colonial civilization at this epoch was Benjamin Franklin, by birth and education a New Englander, by adoption a Pennsylvanian. He cannot be said to have been an offspring

of the theocracy, inasmuch as he was a latitudinarian in
religion and had a natural son. But he was an offspring
of New England Puritanism grown mellow. His commercial shrewdness, his practical inventiveness, his fundamental
integrity, his public spirit, his passion for improvement,
were native to his community in the phase which it had
now reached, no less than were his " Poor Richard " philosophy of life and the absence in him of anything spiritual
or romantic. He it was who in his boyhood had suggested
to his father that much time might be saved by saying
grace at once over the whole barrel of red herrings. He
leads up the mighty army of American inventors. At
the same time though no revolutionist by nature he was the
destined harbinger of the Revolution. He had been the
first projector of a general union of the colonies. His figure
marks the transition to the revolutionary and national
period which is now opening from that of the Puritan
commonwealth.

CHAPTER II

REVOLUTION, INDEPENDENCE, AND UNION.

IT cannot be too often repeated that the relation between the imperial country and a colonial dependency was radically false. It became more manifestly false as the colony grew in strength and every conceivable need of tutelage passed away. Separation was sure to come. It was visibly approaching. But its arrival was delayed, the tie of affection between the mother country and her offspring was for a time renewed, and the shadow on the dial which hastened towards the fatal hour was turned 1689 backward by the series of struggles in which Great to Britain and her colonies were together engaged with 1759. France, the long arm of whose ambition reaching from Quebec round to the valley of the Mississippi threatened, or seemed to threaten, not only the ascendancy but the security of Englishmen in the new world, while native savages under French Catholic instigation were always harassing the Protestant settlements of New England. The population of French Canada compared with that of the English colonies was very small, but all French Canadians of military age were fighting men. Their force was wielded by the single will of a military governor such as Frontenac or Montcalm, and with them were the regular troops of conquering France. (The

Indian was mainly on the side of the Frenchman, who amalgamated with him more easily than the Englishman, nor did the Jesuit shrink from launching his savage convert with tomahawk and firebrand on the villages of the heretic.) (The English colonies had no sufficient bond apart from their common allegiance to the empire to unite them against a foe whose union was complete.) Besides their disputes with the royal governors they had quarrels among themselves about boundaries, about relations with the Indians, about shares of responsibility for the cost of colonial wars. Even their commercial union was imperfect. It was difficult to induce such of them as were remote from the point of danger to contribute to the common defence. An attempt was made to bring about a defensive union. It was earnestly supported by Franklin who to his account of the loss of a fort added a picture of a rattle-snake cut into thirteen pieces with the motto "Join or Die." But the plan when framed pleased neither the colonists, who thought there was too much in it of royal supremacy, nor the crown, which thought there was too much in it of independence. In fact the colonies could not fully feel the necessity, so long as they were united under the imperial government and led by its commanders. (Nor were English colonists military like the French, but agricultural and commercial, though, as the stormy waters witnessed, they were strong and brave.) Wolfe said of his North American Rangers that they were the worst soldiers in the universe, a censure which, however, must have referred more to lack of discipline than of valour and was inapplicable to bush-fighting with Indians, as the rout of Braddock's regulars and the protection of their retreat by Washington's Virginian Militia had shown. (Ships of war the colonies had none. Hardly without the aid of British armies. fleets, and commanders would colonial prowess have prevailed over the warlike bush rangers of Quebec with the 1744. armies, fleets, and generals of France.) A colonial expedition took Louisbourg. the Gibraltar of North America, without the aid of British troops; but the works of Louisbourg were then weak, the garrison was ill-provided and mutinous, the commandant was irresolute, and when his supplies were cut off by a British fleet he surrendered. Otherwise this famous enterprise, undertaken in a fit of enthusiasm, religious as well as military, and led by crusaders ignorant of war, would probably have failed. Better for the colonists than British protection against France. for which they paid by entanglement in European quarrels, would have been a compact of colonial neutrality. exempting the American colonies of European powers from wars between the imperial countries. Such a project had been framed and even embraced, but it proved abortive. (As it was, New England might have been worsted in the struggle with New France had not the protecting arm of Old England been stretched over her.) Though the war was European, it was in no merely British quarrel that British blood was poured out and British treasure lavished on the American field. Braddock may have been arrogant and blundering. but the fact remains that he and his soldiers were there at England's cost to defend her American children against the French and their Indian allies. Not for Great Britain alone, but for the British race and for its ascendancy on this continent the red coats conquered on the heights of Abraham 1759. and Wolfe died. >

⟨That colonial loyalty was in a great measure fear of France and that the colonists, as soon as England had rid them of that fear, would break the tie, was the surmise of shrewd and cynical observers at the time.⟩ Yet Americans will hardly upbraid the mother country with blindness in not foreseeing that result. ⟨When the question arose whether Great Britain should retain Canada or take a sugar island which to herself would have been more valuable, Franklin pressed on her the retention of Canada.⟩ Assuming his advice to have been sincere he must have trusted colonial gratitude. ⟨There was at all events a transient renewal of love.⟩ When Quebec fell the bonfires of loyalty were lighted.   England and Chatham were in all colonial hearts.   If only that happy moment could have been seized for parting in peace! ⟨If when the British flag was run up on the great stronghold of France, the mother country could have said to the child, "I have done for you all that a parent could do, I have secured to you the dominion of the new world, you have outgrown my protection and control, follow henceforth your own destiny, cultivate your magnificent heritage and be grateful to the arm which helped to win it for you!"   Had those unuttered words been spoken, how different might have been the history of our race, perhaps to the end of time?⟩

1759.

It is needless and would be painful to recount to Englishmen the annals of a quarrel which fills a too familiar page in English history, and wretched as it was on both sides, went nearer through its European extension than even the domination of Louis XIV or the conquests of Napoleon to bringing the head of England low among the nations. Few require to be again told how when England was burdened by a heavy debt contracted in the war, George

Grenville in an evil hour bethought him of making the
colonies contribute to their own defence, while he enforced
at the same time with calamitous industry the fiscal laws
and the restrictions on trade; how to raise revenue for a
1764. colonial army he imposed the stamp duty; how the colonists resisted and Chatham applauded their resistance;
how by Rockingham with Burke at his side the stamp
1766. duty was repealed, while with the repealing act was unhappily coupled, to save imperial honour, a declaration of
the power of Parliament to bind the colonies by its
legislation in all cases; how peace and a measure of
good feeling were thereby restored; how Townshend
usurping command of the government during an eclipse
of Chatham madly re-opened the fatal issue by the im-
1767. position of a number of import duties / how Parliament
gave a careless assent to Townshend's proposal; how
colonial resistance was renewed; how while the other
duties were repealed pride and obstinacy retained the tea
duty as a proof of power; how strife again broke out and
ended only with the destruction of the unity of the British
race. > Nor would it be profitable to rehearse arguments
which were mostly in the air, though they had too practical an influence on the conduct of statesmen and of political assemblies. A sovereign power there must have been
somewhere. Where could it be but in the Imperial Parliament? Had not the colonists just acquiesced in an act
declaring the power of Parliament to bind them in all
cases? Out of the jurisdiction of Parliament they could
not pretend to be, since they had submitted to laws made
by Parliament respecting navigation, trade, naturalization,
and other imperial matters, not to mention the Habeas
Corpus Act, or the common law which was recognized in

he colonies, and must have had for its basis the legislative
upremacy of the parliament of Great Britain.   That there
vas an essential difference between internal and external
axation, as Chatham in the interest of peace and unity
ontended, few will now maintain.   The sovereign power
must include the power of taxation, and taxation is but an
xercise of the legislative power in the form of a law enact-
ng that the impost shall be paid.   We rely for our judgment respecting these questions mainly on Burke.   But
Burke though of all rhetoricians the most philosophic was
till a rhetorician and presented only one side of a case.
Of this his essay on the French Revolution is the memo-
able and disastrous proof.   Though he goes deep into
everything he seldom goes to the bottom.   You cannot
xtract from him any definite theory of the colonial rela-
ion, of the authority which an imperial country was
ntitled really to exercise over colonial dependencies, or
f the use of such dependencies if authority really to be
xercised there was none. ⟨Was Great Britain bound to
lefend the colonies and were the colonies not bound,
unless they chose, to contribute to the defence?⟩ Was
ach colonial legislature in the case of a peril calling for
ommon effort to be at liberty to renounce its share of the
urden?   It is said that if England had then done by the
American colonies as she has since done by her other
olonies, the result would have been equally happy.   The
esult is that she bears the whole burden of imperial
lefence and all other expenses of the Empire while the
olonies lay protective duties on her goods.   Of such an
mpire neither Burke nor anyone else at that time dreamed.
They all, however indistinct their vision might be, had in
heir minds an empire of real power and solid gain.⟩

Would Chatham have thought of allowing the colonies to lay protective duties on British goods, he who talked of forbidding them even to make a nail for a horseshoe? Wisdom spoke, albeit in a crabbed way, by the mouth of Dean Tucker, on whose mind. Tory as he was, the truth had dawned that colonial dependencies were of no real use commercially, inasmuch as you might trade with a colony just as well when it was independent, and of less than no use politically when they were in a chronic state of smothered sedition and refused to contribute to the defence of the Empire. The Dean advised, if the colonies persisted in their refusal, to bid them begone in peace, an invitation which at that time they would almost certainly have declined. But the voice of wisdom was not recognized even by the philosophic Burke. ⟨On the other hand Burke was surely right in rejecting the plan countenanced by Adam Smith of colonial representation in the Imperial Parliament. The difficulty of distance would have been very great, that of the appointment of representatives still greater, especially as the House of Commons was then constituted; that of a total want of community of interest between states on opposite sides of the Atlantic would have been the greatest of all. The plan of a federal union between the American colonies and Great Britain floated as some think before the mind of Chatham. Such a union might have lived with Chatham; with Chatham it would have died.

At the same time we must recognize the natural sentiment of empire. When Chatham speaks with pride of that " ancient and most noble monarchy " which his genius had raised to the height of glory, and with anguish of its possible dismemberment, his emotion is surely not less generous than any that swelled the bosom of Samuel or

John Adams, Patrick Henry, or Thomas Paine. It may
even be said that the determination of George III to hold
the colonies at whatever cost of blood and treasure, at
whatever risk to his crown, was more complimentary to
them, if it was less kind, than the proposal of Dean Tucker
at once to show them the door. This controversy to
Americans is dead. For England it will retain something
of a living interest so long as the tie of colonial dependence, though attenuated, continues to exist with difficulties and liabilities reduced yet not annulled.

⟨That the cause of the revolt was not general oppression
of the colonies by the mother country seems clear. We
have seen that when a governor of New York charged his
assembly with a tendency to independence, the assembly
responded by a vehement protestation of attachment to
the government under which they lived. Franklin declared that having travelled over the whole country and
kept company with people of all sorts he had never heard
from any person, drunk or sober, the expression of a wish
for separation or a hint that such a thing could be advan-
tageous to America⟩ John Adams said as late as March,
1775, of the people of Massachusetts itself, "that there
are any that hunt after independence is the greatest slander on the province." ⟨Jefferson averred that before the
Declaration of Independence he had never heard a whisper
of disposition to separate from Great Britain. Washington said in October, 1774, "I am well satisfied that no
such thing as independence is desired by any thinking
man in all North America; on the contrary that it is the
ardent wish of the warmest advocates for liberty that
peace and tranquillity on constitutional grounds will be
restored, and the horrors of civil discord prevented."⟩

⟨The New York Congress, in an address to Washington
after his assumption of the command, declared that the
fondest wish of every American soul was an accommodation with the mother country; and Washington in his
reply recognized the re-establishment of peace and harmony between the mother country and the colonies as
the ultimate object of his undertaking.⟩ New Hampshire,
Pennsylvania, Virginia, South Carolina, New Jersey, spoke
in the same strain as New York. Massachusetts, the very
hotbed of revolution, in her address to the king, spoke of
the restoration of union and harmony between Great
Britain and her colonies as indispensable and necessary
to the welfare and happiness of both. John Adams was
warned by his associates in the movement at Philadelphia
that if he uttered the word independence he was undone,
for the idea was as unpopular in Pennsylvania and in all
the middle and southern states as the Stamp Act itself.
He confesses that when he broached the idea he was
avoided as a man infected with leprosy. Even years after
he said, " For my own part there was not a moment
during the revolution when I would not have given all
I possessed for a restoration to the state of things that
existed before the contest began, provided we could have
a sufficient security for its continuance." If some of these
professions were hollow, that only proves the strength of
the general feeling which demanded the tribute. Did the
authors of the revolution aim at independence, or did
they not? If they did not, they could hardly have been
groaning under systematic oppression; nothing less than
which, moderate men would say, can justify revolution
and civil war. If they did, the British government apparently may claim to be absolved so far as they are

concerned, since what they sought was a thing which by
their own showing the vast majority of their own people
abhorred, as well as a thing which by its recognized duty
the British government was bound to refuse. In fact the
panegyrical historians stand not for two pages on the
same foot; in one page they applaud the patriot for aim-
ing at independence, in the next they represent constitutional redress as his sole aim.

⟨ Separation, again be it said, was inevitable. It was too
likely that, the vision of statesmanship being clouded as
it was respecting the relation of colonies to the mother
country, the separation would be angry and violent.⟩ Still
it might conceivably have been amicable, and that dark
page might possibly have been torn from the book of
destiny. Woe, we must say, to them by whom the offence came and through whose immediate agency, culpable in itself, the two great families of our race were
made and to a deplorable extent have remained enemies
instead of being friends, brethren, and fellow-workers in
the advancement of their common civilization. Woe to
the arbitrary and bigoted king whose best excuse is that
he had not made himself a ruler instead of being what
nature intended him to be, a ploughman. Woe to Grenville, who though not wicked or really bent on depriving
the colonies of their rights, but on the contrary most
anxious after his fashion to promote their interests, was
narrow, pedantic, overbearing, possessed with extravagant
ideas of the authority of Parliament, and unstatesmanlike
enough to insist on doing because it was technically lawful that which the sagacity of Walpole had on the ground
of practical expediency refused to do. Woe above all to

Charles Townshend, who, with his vain brilliancy and his
champagne speeches, repeated in the face of recent and decisive experience the perilous experiment and recklessly
renewed the quarrel. Woe to Lord North, and all the
more because in stooping to do the will of the king he
was sinning against the light of good nature and good
sense in himself. Woe even to Mansfield, whose supremely
legal intellect too ably upheld the letter of the law against
policy and the right. Woe to the Parliament — a parliament be it ever remembered of rotten boroughs and of
nominees not of the nation — which carelessly or inso-
lently supported the evil resolution of the ministry and
the court. Woe to the Tory squires who shouted for the
war, to the Tory parsons who preached for it, and to the
Tory bishops who voted for it in the House of Lords.
Woe to the pamphleteers of prerogative, such as Johnson,
whose vituperative violence added fuel to the flame. But
woe also to the agitators at Boston, who, with the design
of independence unavowed and of which they themselves
were perhaps but half conscious, did their utmost to push
the quarrel to extremity and to quench the hope of
reconciliation. Woe to the preachers of Boston, who
whether from an exaggerated dread of prelacy or to win
the favour of the people made themselves the trumpeters
of discord and perverted the gospel into a message of
civil war. Woe to contraband traders if there were any,
who sought in fratricidal strife relief from trade restrictions; to debtors if there were any, who sought in it a
sponge for debt. Woe to all on either side who under
the influence of passion, interest, or selfish ambition
fomented the quarrel which rent asunder the English
race.

⟨Of the fomenters of the quarrel in New England the chief was Samuel Adams, who, we can scarcely doubt, whatever might be his professions, had set his heart on the achievement of independence; had been laying his plans and enlisting his associates, such as the wealthy Hancock and the impetuous Otis, for that purpose; had welcomed rather than dreaded the dispute, and preferred the mortal issue to a reconciliation.⟩ This man had failed in business as a maltster and as a tax collector, but he had succeeded as a political agitator and has found a shrine in American history as a patriot saint. Though an enthusiast, he was not wanting in the astuteness of the politician. The latest of his American biographers cannot help surmising that his Puritan conscience must have felt a twinge when in the very time at which he had devoted himself body and soul to breaking the link that bound America to England, he was coining for this or that body phrases full of reverence for the king and rejecting the thought of independence. He had a paternal feud with Hutchinson, afterwards Governor of Massachusetts, a man whose reputation long lay buried under patriot vituperation, but who is now admitted by fair-minded writers to have been himself a patriot, taking the line opposite to that of Samuel Adams, and seeking to the utmost of his power peace with justice.

⟨The chief fomenter of the quarrel in the South, not less glorified than Samuel Adams, was Patrick Henry.⟩ This man also had tried various ways of earning a livelihood, and had failed in all. He was a bankrupt at twenty-three, and lounged in thriftless idleness, till he found that though he could not live by industry, he could live by his eloquent tongue. The circle in which as a Virginian

not of the highest class he formed his statesmanship is
described by an American biographer as "having comprised an occasional clergyman, pedagogue, or legislator;
small planters, and small traders; sportsmen, loafers,
slaves and the drivers of slaves, and more than all this the
bucolic sons of old Virginia, the good-natured, illiterate,
thriftless Caucasian consumers of tobacco and whiskey,
who cordially consenting that all the hard work should be
done by the children of Ham, were thus left free to com-
mune together in endless debate in the tavern porch, or
on the shady side of the country store." In Virginia
admission to the legal profession might be gained without
laborious study of the law. Henry's first exploit as a
barrister was a successful defence of the spoliation of the
clergy, an unpopular order, by an appeal to public passion
against legal right. Civil discord brought him at once
1765. to the front. His famous speech against the tyranny of
George III is often recited:— "Is life so dear, or peace
so sweet, as to be purchased at the price of chains and
slavery? Forbid it, Almighty God. I know not what
course others may take, but as for me, give me liberty
or give me death." When he said, "Is life so dear, or
peace so sweet, as to be purchased at the price of chains
and slavery," he stood, as an eyewitness has told us, in the
attitude of a condemned galley slave, loaded with fetters,
awaiting his doom; his form was bowed, his wrists were
crossed, his manacles were almost visible as he stood like
an embodiment of helplessness and agony. After a
solemn pause he raised his eyes and chained hands
towards heaven, and prayed in words and tones that
thrilled every heart, "Forbid it, Almighty God." Men-
tally struggling with the tyranny, he looked, the same

witness tells us, like "Laocoon in a death struggle with
the coiling serpents." "The sound of his voice was like
that of a Spartan pæan on the field of Platæa, and as each
syllable of the word 'Liberty' echoed through the building his fetters were shivered, his arms were pulled apart,
and the links of his chain were scattered to the winds.
He stood like a Roman Senator defying Cæsar, while the
unconquerable spirit of Cato of Utica flashed from every
feature, and he closed the grand appeal with the solemn
words, 'Or give me death,' which sounded with the awful
cadence of a hero's dirge, fearless of death, and victorious
in death ; and he suited the action to the word by a blow
upon the left breast with the right hand, which seemed to
drive the dagger to the patriot's heart."

It is no wonder that Patrick Henry could so vividly
portray to his audience the attitude of a slave. From the
beginning to the end of his life he was a slaveholder, he
bought slaves, he sold slaves, and by his will, with his
cattle, he bequeathed slaves. A eulogist says of him that
he could buy or sell a horse or a negro as well as anybody.
That he was in some degree conscious of the inconsistency does not alter the fact. Other patriot orators besides Patrick Henry, when they lavished the terms slave
and slavery in their revolutionary harangues, might have
reflected that they had only to look round them in order
to see what real slaves and slavery were.

Massachusetts, where the fire broke out, was in a specially
inflammable state. John Adams in a paper embodied in
his diary describes the multitude of taverns swarming with
busy politicians, who he says were more in number than
the people who attended to their own business. The
constitutional sensitiveness and contentiousness called

forth by the dispute about the Stamp Act had upon the
repeal of that act calmed down but had not died out.   By
this time the legal profession was fully fledged. Lawyers
had taken the lead in political life and they carried into
it the spirit of litigation.   A great many law suits were
going on.   Even the discourses on polemical theology
which the people constantly heard from the pulpit would
tend to make them argumentative and contentious.   Patriotism of the classical type was fashionable in England,
and the fashion had spread to the colony.   Brutus and
Cassius were the model patriots of the hour : rhetoric was
always conjuring with their names.   Wilkesbarre, the
name of a town in Pennsylvania, is a quaint memorial of
the settlers' reverence for those two great tribunes of the
people, Wilkes and Barré, on the moral glories of the first
of whom it is needless to dwell ; while the second, the
author of a famous stroke of rhetoric against the false
claim of the mother country to colonial gratitude, made
his way through a career of fiery patriotism to the Clerk-
ship of the Pells, one of the fattest sinecures of corruption.
The Puritan clergy were angered by the concession of
legal toleration to Roman Catholicism in Quebec and were
always in dread of prelatic invasion.   There was a daily
source of irritation in the tightened pressure of commercial
restrictions and the demeanour of royal officers engaged in
enforcing them.   The disputes about fixed salaries for
governors and other crown officers were also in an angry
state.   The presence of a soldiery, alien to a city of
Puritan merchants like Boston, filled up the measure of
exasperation, for such a garrison was sure to bear itself
haughtily towards the people.
   When fortune frowns everything goes wrong.   Of all

the disasters the greatest was the eclipse of Chatham which
left the political firmament to Townshend's malignant star.
Next to this was the social catastrophe of Franklin, the one
man who being revered in England as well as in America
might have mediated with some chance of success, and
to whose advice George Grenville had in fact resorted.
The private letters of Governor Hutchinson were betrayed 1773
into his hands. He must have known and he did know
that they had been stolen, or at least improperly obtained,
and that he had no right to use them. When he sent
them to Boston under the formal seal of confidence, he can
hardly have failed to surmise that by the men to whom he
sent them that seal would be broken. His plea that he
acted in the interest of peace, hoping to convince his fellow colonists that evil counsels came not from England
but from their own quarter, cannot be seriously enter-
tained. Its hollowness confirms his condemnation. That
he believed himself to be doing good may be admitted, it
cannot be admitted that he believed himself to be doing
right. English gentlemen were licentious and some of
them were politically corrupt, but they had a keen sense
of social honour. To complete the disaster, the duty of
dealing with the case fell not to the lot of a man of character and dignity but of Wedderburn, a low adventurer,
branded at his death by the king himself as the greatest
scoundrel in the realm, whose brutalities made of Franklin
a deadly foe. Another piece of ill luck was the Opposition
leadership of Fox, a debauchee in politics as in private life,
whose reckless violence and revolting displays of sympathy
with the Americans even when they had France for an ally,
could only confirm the obstinacy of the king and his ministers and identify their cause in the eyes of the nation

with that of the honour of the country. Sir Gilbert Elliot
was probably right in saying that North might have fallen
long before if he had not been propped by the unpatriotic
behaviour of Fox.   Burke, as Fox's partner, hardly escapes
a share of the same censure.   Fox behaved in the same
way at the outbreak of the French Revolution.

⟨The restrictions upon colonial trade and manufactures
were a cause for the most reasonable discontent⟩ The
restrictions on trade might be excused by the dominant
fallacies of a protectionist era and palliated by the commercial privileges and bounties which the colonies enjoyed.
Those on manufactures were without palliation or excuse,
imposed solely in the interest of the selfish manufacturer
at home. ⟨These grievances, if redress had been obstinately
refused, would have justified revolt.   But they are not put
forward as a ground of revolt in the American Declaration
of Independence.   The Stamp Act having been repealed,
all the duties except that on tea having been removed, and
a pledge against their re-imposition having been given, the
tea duty was the sole remaining issue.   Was this a sufficient reason for overthrowing a government under which
all admitted that general liberty was enjoyed, for shatter-
ing an empire of the greatness of which all professed to be
proud, and for bringing on a country the havoc, moral as
well as material, of civil war?⟩ It is true that in the case
of the tea duty, as in that of Hampden's assessment to ship
money, what was to be considered was the principle, not
the amount.   But ship money was not merely a wrongful
impost, it was the entering wedge of unparliamentary taxation destined to furnish the means of a system of government in church and state fatal to the political liberties and
to the spiritual life of the nation.   Not Grenville, not even

Townshend, not George III himself had conceived any such design; though the arbitrary tendencies of the king at least were soon called forth by the conflict. ⟨There seems to be no reason for believing that either Grenville's or Townshend's policy was originally inspired by the king.⟩ Nor was there ever a man less likely to play Strafford than Lord North.⟨ Would it not have been right before drawing the fratricidal sword to be sure that no hope of peaceful redress was left? ⟩Why should not the tea duty have been repealed as the other duties and the Stamp Act had been repealed? ⟩Its retention was understood in America to have been carried in the cabinet by a bare majority. A circular from the Home Secretary assured the colonies that the duties would not be re-imposed, and if the ground assigned was that a mere commercial expediency and not that of constitutional principle, the assurance was not the less practically valid. Colonial right had powerful advocates in Parliament. It had Rockingham with Burke at his side. It had Chatham whenever he should emerge from the cloud. British merchants had thronged the lobbies of the House of Commons on the night of the repeal of the Stamp Act and hailed Conway, who moved the repeal, as a delivering angel. ⟨But what those who managed the populace of Boston at heart desired was not constitutional redress, it was independence.⟩ On the passing of the Stamp Act, among other excesses the Stamp Office at Boston was levelled, the house of the stamp distributor was wrecked, and he was compelled by the mob to resign his office and to swear beneath the tree upon which his effigy was hanged never to resume his post: the houses of two officials connected with the Admiralty Court of the Custom House were rifled, the records of the Admiralty

Court burnt; the mansion of Lieutenant Governor Hutchinson was destroyed, his plate, his furniture, his pictures,
and his fine library were plundered and burnt, and the
owner scarcely escaped with his life.〈On the passing of
the tea duty outrage was renewed.〉 The custom house
officers were assailed by parties armed with bludgeons and
compelled to fly, officers were tarred and feathered, commissioners were hung in effigy. The "Tories," as the
friends of government were nicknamed, were everywhere
pursued with insult by the Patriot party who borrowed
from the party of the English Revolution the honoured
name of Whigs. 〈A reign of terror was directed against all
the ministers of the law; merchants who had imported
goods from England were compelled by the populace to
give them up to be destroyed or to   re-shipped. One
who sold English goods was stoned through the streets.
Sedition was preached from the popular pulpit. Under
extraordinary provocation a party of soldiers fired, killing
five rioters and wounding six. This was the "Boston
Massacre," celebrated by mourning services in chapels
hung with crape. Praise is claimed for the citizens because
they forbore to hang the soldiers. But had they hanged a
soldier, it was clear that to avenge his blood the last powder of the empire must have been burned; and John
Adams showed not less of policy than of chivalry in
appearing for the defence. Presently a revenue cutter
was fired, after shooting and badly wounding the com-
1773. mander.- At last came the "Boston Tea Party" in which
a cargo of tea, the property of merchants trading under
the imperial flag, was thrown into the bay. A government
thus bearded and insulted has its choice between abdication and repression. In this case abdication would have

been the wiser course, but repression was the more natural. Americans at the present day would not applaud violence as their historians applaud the "Boston Tea Party." If the temper of the English Tory was tyrannical, neither that of the New England Puritan nor that of the Virginian slaveholder was mild.

In what order and degree the various causes of the catastrophe for which the government or the mother country was responsible — resentment at illegal taxation, soreness under commercial restraints, anger aroused by violent measures of repression, the galling presence of an unwelcome soldiery, and imperial arrogance — may have combined with republican aspiration on the part of colonial leaders and the spread of a revolutionary spirit, it is impossible to say. All that can be said is that the catastrophe was sure to come and sure to be disastrous. The measures of repression, in any view, deserve the censure which has been passed on them. They were passionate, indiscriminate, and insulting; bolts of blind wrath launched across the Atlantic by men imperfectly informed as to the situation and ignorant of the character of the people, as transoceanic rulers must always be. By closing the port of Boston scores of traders faithful to the government were struck. By the abrogation of the charter of Massachusetts every colony was made to feel its chartered rights imperilled. Worst of all was the revival 1774 of a law passed in the hateful reign of Henry VIII, under which subjects accused of treason anywhere could be transported to England for trial. This not only threatened all colonists with the loss of safeguards for personal liberty but outraged their self-respect. Shoot people if you must, but do not hurt their feelings. If there was to be repression at all, troops enough should have been sent, and the law should have been enforced against its violators at Boston without inflicting penalties on the innocent or menacing colonial liberties in general. However, no repression could have been final; its temporary success would have been the beginning not the end of woes.

In entering on his attempt at coercion the King was assured that there was a strong party in the colonies on his side. There was without doubt a party opposed to revolution, and at the outset it included a large portion of the wealth and intelligence and probably a large majority of the entire people. But the adherence of much of it to the crown was rather passive than enthusiastic, the commercial Quaker of Philadelphia desiring not to fight on either side but to be at peace. It was unorganized, and when the royal governors had been expelled it was without leaders. Still in the struggle which ensued as many as twenty-five thousand loyalists at the lowest computation, according to the best authority, were in arms for the crown, a number sufficient to give the conflict the character of a civil war between the parties in America as well as between the British and American sections of the Anglo-Saxon race. By the unwise violence of the king's ministers, and afterwards by the blunders of his commanders and the excesses of his mercenary troops, the numbers of his party were much reduced. The military obstacles were great. The colonies were three thousand miles off, which in those days made supply, communication, and the direction of operations from a centre very difficult. They extended from north to south along nine hundred miles of country, woody for the most part and tangled, unfavourable to regulars, favourable to a sharp-shooting militia.

Those who said that the American militia would not stand
before regulars had ground for what they said. In the
open field the regulars won, generally with ease, but most
of the fighting was not in open field, it was in wooded
country, and the Americans were excellent marksmen.
The king had no general. Wolfe and Clive were gone,
Moore was a boy, Wellington a child, and India claimed
Eyre Coote. Cornwallis was energetic and enterprising,
he reaped laurels afterwards in India. Had he or Sir
Guy Carleton commanded in chief there might have been
a different tale to tell. Howe, who did command in chief,
though brave was torpid; probably he was not only torpid
but half-hearted. As a member of parliament he had
pledged himself to his constituents not to fight against
the Americans, and he must have been fettered by that
pledge. He was inspired also, it may be surmised, with
the secret misgivings of North, whose conscience was all
the time accusing him, and who sent forth his commander
with a sword in one hand and the olive branch in the
other, to the detriment alike of the olive branch and the
sword. Nor had the king a war minister. The place of
Chatham was filled by the narrow mind and bad temper
of Lord George Germaine. Without a general or a war
minister, the king was also without an army. Unable to
raise soldiers enough in England he had to buy Hessians,
who, though good troops, well-commanded, and not devoid
of a certain sympathy with the cause of a king against
rebels, were foreigners torn by sordid masters from their
homes, and, as aliens and hirelings, hateful to the people
whose homes they were sent to destroy. Such a necessity,
ignominious in any war, worse than ignominious in a war
with his own subjects, ought to have shown him that

though the pride of the nation might be stung by Boston-
ian insult and its pugnacity aroused, the object for which
he fought was not truly national nor was the heart of the
nation with him. ⟨Never, not even under Newcastle, did
England make a worse show in the field.⟩⟨The court had
also to contend with an opposition in parliament, weak
at first in numbers but sure to be swelled by every reverse,
and embittered enough by faction to strike at the ministry
even through the honour of the country.⟩⟨It might have
been known, too, that France and the other European
enemies of England were watching the growing trouble
with eager eyes.⟩ Yet events proved that success in the
war, though unlikely, was not impossible. ⟨That which
was impossible was to continue to rule thirteen British
communities subjugated by arms on the other side of the
Atlantic.⟩ The forces of one part of the empire would
have been forever expended in holding down the other
part. In this, to say nothing of the colonists, the people
of Great Britain would never have acquiesced. Had the
colonies been really dependencies and the king absolute
he might, like a Spanish or French despot, have sent out
a viceroy with sufficient power. But the colonies being
free and British government having become parliamentary, dominion was at an end. √

⟨War evidently impending, the colonies obeyed a manifest necessity in federating for the purposes of mutual
defence.⟩ Thus the American Federation was born in the
same way as the Achaean League, the Swiss Bund, and the
United Netherlands. ⟨The powers which provincial jealousy would allow the Congress under the articles of confederation were insufficient even for the limited object,
since Congress had no authority itself to levy men or

1774
to
1775.

impose taxes, but could only address requisitions to the several colonies without the means of enforcement. The voting was by states, and the assent of nine states was required, so that five states could paralyze action. The Federation in fact was little more than a league. Congress, however, assumed in a feeble way the character of a national government. It raised a continental army with officers bearing its commission and wearing its uniform of blue and buff. In time it unfurled its flag, the stars and stripes, the harbinger of the tricolour. Advice was given by it to the several colonies to erect themselves into states on a republican footing. This advice they easily followed. Already their constitutions were essentially republican, already their political spirit was essentially republican, and they had only, where it was needed, to strike off the monarchical apex of the structure and substitute an elective governor for the governor sent out by the crown. In a hall at Philadelphia, rendered sacred to all American hearts by the act, was signed a declaration of independence; it was signed with sorrow and reluctance at the time even by some of those who had been foremost in the constitutional fray, though descent from one of those who subscribed it is now a title of nobility. Colonial resolution had been screwed to the sticking point by Tom Paine, the stormy petrel of three countries, with his pamphlet "Common Sense," issued in the nick of time, coarsely but forcibly written and well spiced with rhetoric about the "royal brute." The Declaration of Independence, one of the 1776. most famous documents in the muniment room of history, bespeaks the hand of the philosophic Jefferson. It opens with sweeping aphorisms about the natural rights of man at which political science now smiles, and which, as Amer-

ican abolitionists did not fail to point out at a later day,
might seem strange when framed for slave-holding communities by a publicist who himself held slaves. It pro-
ceeds to recount in a highly rhetorical strain all the offensive acts of George III and his government, designating
them as "a long train of abuses and usurpations pursuing
invariably the same object and evincing a design to reduce
the colonists under absolute despotism" and asserting that
"they all had as their direct object the establishment of an
absolute tyranny" — propositions which history cannot
accept. It blinks the fact that many of the acts, styled
steps of usurpation, were measures of repression which
however unwise or excessive had been provoked by popular outrage. It speaks of the patient sufferings of colonists
who had sacked the houses and maltreated the persons of
the king's officers, burnt his revenue cutter, and flung the
goods of merchants trading under his flag into the sea.
One count in the indictment is the Act declaring the British Parliament invested with power to legislate for the colonies in all cases. Yet in this Act, framed by Rockingham
and Burke as a pendant to the repeal of the Stamp Act
the colonists had certainly acquiesced. The archives of
English Puritanism it seems had been searched for a precedent, and the precedent adopted was probably the Grand
Remonstrance. But the Grand Remonstrance was founded
on fact, since the violent acts of Charles I, Strafford, and
Laud were really steps in the execution of a plan for the
establishment of arbitrary government. The author of the
Declaration of Independence proposed to insert a clause
denouncing George III as responsible for the slave trade,
and accusing him of "thereby waging cruel war against
human nature itself, violating its most sacred rights of life

and liberty in the persons of a distant people who never offended him, captivating them and carrying them into slavery in another hemisphere, or to more miserable death in the transportation thither." "This piratical warfare," so ran the clause, "the opprobrium of Infidel Powers, is the warfare of the Christian King of Great Britain." But this was too much not only for the slave-owners of Virginia but for the slave-traders of New England. Had George III framed the Virginian or Carolinian slave codes? Such checks as had been put by Virginia or as she had proposed to put on the importation of slaves are admitted by candid American historians to have had not a moral but an economical motive. (Jefferson himself, though an opponent and doubtless a sincere opponent of slavery, never emancipated his own slaves.)

The war opened at Boston, where General Gage, now its military governor, lay with a small army of occupation and repression, and it opened in a way ominous of the final result and significant of the means by which the result was to be brought about. (Gage sent out a detach- April 19, 1775. ment to seize rebel stores at Lexington. The militia of the country, called Minute Men because they were always to be in readiness, excellent sharp-shooters, swarmed out, surrounded the detachment, and forced it to fall back with loss on Boston.) The next engagement was more ominous still. The patriots occupied Breed's Hill (not Bunker's June 17, 1775 Hill, but an adjoining height), which commanded Boston, and fortified it with a redoubt and breastwork.) It seems that they might have been dislodged by manœuvring. But the royal commander, in his pipe-clay pedantry and pride, chose to lead his men on a hot summer's day with heavy knapsacks on their backs up the front of the hill against the breastwork. ⟨Thrice they mounted in face of the fire of the sharp-shooters, who from under cover securely shot them down. The third charge took the position, and a captured gun stands on the citadel of Quebec as the trophy and proof of royalist victory; but the loss had been immense and the moral advantage was with the insurgents.⟩ Gage now gave place to Howe, and Howe found himself surrounded in Boston by swarms of Minute Men who were presently under the command of a good

1775. general. ⟨The appointment of Washington as commander-in-chief of the Continental forces was a politic compliment to Virginia, but it was also by far the best appointment that could be made. Washington when a stripling had made a wonderful mark, not only as a soldier in border war against the Indians, but as a negotiator; while in Braddock's disaster he had shown a fortitude and steadfastness in defeat which were to be inestimable in his present place.⟩ Having suffered in military grade and in feeling so as to be led to resign his position by the exclusive precedence of the royal officers, he would not be unwilling to measure swords with them in the field. ⟨He found an army undisciplined, impatient of control, ill-equipped, unprovided with ammunition. But he managed to hold this army together, to present a front which to his surprise his unenterprising enemy respected, and at last on a dark night to seize and fortify an eminence which commanded the place and rendered it no longer

March tenable. Howe evacuated Boston, where redcoats never
1776. appeared more.⟩

In leaving Boston the royal fleet took with it, according to Mr. Sabine, eleven hundred loyalists, including women and children, the first instalment of a great loyalist migra-

tion. The number included, of members of the Council
and officials, one hundred and two ; of clergymen, eighteen ;
of inhabitants of country towns, one hundred and five ; of
merchants and other residents in Boston, two hundred
and thirteen ; of farmers, mechanics, and traders, three
hundred and eighty-two. The case of these people is not
to be settled, nor is the witness which they bore to their
cause to be annulled, by designating them as Tories. Was
it just that they should be outlawed, pillaged, driven from
their homes, maltreated, condemned to the death of traitors by men who had but yesterday been conspirators, out-
wardly professing allegiance to the government to which
the loyalists adhered, and were still without any recognized
government of their own? Were not the loyalists Americans, and did not their wrongs exceed any of those done
to Americans by the king? On the eve of the civil war
in England, Sir William Waller the Parliamentarian,
wrote to Sir Ralph Hopton the Royalist: " My affections
to you are so unchangeable that hostility itself cannot
violate my friendship to your person, but I must be true
to the cause wherein I serve. The old limitation of *usque
ad aras* holds still. . . . The great God, who is the searcher
of my heart, knows with what reluctance I go upon this
service, and with what perfect hatred I look upon war
without an enemy. But I look upon it as *opus domini*,
and that is enough to silence all passion in me. The God
of Peace in His good time send us peace, and in the meantime fit us to receive it! We are both on the stage and
we must act the parts that are assigned us in this tragedy.
Let us do it in a way of honour, and without personal
animosities." Such was the spirit of men mournfully
obeying in a great cause the inevitable call of civil war.

There was little of it on either side in the American Revolution.

⟨The loyalists retaliated when they could; where they were strong they became the aggressors, and as their party included, with some of the chiefs of society, many of the lowest and wildest class, they rivalled and probably outvied their opponents in atrocity. The civil strife grew more murderous and viler as it went on.⟩ "The animosities between Whigs and Tories," wrote the worthy American General Greene, "render their situation truly deplorable. The Whigs seem determined to extirpate the Tories and the Tories the Whigs. Some thousands have fallen in this way in this quarter and the evil rages with more violence than ever. If a stop cannot be put to the massacres, the country will be depopulated in a few months, as neither Whig nor Tory can win." "The people of the South," says Chief Justice Marshall, "felt all the miseries which are inflicted by war in its most savage form.⟨ Being almost equally divided between the two contending parties, reciprocal injuries had gradually sharpened their resentment against each other and had armed neighbour against neighbour until it had become a war of extermination.⟩ As the parties alternately triumphed, opportunity was alternately given for the exercise of their vindictive passions." Even in the Wars of the Roses, amidst the mutual butcheries of the aristocratic factions the common people had been spared and had spared each other. Nor were the royal officers now behind in cruelty. They bombarded seaboard towns, and in their executions of relapsed rebels violated the humanities if not the laws of ordinary war. Between rebellion and belligerency there is a doubtful period during which the agents of government think themselves licensed to give way to their passions under the name of crushing treason. Among the loyalists of the baser sort some exercised brigandage in the name of the crown. ⟨ The devilry was completed by the introduction of Indians, whose ferocity no commander could restrain, though Carleton and Burgoyne did their best⟩ They had been enlisted first by the colonists, so that Chatham's tremendous invective was misplaced saving as such a policy might be more disgraceful to a government than to rebels. The horrors of Wyoming, painted both in verse and prose, were the work of Indians led on by a band of Tories who had themselves been driven from their homes.

John Adams has given us an account of the doings at Philadelphia while the politicians were hatching the revolution. In the evening at Mr. Mifflin's there was "an elegant supper and we drank sentiments till eleven o'clock. Lee and Harrison were very high. Lee had dined with Mr. Dickenson and drank Burgundy the whole afternoon." From nine in the morning till three in the afternoon the delegates attended to business, "then they adjourned and went to dine with some of the nobles of Pennsylvania at four o'clock, and feasted upon ten thousand delicacies, and sat drinking Madeira, Claret, or Burgundy till six or seven, and then went home fatigued to death with business, company, and care." It is a pity that in such cases there cannot mingle with the flavour of the Claret and Burgundy a foretaste of the bitterness of civil war. But the politicians who quaff the wine too seldom drink of the other cup.

⟨Meantime the colonists had grasped at Canada, which they thought would fall into their arms. Among the charges originally levelled by New England against the

king's government was that of having by the Quebec Act
established in Canada Roman Catholicism, which New
England stigmatized as a religion that had "drenched
Great Britain in blood and disseminated impiety, bigotry,
persecution, murder, and rebellion through every part of
the world." Afterwards the colonists, desiring to draw
Canada into their league, addressed her in a different
strain, setting forth how under the blessed influence of
republican liberty Roman Catholicism and Protestantism
might dwell together in the sweetest peace. But the
Canadian clergy, having both manifestoes before them,
believed in the genuineness of the first, which was more
in accordance with the practice and even with the laws of
Massachusetts. They advised their people to adhere to
Great Britain or at least to be neutral, and their influence
was seconded by the conduct of Sir Guy Carleton, a wise,
brave, and popular governor. The Americans finding
honeyed words unavailing, invaded Canada and took Montreal, but they were repulsed in a daring attack to storm
Quebec in which their general, Montgomery, fell and
Canada was lost to the Union.

Dec. 1775.

From Boston the scene of war shifted to New York,
where royalism was strong, and neutrality still stronger,
especially in the commercial class, while by occupying that
position the confederacy might be cut in two. Washington
had here concentrated his forces and fortified himself. On
Long Island patriotism for the first time met discipline in
the open field and was driven in flight before it. Had
Howe followed up his victory there probably would have
been an end of the Continental army, whatever local
resistance might have survived. But Howe, there can be
little doubt, was wavering as well as lethargic and instead

Aug. 1776.

of pressing his enemy he went to luncheon. New York
was taken. Some of the patriots had proposed to burn it,
"since," as General Greene said, "two-thirds of the property of the city and suburbs belonged to the Tories." It
was fired, but was saved by the captors and remained the
centre of royal operations to the end of the war. Howe's
subsequent conduct seems to have been marked with a
sluggishness and irresolution which the energy of his
lieutenant, Cornwallis, could not redeem. Washington
was allowed to pluck victory and reputation out of the
jaws of defeat by surprising two battalions of Hessians
who were sleeping off their Christmas debauch at Trenton,
and overwhelming after a masterly movement two isolated
regiments at Princeton. All this restored the confidence
of the revolutionists and raised their military character in
Europe, notably in France, while the excesses of Howe's
mercenaries turned the Jerseys back from royalism to revolution. At last Howe moved, and having defeated Wash- Sept.
ington at the battle of the Brandywine entered Philadel- 1777.
phia, the capital of the confederacy, where he was well
received and passed a highly festive winter. Washington
attempted a surprise but was again defeated, though not
with ease, at the battle of Germantown. Notwithstanding
Washington's reverses, with him remained the honours of
the campaign.

Howe, feeling, probably, that in spite of his successes
in the field the attempt to subdue the colonists was a failure, and having achieved as little by diplomatic offers of
reconciliation as by force, went home and was succeeded
by Sir Henry Clinton. Washington had taken up his
quarters for the winter near his enemy, in an unassailable
position among the hills at Valley Forge. This winter at 1778.

Valley Forge is the most heroic episode of the revolution. Washington's men, more the men of Washington than the men of the revolution or the Congress, were left without meat for days together, sometimes without bread; without blankets, so that they had to sit up by their camp-fires to keep themselves warm; and without sho█████ ██at the traces of their march over the sn██ ████ere ma██████ ██h blood. Yet they showed of what race they were by holding together and making their foe beware of them. During the winter they went through a course of drill under Steuben, a Prussian, and other foreign officers, which put them on a level with the king's soldiers, their natural qualities being the same.

Washington was to the confederacy all in all. Without him it would have been ten times lost, and the names of the politicians who had drawn the country into the conflict would have gone down to posterity linked with defeat and shame. History has hardly a stronger case of an indispensable man. His form, like all other forms of the revolution, has no doubt been seen through a golden haze of panegyric. We can hardly number among the greatest captains a general who acted on so small a scale and who, though he was the soul of the war, never won a battle. In that respect Carlyle, who threatened "to take George down a peg or two," might have made good his threat. But he could not have stripped Washington of any part of his credit for patriotism, wisdom, and courage; for the union of enterprise with prudence; for integrity and truthfulness; for simple dignity of character; for tact and forbearance in dealing with men; above all for serene fortitude in the darkest hour of his cause and under trials from the perversity, insubordination, jealousy, and perfidy of those around him severer than any defeat.⟩ Some American writers seem anxious to prove that Washington's character is essentially different from that of an English gentleman. About this we need not dispute. The character of an English gentleman is certainly devoid of any traits that might be derived either from a plantation or from war with Indians in the backwoods. Yet an English gentleman sees in Washington his ideal as surely as he does not see it in Franklin, Samuel Adams, or Patrick Henry. It has been truly said that Washington and Wellington have much in common. Wellington contending with Spanish perversity and ministerial incompetence reminds us by his calmness and self-control of Washington contending with the folly and dishonesty of Congress and the fractiousness of the state militia. They write in the same even, passionless, and somewhat formal style, the expression of a mind always master of itself. In both of them there was, though under control, the strong temper which is almost inseparable from force. Wellington might be more of an aristocrat than Washington, less of a democrat he could hardly be. ⟨Washington insisted that his officers should be gentlemen, not men fit to be shoeblacks⟩ He drew a most undemocratic distinction between the officer and the private soldier. His notions about the private soldier are those of an old world disciplinarian. He says that the soldier should be satisfied to serve for his food, clothes, and pay, and complains that he cannot lay on the back of the insubordinate patriot more than one hundred lashes, holding that five hundred are not too many. The other army leaders, Gates and Lee, caballed against him and were abetted by politicians morbidly or perhaps selfishly jealous of military ascendancy. It appears

that both Samuel and John Adams, if they did not intrigue, were unfriendly to Washington and would willingly
have seen him superseded. Washington bore the attacks
on him magnanimously, never allowing his personal wrongs
to interfere with his duty nor ever thinking of abandoning
his post. ⟨Perhaps in the whole conflict the three noblest
things are the character of Washington, the behaviour of his
army at Valley Forge, and the devotion of the better class
of loyalists. On Washington's death the flags of the British fleet under Lord Bridport were half-masted. We owe
the American Hildreth thanks for recording the fact.⟩

⟨A plan had been formed by the British war office for
a movement from Canada down the valleys of the Mohawk
and the Hudson, so as to break the centre of the confederacy. Burgoyne, who seems to have been the originator
of the plan, was put in command. He had won some
distinction in war, but was more of a wit, a playwright,
and a social star than a captain. Down the Hudson and
Mohawk he came with six or seven thousand regulars,
British and German, some Canadian auxiliaries, and a
train of Indians. The royal general at New York was to
have moved out to meet him, but the despatch was not
sent in time because, as tradition has it, Lord George
Germaine had chosen to hurry off to his pleasures instead
of waiting till the clerks had done their work. Burgoyne
took a wrong course, lost himself in a tangled country,
found no Clinton to meet him, was deserted by his Canadians and Indians, and was surrounded by the local militia,
famous bush-fighters and riflemen, who poured out in
defence of their own states. Here was seen the strength
of the local resistance in contrast with the weakness of
the confederation. Hemmed in by swarms of sharp-

Sept.
1777.

shooters, whose number was four times his own, and unable to get open battle, Burgoyne was forced to surrender. This he did under a convention providing that he and his troops should be sent to England under parole not to serve against America. It occurred to Congress that the troops, though they could not be used against America, might be used in setting other troops free for that service. On pretexts utterly frivolous and disowned by the American commander Congress broke the convention, detained the troops, and against the laws of war tried to entice the men into its own service. It was a violation of public faith for which no real excuse has been offered. Nor did Congress stop here. It insisted that the sum which had been expended in provisions for the captured army in Continental paper should be repaid in gold three times the paper's worth, and this while it was treating the refusal of the paper as a crime. "Jay," ejaculated Gouverneur Morris thirty years afterwards, "what a set of d—d scoundrels we had in that second Congress!" "Yes," said Jay, "we had," and he knocked the ashes from his pipe. It seems that when Congress had sunk into impotence and discredit some of the best men left it to employ their energies in their own states, probably the best of all were in the field. From Gates and from Schuyler of New York, to whom Burgoyne surrendered, he and his troops received chivalrous treatment. When they got to Boston there was a change. Madame de Riedesel, the wife of the German general, complains that she was cruelly insulted by the Boston women. In her memoir we are told that the wife and young daughter of Captain Fenton, a royalist absentee, were stripped naked, tarred and feathered, and paraded through the city. The Americans on their side

Oct.
1777.

had too much reason to complain of the cruel treatment of prisoners at New York by royal commanders at New York who had no pity for those whom they still deemed rebels, or Tory officials made merciless by the rage of faction. Such is civil war. ⟨There is no test of the humanity of a nation so trying as civil war.⟩ We have to wait till a later period to see that the test might be borne.

⟨Clinton presently evacuated Philadelphia and fell back
1778. on New York, which remained in the king's hands to the last.⟩ On the march he fought a drawn battle with Washington at Monmouth Court House, in which the improved drill of Washington's soldiers showed its effect.   He took with him from Philadelphia three thousand loyalists who dared not fall into the hands of the Whigs. Of those who remained behind a number were condemned to death, but two Quakers only were hanged.

The Netherlands, when they rose against Spain and the Inquisition, had a cause terribly great and showed spirit as great as their cause. The cause in which the Americans rose against the imperial government was not so great if it was not largely rhetorical, and the amount of spirit which they showed was proportional. When from drinking patriotic toasts, declaiming against tyranny, tarring and feathering Tories, and hanging stamp collectors in effigy, it came to paying war contributions and facing the shot, enthusiasm declined. Of this Washington became sensible as soon as he had assumed the command. From the lines before Boston, 28th November, 1775, he writes : "Such a dearth of public spirit and such want of virtue, such stock-jobbing and fertility in all the low arts to obtain advantages of one kind or another, in this great change of military arrangement, I never saw before, and pray God's mercy that I may never be witness to again." This wail runs through his letters, growing more and more mournful to the end of the war, or at least till the arrival of French aid. From Valley Forge in 1778 he writes: " Men are naturally fond of peace, and there are symptoms that may authorize an opinion that the people of America are pretty generally weary of the present war. It is doubtful whether many of our friends might not incline to an accommodation on the grounds held out, or which may be, rather than persevere in a contest for independence." From Philadelphia, 30th December, 1778, he writes: " If I were called upon to draw a picture of the times and of men from what I have seen, heard and in part know, I should in one word say that idleness, dissipation, and extravagance seem to have laid fast hold of most of them ; that speculation, peculation, and an insatiable thirst for riches seem to have got the better of every other consideration, and almost of every order of men ; that party disputes and personal quarrels are the great business of the day ; while the momentous concerns of the empire, a great and accumulating debt, ruined finances, depreciated money, and want of credit which in its consequences is the want of everything, are but secondary considerations and postponed from day to day, from week to week, as if our affairs wore the most promising aspect." John Adams had oratorically decreed that the war should be violent and short, but oratory does not shorten war or make anything violent but passion. The eloquent opponents of the tea duty did not, like the opponent of ship-money, take the field. They were content with the part, to use a phrase adopted by Washington, of chimney corner heroes. If John Adams could

sigh as he said he did for things as they had been before
the war, the people were not likely to feel that the change
was worth much of their money or their blood. When
the war came their way they would readily turn out, and
fight well in their own sharp-shooting fashion in defence
of their own states, but they would not readily turn out
in the Continental cause even though the assembly of
Virginia might offer to any patriot who would take arms
to deliver the country from slavery three hundred acres of
land and a healthy sound negro. If they did turn out it
was for a fixed term, and at the end of that term they
insisted upon taking their departure, notwithstanding it
might be the eve of a battle, carrying with them their
arms and ammunition, not assuredly because they lacked
courage, but because they lacked zeal in the cause. ❮ "Soldiers absent themselves from their duty in numbers, stay-
ing at their homes, sometimes in the employment of their
officers; drawing pay, while they are working on their
own plantations or for hire.❯ The troops of Connecticut
at one time were mostly on furlough, and Washington
finds such a mercenary spirit pervading them that he could
not be surprised at any disaster. ❮Regiments are expected
in vain, harvest and a thousand other excuses being given
for delay. At a critical moment a militia is reduced
from six thousand to less than two thousand. It takes
all the exertion of the officers to induce a corps to stay
six weeks on a bounty of ten dollars. Washington's
army in short is always moulting; there is not time
to drill the men before they are gone, and discipline is
impossible because if it was enforced they would go.
Washington complains also of the want of patriotic feeling among the people.❯ The conduct of the Jerseys, he

says, " is most infamous ; instead of aiding him they are
making their submission as fast as they can.   Pennsylvanian militiamen, instead of responding to the summons of
the Council of Safety, exult at the approach of the enemy
and over the misfortunes of their own friends.   The disaffection of Pennsylvania is beyond conception.   The
people bring supplies as readily to the royal army as to
their own ; more readily in fact, since the royal army pays
not in paper but cash."   Officers appropriate the money
for the payment of the troops.   Cabals and intrigues
about appointments, jealousies between soldiers from different states, selfish interests of all kinds are stronger
than adherence to the cause.   There was the pride too,
though Washington does not mention it, of the Virginian
gentlemen who looked down on the New England trader
not less than the officers of the royal army had looked
down on those of the colonial militia.   All this goes far
towards justifying the king's judgment and that of his
informants as to the strength of the resistance and the
chances of the war.   (The army, Washington says, was
at one time losing more by desertion than it gained by
recruiting.) (Deserters, defaulters, and malingerers, of
whom there were also plenty, had every excuse that the
failure of the commissariat and the arsenals could give.)
(Two thousand men at one time were without firelocks,
and the supplies of food and clothing seem to have
been always most defective.) That his men should be
starving, shivering, and marking their marches over the
snow with their blood, while forestallers, regraters, and
monopolists are flourishing, stings Washington to the soul.
(The end of the dealings of Congress with the army was
that the army became a skeleton, and there was at last a

mutiny of the Pennsylvanian militia which was prevented
from being fatal only by the personal ascendancy of the
general. A sufficient force of regular troops, serving for
adequate pay and pensions, was Washington's constant
desire. Cromwell's insight taught him, after Edgehill,
that instead of men serving only for pay he must form
an army of men whose hearts were in the cause. Washington's insight after a few months of command taught
him that when enthusiasm had grown cold an army must
be formed of men serving for good pay. "When men,"
he says, "are irritated and passion inflamed they fly
hastily and cheerfully to arms; but after the first emotions
are over to expect the bulk of an army to be influenced by
anything but self-interest is to look for what never did
happen." Cromwell and Washington alike recognized
the supremacy of discipline. "To lean on the militia,"
says Washington, " is to lean on a broken reed. Being
familiar with the use of the musket they will fight under
cover, but they will not attack or stand in the open
field."

States refused to tax themselves and Congress had no
power to tax them. Its war budget was one of confisca-
tions, forced requisitions, and paper money. From the
printing press, its mint, issued ever increasing volumes of
paper currency, the value of which as usual rapidly declined, and all the faster the more Congress and its partisans, like the French Jacobins after them, had recourse to
violence to make bad money pass for good. A hotel bill
of seven hundred pounds was paid with three pounds cash.
The phrase came into vogue, "Not worth a continental."
At last, as Washington said, there was almost a stagna-
tion of purchase. There could not fail to ensue a fearful

disturbance of commerce and of commercial morality. Debts contracted in good money were paid in worthless paper. Washington was himself thus defrauded while he was serving the country without pay, a wrong of which he speaks with his usual magnanimity. Gambling and speculation naturally followed. Fortunes were made by knaves and riotous living went on while the army suffered and dwindled to a shadow. Years afterwards Tom Paine, no straight-laced economist, seriously demanded that any one who proposed to return to paper money should be punished with death. The inestimable clause in the American constitution forbidding legislation which would impair the faith of contracts, may perhaps be regarded in part as a memorial of those evil times.

A fleet, Congress can scarcely be said to have had. But what local assistance, independently of the armies of the central government, did on land, privateers manned by the hardy seamen of New England did at sea. A number of English merchantmen were captured in American waters, and Paul Jones in his *Bonhomme Richard* made himself the terror of the English coasts. The royal navy however presently asserted its superior power, and American commerce was swept from the sea.

The surrender of Burgoyne proved decisive, as it brought France to the aid of the Americans. Ever since her loss of Canada she had been intriguing through her agents in the colonies. From the outset of the war she had been sending secret aid to the revolutionists, and lying when expostulations were addressed to her. The motive of her government was enmity to England. But there was a section of her aristocracy which had embraced political reform and even begun to dally with revolution, a

pastime for which the salons afterwards paid dear. A
youthful scion of this section, Lafayette, fired at the sight
of American revolt, had gone forth on a republican crusade
Feb. and become the companion in arms of Washington.⟩⟨After
1778. Burgoyne's surrender American envoys were able to per-
suade the French government to make a treaty with the
colonies and go to war with Great Britain, from whom
1779. France had received not the slightest provocation⟩⟨Spain
was afterwards drawn in, not by sympathy with the Americans whom she regarded as dangerous neighbours to her
      American dependencies, but by the hope of recovering
1780, Gibraltar; Holland by maritime jealousies and disputes.⟩
⟨Thus England, in addition to her revolted colonists, had
the greatest military power in Europe and the three greatest naval powers on her hands. She lost that command of
the sea which had enabled her to crush the commerce of
the colonists, to wear them out by pressure on the seaboard,
and to choose her own point of attack. On the other hand
her national spirit was aroused to do battle with her
ancient foe. Chatham would have dropped the colonies
and turned on France. Lord North, being no Chatham,
sent out commissioners with overtures of reconciliation,
offering the colonies representation in Parliament. Of
course his attempt proved worse than vain.⟩ A great
French fleet under d'Estaing soon appeared on the scene.
A French army was to follow, and the French treasury
supplied Congress with the hard cash of which it was by
this time in the sorest need. Incompatibilities and mis-
understandings between the French and their colonial
allies put off the catastrophe, but the balance was decisively
turned and the result was no longer in doubt. "To me,"
said Washington, August 20th, 1780, "it will appear

miraculous if our affairs can maintain themselves much longer." "If," he added, "the temper and resources of the country will not admit of alteration, we may be reduced to seeing the cause in America upheld by foreign arms." That time had now come.

〈 It was in the dark hour before the arrival of French aid that treason entered into the heart of Benedict Arnold, the commander of the all-important lines upon the Hudson. Arnold had been one of the best of the American commanders, perhaps the most daring of them all. He had reason to complain of slights and wrongs, not at the hands of Washington who valued and trusted him, but at the hands of the politicians. He seems to have despaired of the revolutionary cause and to have shrunk from the French alliance, suspecting as did others that the French had designs on Canada, and to have made up his mind to play Monk. He opened clandestine negotiations with Clinton, whose adjutant and envoy was the ill-starred André, a young man of culture and sensibility. By Arnold's invitation André visited the American lines, and on his way back fell into the hands of the enemy while Arnold had just time to escape. Whether having been drawn into the American lines by their commander he was guilty of having acted as a spy must be decided by martial law, which has rules and a phraseology of its own.〉 But it can hardly be said that he was tried. 〈He was convicted and sentenced solely on his own statement, of which the incriminating part was taken, while to the exculpating part, his averment that he had been unwittingly drawn by Arnold within the lines, no weight was allowed, though the evidence for both was the same.〉 Greene, who presided over the court, had written before the trial: " I wrote you a letter by the post

1780.

yesterday respecting General Arnold. Since writing that
letter General Washington is arrived in camp and the
British Adjutant General and Joshua Smith, both of whom
are kept under strong guard. They are to be tried this
day and doubtless will be hung to-morrow." It seems vain
to cite the foreign officers who sat in the court of inquiry
as impartial judges ; they were enemies of England and of
2d Englishmen. André was hanged with great parade, his
Oct. prayer that he might be shot having been refused by
1790. Washington, and as his enemies denied him a soldier's
death his country did right in giving him more than a
soldier's tomb. It seems certainly to have been hinted to
Sir Henry Clinton that André might be exchanged for
Arnold. If the hint came from any important quarter a
dark shade is cast upon the execution of André.

1779. ⟨After Burgoyne's disaster and the proof which the
Northern States had on that occasion given of their spirit,
the royal commanders turned to the South, which they
might hope to detach and save for the king, even if the
North was lost. In the South there was reason to believe
that Royalism was stronger than in the North. The people
were not Puritan, they were more monarchical than those
of New England, more simple-minded, and being not
traders or manufacturers but husbandmen, they had been
13th less galled by the laws of trade. Clinton took Charleston,
May, the chief southern port and city, with a large garrison
1780. and great stores.⟩ Cornwallis, left in command while
Clinton returned to New York, gained an easy and complete victory over very superior numbers at Camden in
16th South Carolina, the militia giving signal proof of the
Aug. truth of Washington's saying that they would not stand
1780. against regulars in the open field. He afterwards gained

a victory less easy or complete over Greene, the best of the American generals save Washington, at Guildford. Tarleton, a local royalist, also did wonders with his light horsemen, though he soon found his match in the American Marion. But Tarleton, with a detachment of Cornwallis' force under his command, attacking in his over confidence with weary troops, was defeated at the Cowpens; the only battle, if an engagement on so small a scale can be called a battle, lost in open field by the king's troops during the war. The local loyalism, though fiery and too often cruel, proved not staunch, and the effect of the incursion was rather to let loose mutual massacre and plunder amongst the motley population of Dutch, Germans, Quakers, Irish Presbyterians, and Scotch Highlanders, than to bring the colonies back to their allegiance. A combined French and American attack on New York appearing imminent, Cornwallis, recalled by Clinton, fell back into Virginia and intrenched himself on a neck of land at Yorktown on the Chesapeake Bay, in a position which so long as his own fleet commanded the bay was a stronghold, but when the command of the sea was lost became a trap. The command of the sea was lost by the arrival of a French fleet under De Grasse, with which there was no British fleet to cope. Washington uniting his army to that of Rochambeau, they moved together on Yorktown, while some misunderstanding, as it appears, between Cornwallis and Clinton retarded Clinton's aid. Cornwallis, in a desperate position and beleaguered by an army four times outnumbering his effective force, after turning his eyes for some days to the sea in the vain hope of discerning British sails, was compelled to capitulate and march out, as the painting in the hall of the Capitol depicts him, between the lines of French and American troops.) Washington had the modesty and generosity to keep off spectators. ⌐This was the end.⌐ It would not have been the end if America had been a foreign enemy and the heart of the British nation had been really in the struggle. It was not the end of the contest with France, Spain, and Holland.⟩ But of the contest with the colonies it was the end.⟩ The American farmers might go home, hang up their muskets and follow the plough as they had in "the old colony days," which probably not one in a hundred of them regarded with abhorrence and to which most of them, we may be pretty sure, had been looking back with regret. ⟨ No conflict in history has made more noise than the Revolutionary War.⟩ It set flowing on every fourth of July a copious stream of panegyrical rhetoric which has only just begun to subside. Everything connected with it has been the object of a fond exaggeration. Skirmishes have been magnified into battles and every leader has been exalted into a hero.⟨ Yet the action and, with one grand exception, the actors were less than heroic, the ultimate conclusion was foregone, and the victory after all was due not to native valour but to foreign aid. ⟩

Civil war as well as international war there will sometimes be, but it ought always to be closed by amnesty. For amnesty Cromwell declared on the morrow of Worcester. Amnesty followed the second civil war in America. ⟨ The first civil war was followed not by amnesty, but by an outpouring of the vengeance of the victors upon the fallen. Some royalists were put to death. Many others were despoiled of all they had and driven from their country. Several thousands left New York when it was evacuated by the king's troops.⟩⟨ Those who remained underwent

virulent persecution.) Massachusetts banished by name
three hundred and eight of her people, making death the
penalty for a second return; New Hampshire proscribed
seventy-six; Pennsylvania attainted nearly five hundred;
Delaware confiscated the property of forty-six; North Carolina of sixty-five and of four mercantile firms; Georgia
also passed an act of confiscation; that of Maryland was
still more sweeping.   South Carolina divided the loyalists
into four classes inflicting a different punishment upon
each.   Of fifty-nine persons attainted by New York three
were married women, guilty probably of nothing but
adhering to their husbands, and members of the council or
law officers who were bound in personal honour to be
faithful to the crown.(Upon the evacuation of Charleston,
as a British officer who was upon the spot stated, the loyalists were imprisoned, whipped, tarred and feathered,
dragged through horse ponds, and carried about the town
with "Tory" on their breasts.   All of them were turned
out of their houses and plundered, twenty-four of them
were hanged upon a gallows facing the quay in sight of
the British fleet with the army and refugees on board.)
Such was the statement of a British officer who was upon
the spot, ashore and an eye witness to the whole.   Some
of these men, such as Johnson the guerrilla leader and
Butler the author of the attack on Wyoming, had been
guilty of crimes for which they might justly have suffered
under the common law, though they could not have suffered more justly than some ruffians on the other side.
But the mass had been guilty of nothing but fidelity to
a lost cause.   Honour, we will say with Mr. Sabine, to
those who protested; to General Greene, who said that it
would be "the excess of intolerance to persecute men for

opinions which twenty years before had been the universal
belief of every class of society"; to Alexander Hamilton,
who nobly stood up against the torrent of hatred as the
advocate of its victims in New York; to John Jay, who
said that he "had no desire to conceal the opinion that to
involve the Tories in indiscriminate punishment and ruin
would be an instance of unnecessary rigour and unmanly
revenge without a parallel except in the annals of religious
rage in the time of bigotry and blindness." ⟨The loyalist
exiles peopled Nova Scotia, New Brunswick, and Upper
Canada with enemies of the new Republic, and if a power
hostile to the Republic should ever be formed under
European influence in the north of the continent, the
Americans will owe it to their ancestors who refused
amnesty to the vanquished in civil war. ⟩

1783.   ⟨ By the treaty of peace, Great Britain not only recognized
the independence of her colonies but gave them, what
France was not very willing and Spain was very unwilling
to give, unlimited extension to the westward over the
territory which her arms had won from France.   Canada,
her bond of honour to the loyalists compelled her to
retain.⟩ In the course of the negotiations the hollowness
of the league of hatred between America and the European
enemies of England appeared.   France, as the American
envoys thought, played America false, and the Americans
were guilty towards France of what they admitted to be
a breach of diplomatic courtesy while France called it by
a harder name.   "It is now substantially proved," says a
recent American writer of eminence, "that the unmixed
motive of the French cabinet in secretly encouraging the
revolted colonies, before open war had broken out between
France and England, had been only to weaken the power

and sap the permanent resources of the natural and apparently eternal enemy of France." To seize the opportunity of crippling a powerful enemy was the avowed aim of Vergennes in urging his king to go to war. The conduct of negotiations on the British part fell at first to the lot of Shelburne, the most liberal statesman of his day, who had ardently desired re-union and who now, with young Pitt by his side, sought to make the settlement with the colonies a treaty not of peace only but of reconciliation, dividing the imperial heritage without destroying the moral unity of the race. Had Shelburne's policy prevailed, there would have been no war of 1812, there would have been no fisheries question, nor Behring Sea controversy. But Shelburne's government was overthrown by the factious ambition of Fox, with whom it is painful to say went Burke. ⟨A demand for compensation to the loyalists Congress, unable to deny its justice, put off with an ironical recommendation of compliance to the States, whose resolution it knew. England gave the loyalists more than three millions and a half sterling if we include the pensions and half pay, and new homes to those that chose them under her flag. The recognition of private debts was, thanks to the honesty and wisdom of John Adams, though not without great difficulty, obtained.⟩

⟨The political separation of the colonies from the mother country, once more, was inevitable.⟩ Not even the most fervid imperialist can imagine the sixty-five millions of the United States remaining dependent on the thirty-five millions of the British Islands. No English statesman in the present day could think without shuddering of such a task as that of governing New England across the Atlantic. But by right-minded men the violence of the separation must ever be deplored. The least part of the evil was the material havoc. Of this the larger share fell as usual upon the country which was the scene of war. ⟨ England came out at last with her glory little tarnished. ⟩ She had yielded not to America, but to America, France, Spain, and Holland combined. ⟩ That tremendous coalition she had faced, the national spirit of her people which had not been thoroughly awakened by the war against her own colonists rising to do battle with her foreign enemies ; and her flag floated in its pride once more over the waters which were the scene of Rodney's victory, and on that unconquered rock beneath which the Spaniard received his share of the profits of the league. While she was losing nominal empire in America, illustrious adventurers had enlarged her real empire in Hindustan. Of all the consequences, the worst to Great Britain was that the oligarchy which ruled in Ireland was enabled, by taking advantage of her peril, for a time to cast off imperial control and to set up an independence which ended in the catastrophe of '98. The loss of her colonial dependencies in itself was clear gain, political, military, and commercial. Their trade, her share of it, and her profit from it, increased after their political emancipation. She was thus repaid what she had expended in the war. But she lost what was more valuable than glory, empire, or the profits of trade, the love of her colonists, and in place of it incurred their intense and enduring, though unreasonable and unworthy, hatred. The colonists by their emancipation won commercial as well as fiscal freedom, and the still more precious freedom of development, political, social, and spiritual. They were fairly launched on the course of their own destiny, which diverged widely from that of a monarchical and aristocratic

realm of the old world. But their liberty was baptized in
civil blood, it was cradled in confiscation and massacre, its
natal hour was the hour of exile for thousands of worthy
citizens whose conservatism, though its ascendancy was
not desirable, might as all true liberals will allow have
usefully leavened the republican mass. A fallacious ideal
of political character was set up. Patriotism was identified
with rebellion, and the young republic received a revolutionary bias, of the opposite of which it stood in need.
The sequel of the Boston Tea Party was the firing on Fort
Sumter.

⟨ Another consequence was the severance of Canada from
the United States and a schism of the English-speaking
race on the North American continent, opening the way,
which unity would have closed, for the introduction of
international enmities, of a balance of power, and of war.⟩
Statesmanship is now labouring against an accumulation
of difficulties to undo the evil work done a century ago by
denial of amnesty to the vanquished in civil strife.

⟨France in gratifying her hatred of England became
bankrupt. Bankruptcy brought revolution, and the French 1789.
revolution brought a deluge of woe, not only on France
but on mankind. Up to that time the spirit of philosophy,
philanthropy, and reform had by a peaceful movement
been gaining possession of the governments of Europe.⟩
An era of improvement without convulsions seemed to be
dawning. Young Pitt when he came into power saw noth- 1784.
ing before him but peace and reduction of taxes. He
looked forward to the total abolition of customs and to
free trade, within sight of which the world has never since
come. The American revolution by the financial ruin
which it brought on France, by the revolutionary spirit

which it infused into her, and by the violence for which it
gave the signal, changed the scene, and Jacobinism, terror-
ism, reactionary despotism, militarism, incarnations of the
same malignant spirit, were let loose upon a world which
they still distract and ravage. Misfortune pursued even
the persons of those most concerned. The French king,
whose weakness had consented to the war, and his queen,
1793. whose folly had encouraged it, mounted the scaffold before
the unpitying eyes if not amid the plaudits of the American democracy which they had saved. D'Estaing having
helped the queen to her doom, himself followed her, and
Lafayette, after dancing for a moment on the top of the
revolutionary wave, was overturned by genuine revolutionists and flung out into disappointment and impotence.

The good effects of the American revolt on British
politics have it would seem been overrated. Whatever
Chatham or any one else might say in his oratoric mood,
there was little danger of the enslavement of Britain by
means of a colonial stamp act or a colonial duty on tea.
For that the Whigs and the people were too strong. On
the other hand, a few years after Yorktown the king was
able to set his foot on the neck of the Whig party by his
1784. personal nomination of Pitt, and Toryism reigned thenceforth with hardly a break for forty years. England's
colonial system also remained unchanged till with all the
other parts of British government it felt the tide of returning Liberalism, which carried the Reform Bill. In truth,
defeat in anything like a British cause was not likely to
entail on the monarch a forfeiture of British hearts, and it
was in a British cause that Rodney and Eliot at all events
had conquered, while it was before French arms that Cornwallis had fallen.

What is called the American revolution was not truly a revolution but a separation. The colonists had taken up arms as they averred for chartered right, not for constitutional change. Nevertheless a gradual revolution ensued. The colonists had broken away from monarchy, they had learned to hate it and everything connected with it, they had been steeped in republican sentiment; they had expelled the monarchical, aristocratic, and hierarchical elements and tendencies of the community. So strong had the feeling already become against anything hereditary or aristocratic, that the foundation of "The Cincinnati," an hereditary brotherhood of the officers who had fought in the war and their descendants, brought on a storm. From the British Parliament supreme power had passed to the legislatures of the several States. The States had reorganized themselves in the cases where it was necessary on a republican footing. Their constitutions after some experimental oscillations assumed in process of time nearly the same form, each having as its executive, in the place of a royal governor or the vice-regent of its proprietary, an elective governor with a veto not absolute like that of the crown but suspensive, and a legislature consisting of two houses, a Senate which succeeded to the old Council, and an Assembly; both houses being elective, but the conditions of election to the Senate and the tenure of seats in it being such as to render it rather a conservative and revising body, while the Assembly was the direct expression of the popular will. This was in fact the old English model as it was understood to be, with the omission of the hereditary element. In almost all the states there had been up to that time a property qualification of some sort for the franchise. Gradually in the succeeding years these

qualifications were abolished and manhood suffrage prevailed. This, apart from deliberate policy, the bidding of
politicians against each other for popular support was sure
to bring to pass. The elective principle was unhappily extended in time by most of the states to the judiciary,
Georgia setting the bad example which Massachusetts was
wise enough always to refuse to follow. The common law
of England remained and still remains the basis of American law. Even the technicalities of its pleading system
have in some American states partly survived their abolition in the old country. But the legal supports of territorial aristocracy, primogeniture and entail, disappeared.
With them departed the last relics of the manorial system;
that of freehold farms — territorial democracy, as it has
been called — everywhere prevailed, and New York ceased
to pay homage, ultimately she ceased to pay quit-rents, to
her patroons. The Church establishments, alike that of
Congregationalism in Massachusetts and that of Anglicanism in the Southern and Middle States, passed away
and gave place to religious equality, though a state profession of Christianity with some legal safeguards for religion
lingered on and lingers still, especially with regard to
the observance of Sunday. Congregational establishment
in the North somewhat survived Anglican establishment
in the South, because the first was popular, the second
aristocratic. Churches which had been established took up
their position as free churches, a process in which the
Church of England marked her singularly political character, for the English episcopate could consecrate no one as
bishop who had not taken the oath to the crown, and for
the consecration of an American bishop it was necessary to
have recourse to the free Anglican episcopate of Scotland.

〈 Apart from specific change, constitutional, legal, or ecclesiastical, there was a general change of ideas as to the origin, foundation, and authority of government.〉 The court which had been paid to the king was henceforth to be paid to the sovereign people. 〈To the sovereign people all loyalty was henceforth due.〉 Against the sovereign people only could treason be committed. That treason could be committed against the sovereign people even more easily than against a king, was the opinion of Samuel Adams, who in opposing the extension of mercy to some convicted insurgents laid it down that in monarchies the crime of treason or rebellion might admit of being pardoned or lightly punished, but the man who dared to rebel against the laws of a republic ought to suffer death.

The five years which followed the final separation of the colonies from the mother country have been justly called the critical period of American history. Imperial unity had departed, national unity had not taken its place.〈The bond of mutual danger, weak enough even while the danger lasted, had departed with the return of peace.〉 Congress, originally the organ of a war league and invested only with war or diplomatic powers, was politically a shadow. 〈Its army had been broken up, its currency had lost all value, to raise money it was driven to such expedients as drawing on its foreign ministers and selling the drafts for cash. It was unable to keep its word to the scarred veterans who had fought for it.〉 Its financier, the banker-statesman Robert Morris, struggled with its embarrassments nobly but in vain. 〈It had not the means of protecting the lives or property of its citizens on the high seas.〉 A handful of mutineers turned it out of doors. Reduced to ignominious impotence at home it could not command respect abroad, nor could England or any foreign nation be justly upbraided by Americans with slighting a government which Americans themselves almost spurned. Valid treaties could not be made with a government which had no means of punishing their infraction. Seeing the confusion, some of the army officers would have made Washington king, but he more decisively and sincerely than Cæsar or Cromwell put away the crown. The States were scattered along nine hundred miles of coast, broken by many impediments to travel. They had little intercommunication. Their interests and feelings were still strongly local in spite of their partnership and the comradeship of their soldiers during the war. Among the public men who had taken a leading part in the struggle for independence and among the Continental veterans there might be a community of sentiment, but on the whole the centrifugal forces prevailed and were gaining strength. State selfishness manifested itself with violence, especially in the case of New York. It was becoming fatal even to commercial unity. States fell foul of each other. There were disputes about territory, and in a contest between Pennsylvania and Connecticut for the possession of Wyoming that hapless settlement was a second time devastated, and with cruelty only less than that of the Indians and Tories. Such a dissolution and such a collapse of public spirit are not the usual sequel of a struggle for a great cause, the tendency of which on the contrary is to elevate, brace, and unite. Grievances and discontent were rife. Commerce, almost ruined by the maritime war, was now weltering in the slough of a debased paper currency into which individual States were wading deeper still. There was a heavy burden of private

1784.

as well as of public debt. Men were being dragged to
debtors' prisons.⟩ The community was vexed by litigation
and the enforcement of odious claims. Gambling speculation flourished, as it always does when the currency is
deranged, and the people were incensed by the sight of its
shameful gains. The spirit of repudiation was abroad.
Scarcity appeared and food riots with it. At length law-
loving Massachusetts became the scene of a dangerous
rebellion of the indebted and suffering class under the
leadership of Daniel Shays, formerly a captain in the   1787.
Continental army, who in common probably with many of
his comrades had been reduced to want by the failure of
the public faith.

Shays' rebellion gave a salutary shock. ⟨Anarchy was
evidently at hand.⟩⟨To avert it a convention met to
give the country a government by framing a constitution⟩   1787.
The president of the convention was Washington, who,
the war ended, had sought retirement and domestic happiness at Mount Vernon sincerely but in vain. Personal
confidence in him it was in great measure that made the
convention possible and enabled it to do its work. Once
more and not for the last time he saved the state.⟩ When
the servile dread of popular opinion which is the bane of
popular government began to show itself, he rose from his
chair and said, " It is too probable that no plan we propose
will be adopted. Perhaps another dreadful conflict is to
be sustained. If to please the people we offer what we
ourselves disapprove, how can we afterwards defend our
work?   Let us raise a standard to which the wise and honest can repair ; the event is in the hand of God." " These
words," says an eminent writer, " ought to be blazoned in
letters of gold and posted on the wall of every American

assembly that shall meet to nominate a candidate or
declare a policy or pass a law, so long as the weakness of
human nature shall endure." If it could only be shown
how the politician is to act in this spirit, while to him the
pleasure of the changeful multitude is life and its displeasure is death! ⟨The leading minds of the convention were
Franklin, Hamilton, Madison, Rufus King, Robert Morris,
Gouverneur Morris, Pinckney, Oliver Ellsworth, Elbridge
Gerry, James Wilson, and Roger Sherman — sagacious
and experienced men of business, like the men of whom
the American Senate is now composed, and far unlike the
men to whose lot it unhappily fell to frame a constitution
for revolutionary France. Jefferson, the author of the
Declaration of Independence, whose opinions were French
and revolutionary and whose influence had he been present
would have been great, was happily absent as ambassador
at Paris.⟩ The tendency of the American statesmen was
conservative, their mission being to avert dissolution. That
their work proclaims their wisdom, the world declares.
⟨They founded, if not the first national republic, the first
which was destined to endure.⟩ The republics of antiquity
were cities, and Rome when she became more than a city
ceased to be a republic. In the United Netherlands the
Stadtholderate was a veiled monarchy. The Commonwealth of England lived but for an hour, though it left
what may prove a valuable legacy in the Instrument of
Government. The union of the Swiss Cantons was at
this time not national but federal, in the strict sense of
the term. It has since become national by approximation
to the American model.

⟨The problem which the framers of the American constitution had to solve was that of reconciling a strong na-

tional government, which was the aim of most of them,
with the claims and susceptibilities of separate and in their
own eyes sovereign states. The solution of that problem
was a nation with a federal structure. The federal parts
of the constitution are the recognition of the right of each
state to self-government in regard to all ordinary matters
of legislation or administration; the equal representation
of the states great and small in the Senate, which is placed
beyond the power of amendment; and the election of the
president through state colleges, the verdict of which may
not coincide with that of the majority of votes in the
whole Union; the last provision being however of little
practical importance. It is also declared in the interest of
state right that any power not expressly given to the federal government is withheld and remains in the states or in
the people. In the group of states with which the framers
had to deal there were differences of size or importance
which rendered federation on an equal footing a work of
difficulty.) Yet there was no towering predominance to
excite the permanent jealousy of the rest, as there would
be if England were federally united with Scotland, Wales,
and Ireland. Whether the constitution was a compact, as
parties to which the states retained their independent existence, or an incorporating union in which the independent
existence of the states was merged, was a question left by
the framers to settle itself and which was ultimately decided
by the sword. (What is certain is that Congress was not
made, like the British Parliament, a sovereign power.
The sovereignty remained either in the states or in the
united people.)

The national part of the constitution was not struck out
at a heat as misdirected eulogy avers, but was framed like

the constitutions of the several states on the English
model, as the English model was in law and was still
imagined in fact to be even by the English themselves,
with an executive head and a legislature divided into two
co-ordinate branches. The elective president was the
republican substitute for the hereditary king, and was
invested with the executive powers, political, diplomatic,
and military, which the king was still supposed to possess.
The military command however was to be direct only in
the case of the standing army; of the militia, the commanders were to be the governors of the states, to whom the
president's requisition was to be addressed. The Senate
was the republican and elective House of Lords, and was
like it restrained from originating money bills. The
House of Representatives was the House of Commons, the
direct expression of the popular will, as well as in this
case, the organ of the nation, while the Senate was the organ
of the states. The Senators were to be elected by the state
legislatures for six years, the members of the House of
Representatives were to be elected by the people for only
two years; and the Senate was expected, both from the
mode of its election and from the length of its term, to be
like the upper house of the British Parliament a conservative and revising body. The qualification for the national
suffrage was to be the same as that required for electors
of the most numerous branch of the legislature in each
state, an enactment of which, leaders and parties bidding
against each other for popular support, manhood suffrage
was the certain offspring. The presidency, after much
debate and many changes of mind, was made tenable for
four years with the power of re-election, the exercise of
which was presently limited by fixed custom to a double

term. The election was not intended to be popular; it was vested in colleges of electors, sage citizens it was supposed they would be, one college for each state. But the election of these colleges for the special purpose inevitably became a mandate, and a presidential election practically by manhood suffrage is now the most extensive display of popular sovereignty in the world. The president was invested with a suspensive veto in place of the veto nominally absolute of the British king, while a share was given to the Senate in the executive power by making its consent necessary to official appointments and to treaties. These were deviations from the revered but impracticable principle of Montesquieu, who had laid it down that the complete separation of the executive, legislative, and judicial powers from each other was the only sure pledge of freedom.

On the other hand, whether in deference to Montesquieu or to the political purism which had given birth to place Bills in the old country, ministers of state were excluded from the legislature. Thus a turn was given to the parliamentary system in America different from that which had been taken by the parliamentary system in England, though almost without the knowledge of Englishmen themselves. Cabinet government was precluded. Instead of a ministry responsible to the legislature, and dependent for existence on its vote, America has a ministry independent of the legislature and irremovable during its term of four years. Instead of the control exercised over legislation by the ministers sitting in Parliament, America has controlling committees nominated in the House of Representatives by the Speaker, who is thus not merely the chairman but the party leader of the House. In the Senate there can hardly be said to be any initiative or control, except that of party organization or individual influence.

Of government by party, in which their settlement was destined to result, the framers of the constitution appear not to have thought, though they had an example of it before them in the British Parliament. That organized party would be the dominant force acting under the forms of the institutions which they framed did not, so far as we can see, occur to their minds. In this most momentous respect their foresight failed.

The states were prohibited from laying import or transit duties on each other's goods. Internal free trade was thus secured to the whole of the continent occupied by the United States. This was practically the greatest of all the measures of free trade in commercial history.

For the amendment of the constitution two processes were assigned, the initiative being given either to two-thirds of both Houses of Congress or to the legislatures of two-thirds of the states. Both processes are so difficult, especially when the Union is divided into parties, as to carry conservatism almost to the length of immobility. There was no amendment during a period of sixty years.

The interpretation and legal guardianship of the constitution were vested in a Supreme Court, the judges being appointed by the President with consent of the Senate.

In the constitution, or in additions soon after made to it by way of amendment, are provisions which taken together constitute a republican Bill of Rights. A republican constitution is guaranteed to each of the states, no titles of nobility can be granted, no religion can be established, no religious tests for office can be imposed; speech and the press are to be forever free. liberty of public meeting and of petition are secured, trial by jury is to be every man's right; acts of attainder, *ex post facto* laws, or laws impairing the faith of contracts are not to be passed; no private property is to be taken by the state without compensation; that military usurpation may be rendered impossible, all freemen are permitted to carry arms.〉'

〈The adoption of a <u>federal</u> senate with a <u>national</u> house of representatives was a compromise for the sake of union between the claims of the states and those of the nation.〉 〈The clauses of the constitution respecting slavery were a compromise for the sake of union between the freedom which prevailed in the North and the slavery which prevailed in the South.〉 In the northern and central states since the revolution emancipation had been making rapid progress. Vermont led the way in legislative prohibition. Massachusetts judicially applied to the negro the principle of equal rights embodied in the Declaration of Independence, much as in England slavery had been judicially interdicted in the case of Somerset. Elsewhere liberal sentiment had practically prevailed. In the southern states there were politicians who saw the danger of slavery and philanthropists who condemned its iniquity. But the economical conditions which fostered it were too strong and were destined soon to be fatally reinforced. 〈In the apportionment of representation the South was allowed by the Fathers of the constitution to count three-fifths of its slaves.〉 A fugitive slave law was introduced and the Union is pledged to lend its forces for the suppression of slave insurrection. The existence of the slave trade was secured for twenty years.〉 〈Soon after the adoption of the constitution, Kentucky was admitted as a slave state and two fugitive slaves were arrested at Boston.〉

The names "slavery," "slave," and "slave-trade" are avoided; those of "persons held to service or labour," "importation and migration" are used instead. But the veil of language betrays consciousness without hiding the guilt. Compromises of expediency may well be wise, compromises of principle always fail. We know now of what upas tree the germ was planted here. ⟨This was the first of three great compromises with slavery for the sake of union.⟩

The convention sat with closed doors, as every assembly must if it means really to deliberate, not to talk to the gallery and the reporters. In this case it was most necessary that the debate should be perfectly free, and that the work should come complete before the people. But the substance of the discussion has been preserved in authentic notes and nothing in political archives is more important. In overcoming the opposition, constitutional or arising from the local fears and jealousies of different states, there was abundant work for personal authority, statesmanship, address, and eloquence both of the tongue and pen. ⟨Among the opponents of union were Samuel Adams and Patrick Henry, the latter of whom, if the evidence of his opponents is to be believed, appealed without scruple to all motives.⟩ Pamphleteering abounded on both sides and the controversy gave birth to one memorable work, "The Federalist," of Hamilton, Madison, and Jay. Unluckily "The Federalist" is mainly taken up with allaying the fears, proved by the event to be groundless, of those who fancied that the power of government would be too great, while with the real dangers, democratic passion, demagogism, and factions, it omits to deal.

⟨Provision was made by the constitution for the government. Provision for expansion had been made by a resolution of the old Continental Congress' which declared that the demesne or territorial lands "should be disposed of for the common benefit of the United States, and be settled and formed into distinct republican states, which shall become members of the federal union, and have the same rights of sovereignty, freedom, and independence as the other states." Virginia and other states had conceded to the confederacy the vast tracts to which they laid claim between the Alleghanies and the Mississippi, and for the settlement and political organization of these tracts an ordinance had been made in 1787 second in importance only to the constitution. The nomination of a governor by the president and the election of a rudimentary legislature formed the provisional process by which the territory was to be prepared for admission as a state to the Union by an Act of Congress when its population should have become sufficient, and provided Congress approved its constitution. By a memorable article of the ordinance slavery was prohibited north of the Ohio. Thus marshalled by law and order, the host of settlement and civilization set forth on its westward march. Humanity had advanced since the migrations of the Huns and Tartars. A system of dealing with the public lands which should treat them, in their primary aspect, not as a national estate of which a market was to be made, but as a field for settlement, and open them on the easiest terms to the settler, was needed to complete the policy. In time it came.

CHAPTER III.

REPUBLIC.

1789 to 1797. WASHINGTON became President by acclamation. At the end of his term of four years he with unfeigned reluctance consented to re-election. For eight years he was in power far more of a king than the crowned King of England; he not only reigned, but governed. He even kept something like royal state, he rode in a coach-and-four, at the opening of Congress in a coach-and-six. He treated admission to his levées and parties as a matter of etiquette, unlike his democratic successors, who are compelled to receive all comers at all times and to allow the millions to take them by the hand. His birthday was kept like that of a king. His wife was called Lady Washington, the article in the constitution against titles of nobility notwithstanding. On state occasions he wore court dress. In all this, however, he was not indulging personal pride, but doing what he thought was incumbent on the head of the nation, for he was always a sincere republican, though of the aristocratic type. His state, though modest and certainly covering no designs of aggrandizement, did not fail to give umbrage to jealous democracy, which took arms at once against the proposals to confer on the President such a title as " Highness," or to put his head on the coins.

⟨To the character and authority of the head of the nation must largely be ascribed the success of the constitution, which at first had little hold upon the people.⟩ At the first session of Congress eight weeks elapsed after the appointed day before enough members arrived to form a quorum. ⟨Before the end of Washington's term the constitution had firmly taken root, the authority and dignity of Congress were assured, and it had drawn to it the ability, the ambition, and the political life of the nation.⟩ From the outset there was a full measure of practical sagacity in both houses. The Senate being the upper chamber and the tenure of its members being six years, while that of those of the House of Representatives was only two, it presently drew the higher statesmanship to itself. It was always more conservative and at first sat with closed doors.

⟨Washington's wisdom was that of judgment rather than that of forecast.⟩He seems to have had no inkling of the course which, under the elective system, affairs would really take. Party, the power of the future, his own breast being absolutely free from it, he regarded as a passing malady in others, and thought he could subdue it by uniting in his cabinet the leaders of the opposite schools of politics, Hamilton and Jefferson. But from the irreconcilable enmity of these two men, and the ultimate retirement of Jefferson, he might have seen what would come whenever his own supremacy was withdrawn. Each was the head of a party in course of formation; Hamilton of the Federalists, the party of strong government and English leaning; Jefferson of the democratic republicans, the party of closely circumscribed government, and of sympathy with France.

〈Hamilton, the Secretary of the Treasury, by general consent, ranks first in ability of American statesmen, at least amongst those of the old school.〉 It is to him that hostile critics of American statesmanship have special reference when they say that the transformation of Rome by Augustus has been reversed, and that what was at first an edifice of marble has been turned into an edifice of brick. He was not a native patriot, but had been transplanted to the colony of New York from a crown colony in the West Indies, the sentiments of which were essentially monarchical and aristocratic. At a New York dinner he replied to a democratic sentiment by striking his hand on the table and saying, "Your people, Sir, your people is a great beast." Though he meant beast no doubt in the Platonic sense the sentiment which he expressed was not worship of the people. 〈Ambition, as he frankly admitted to himself, was his guiding star.〉 At the opening of the revolution he seems to have chosen the path to which his star guided him, coolly and without fanaticism, while he showed his moderation as well as his generosity and courage by protecting a royalist against the fury of a revolutionary mob. 〈Joining Washington's staff and becoming military secretary, he displayed precocious ability as a negotiator in delicate affairs and as a writer of despatches, at the same time distinguishing himself in the field.〉 As a witness of the military mal-administration of Congress and the consequent sufferings of the army, he must have had the need of a strong and capable government forcibly impressed upon his mind. The nobleness of his soul was shown in his sympathy with André, and more practically when the war was over by declaring for amnesty and gallantly stemming the tide of vindictive

ersecution in New York. When the time came for
ringing order out of the political chaos which followed
he revolution, his was the leading and informing spirit.
Ie was the most zealous promoter of the constitutional
nion, and as the principal writer in "The Federalist," its
oremost defender. Though New York was his state, not
eing a native of it he could rise above its narrow interests
nd be a citizen of the Union. ⟨To exalt the Union above
he States and enlarge the authority of the central govern-
ient was his steadfast aim.⟩ By his opponents he was
ccused of a design to introduce monarchy and aristocracy.
Ie was a man of too much sense either to suppose this
ossible or to pursue a chimera. ⟨ But though a loyal
epublican he was no democrat.⟩ He would have been
iore at home in the place of Turgot or Pitt than in the
ervice of the multitude. ⟨His belief in the wisdom of the
eople was limited, and he detested mob rule.⟩ He had
nsight enough to discern, and frankness enough to avow
is opinion, that something which was called corruption
ras almost inseparable from the working of parliamentary
istitutions. ⟨ Becoming Secretary of the Treasury under
Vashington, he with wonderful ability got the finances,
he state of which had seemed desperate, into order,
verted bankruptcy and repudiation, induced Congress
iot only to meet the federal debt, but, what was much
iore difficult, to assume the war debts of the States,
unded the entire debt and made provision for the pay-
ient of the interest, restored the national credit, the
oundness of the currency, and with them, commerce and
rosperity. ⟩ Stock-jobbing there could not fail to be in
  great financial transition. "Scripo-phobia" raged for a
eason. But Hamilton did nothing to encourage it, and

his own hands were clean. In Webster's words, for once florid, " he smote the rock of the national resources, he touched the dead corpse of the public credit which sprang upon its feet." "The fabled birth of Minerva from the brain of Jove was hardly more sudden or more perfect than that of the financial system of the United States from the conceptions of Alexander Hamilton."⟨ In doing all this he was called upon to display force of character and ascendancy over men not less than financial skill.⟩⟨Among his measures was the creation of a national bank, and in this, as in his whole policy, he had not only the immediate end but the strengthening of the government in view⟩ His youthfulness at the time of his great success makes him almost a counterpart of Pitt. From the economical fallacies of his day he was not entirely free. His tariff was protectionist, though only to a moderate extent, and it practically affirmed, apparently without constitutional sanction, the power of Congress to impose taxes for the purpose of fostering particular trades as well as for that of raising a revenue. ⟨Otherwise his economical and financial views were sound, and he owed their soundness mainly to his own genius.⟩ His powers of exposition were also of the highest order, though as a popular orator he did not attempt to shine. His purity was above suspicion; the attempts of his enemies to impeach it totally failed. ⟨ Equally above suspicion was his patriotism, and if in the fierce excitement of political conflict he once or twice did what could not be defended, these were but spots on a character otherwise stainless.⟩ ⟨Though not a learned

1804. lawyer he was a great constitutional jurist. He died before his hour, murdered under the form of a duel. But it is not likely that had he lived longer he would ever have been head of the state. Great as was his ascendancy over the men of his own party, he was never popular. His memory never became dear to the multitude, and it was left to his own family at a late day to erect his statue. Jefferson, Washington's Secretary of State, was and still is a popular idol. This man's character is difficult to treat. There is something enigmatic about his portrait, which combines a body large and strong, fitted for horsemanship and athletic exercise, with a face somewhat feminine not to say feline. As governor of Virginia in the war he had shown lack of nerve if not of courage. Few will maintain that he was in an eminent degree truthful, straightforward, free from propensity to artifice and intrigue. Few will contend that he would ever, like Hamilton, have braved unpopularity in defence of righteousness. His own *Ana* remain to confute any admirer who claims for him freedom from malice or greatness of soul. He had unbounded faith in the people, and never doubted the success of the great American experiment in democracy; there lay his strength. The social current of the age was with him; he knew it and steadfastly guided his course on the assumption that, whatever influences might prevail beneath the lingering shadow of the old dispensation, democracy would in the end prove victorious, and bear its votaries on to success. Intently he listened for the voice of the popular will, and surely he caught its every whisper. His political philosophy seems to have been summed up in the belief that all evils having been the work of government, the less of government there was the better. This, it has been said, stood him in the place of religion. Anarchy itself was, or he could fancy that it was, preferable to strong government. Shays'

rebellion in Massachusetts, which frightened the states
into union, was by him regarded as a healthy exercise of
freedom. " A little rebellion," he said on that occasion,
"is a good thing and ought not to be too much discouraged." It was a medicine necessary for the health of
government. " God forbid," he cried, " that we should be
twenty years without such a rebellion. . . . What signi-
fied a few lives lost in a century or two. The tree of
liberty must be refreshed from time to time with the blood
of patriots and tyrants: it was its natural manure." He
affected to believe that the Indians who had no government at all were happier than the people who lived under
the European governments; and of the three conditions,
Indian anarchy, governments wherein every one had a just
influence, and governments of force, it was not clear in his
mind that the first condition was not the best. He did not
think it ridiculous to say that were it left to him to decide
whether they should have a government without newspapers or newspapers without a government he should not
hesitate a moment to prefer the latter. He embraced and
exhorted a disciple to propagate a theory which he shrank
from propagating himself, that no generation had power
to bind its successors; and that as nineteen years were a
generation, national repudiation and bankruptcy would
be lawful after that period. These were his transports,
which in the actual field of politics were controlled by
his good sense. Jefferson, however, was not one of the
people, but a being of a higher order stooping to identify himself with the people who, as they were not yet
conscious of their power, were captivated by his conde-
scension. He was literary, philosophic, scientific. His
love and command of philosophic abstractions appears in

the most momentous and famous of his works, the Declaration of Independence. He planned the University of Virginia. He was in his day the cynosure of classical taste, and the father of that domestic architecture which presented the front of a Doric temple with family and culinary developments in the rear. His agriculture was scientific and experimental. In religion he was a free-thinker, and in his own State an ardent promotor of religious liberty. To him Anglican establishment in Virginia owed its doom. He detested the clergy and by the clergy was detested. He hated England with intense bitterness, was French to the core, and went all lengths in his sympathy with the French revolution. He could palliate the September massacre, rejoice that his friends at home were taking the name of Jacobins, and say that rather than the revolution should have failed he would have seen half the earth devastated; that were there but an Adam and an Eve left in every country things would be better than they were. The clergy, when he taunted them with fanaticism, might have retorted that fanaticism was not confined to religion. Had he been a fellow citizen of Robespierre he would have been in some danger with his enthusiasm, his sentimentalism, and his acquiescence in philanthropic blood-shed, of doing as Robespierre and other sentimental philanthropists did. The danger would have been enhanced by his extreme suspiciousness; for he lived in a perpetual tremor, spying "monocracy," the political demon of his fancy, not only in Hamilton and all Hamilton's associates, but in Washington himself, at whom he glanced in his political correspondence, though he could not directly assail the character of the hero. As to England, she was capable in his imagination of bribing the Algerines to prey upon American commerce. Another of his peculiarities was his tendency, derived perhaps from the mixed influences of a planting state, Rome, Sparta, and Rousseau, to dislike commerce and manufactures, and regard agriculture as the foster-mother of political and social virtue. ⟨Of the abolition of slavery he was a philosophic advocate, but never emancipated his own slaves. As a party leader he was a perfect artist in his way.⟩ But his way was not that of the modern politician, whose first requisite he lacked. ⟨He was no platform orator; he was no orator at all. He seems to have wanted both flow of language and nerve.⟩ He did not even enter the lists as a public writer. He managed his party through its leading men, and its leading men by personal correspondence, which he carried on with boundless industry and consummate tact, always masking his restless and far-reaching ambition beneath professions of devotion to private happiness and distaste for public life. He, however, used the press as his organ, and it is not easy to extricate him from the charge of having countenanced Freneau, a reptile journalist, in attacking the administration of which he was a member. His principal lieutenant was Madison, a man of cultivated mind, a political philosopher, one of the writers of "The Federalist," master of an Addisonian style, free from the extravagances of his leader while destitute of Jefferson's winning enthusiasm and genius for party management, well-meaning and incorruptible, though, as he was destined to show on a fatal occasion, morally weak. ⟨Of all American statesmen, hitherto, Jefferson has left the deepest impression on the character of his people. Their political ideas and hopes, their notions about their own destiny and the part which they are to play in the drama of humanity

have been his.⟩⟨That Jefferson, not Hamilton, rightly
divined the tendency of society and the secret of the
future is so far the verdict of events. It remains to be
seen whether the belief in individual liberty, self-reliance,
and self-help which formed his gospel is to give way as the
creed of the party progress, to belief in socialistic regulation and the paternal action of the state.⟩   //

All that the patriotic appeals of a chief, himself serenely
superior to personal rivalries, could do to hold these two
men together in the public service was done by Washington, but in vain. After explosions and explanations in
which Jefferson failed to produce anything except vague
suspicion artfully expressed against his rival, the Secretary
of State retired from office to Monticello, his hermitage, as
his fancy styles it, to farm, as he said in all his letters, and
at the same time to spin a vast web of party connection by
a correspondence full of personal and political allurement,
while he listened for the footfall of advancing democracy
whose advent was to be the signal for his own rise to
power.

⟨Under Washington's reign and through Hamilton's
measures of financial and administrative reform, the Republic became responsible and respectable. America
entered the community of nations.⟩ She showed it by bold
dealing with the corsairs of Algiers to whom she sent men
of war instead of tribute, laying thereby the foundation of
her national navy. It was hard to expect that she should
be treated as a nation before she had become one, by England or any other power. "Our country," wrote John
Adams, "is grown, or at least has been, dishonest. She
has broken her faith with the nations and with her own
citizens, and parties are all about for continuing this dis-

honourable course. She must become strictly honest and punctual before all the world, before she can recover the confidence of anybody abroad." ⟨The distinguishing qualities of the colonies and their government previously to the union have been described as " faction, jealousy, and discord, infirmity of purpose, feebleness in action, unblushing dishonesty in finance, black ingratitude against the army, and a rapid acquisition of an ever-growing contempt on the part of the rest of mankind." These are the words of a recent American writer of mark.⟩ The conduct of the English government during the years of American anarchy has been harshly judged even by English writers. In the light of what followed it is seen that heartily to take the initiative in the restoration of amity would have been England's wisest as well as her most magnanimous course. But apart from the soreness of defeat upon which people who are themselves at all sensitive ought not to be severe, there was not a little to repel amicable advances. ⟨The Americans refused to pay their debts to their English creditors; some of the States seemed determined to repudiate.⟩ ⟨The treatment of the loyalists, which disgusted Hamilton, Greene, and Jay, could not fail to disgust still more those in whose cause the loyalists suffered, and the complaints of a number of these men who had migrated to England were ringing in English ears. Till the American government had power to enforce treaties, negotiation was bootless and the interchange of ambassadors would have been a farce. In the question of indemnity to loyalists the confederacy had avowed that it had no means of enforcing the concurrence of the States. The north-western posts were held by England practically as a security for the payment of the debts. That the British Government or anybody by its authority was intriguing with the Indians against the Americans is an assertion of which there appears to be no proof. Simcoe, the Governor of Upper Canada, having fallen under suspicion, though an excellent officer, was recalled. Of the narrow mind of George III it would have been vain to expect the magnanimity of greatness. He had suffered enough to be regarded with some indulgence. But he never was discourteous, and he made a manifest effort to be cordial. When John Adams, June, the first American ambassador, addressed him, the King, 1785. as Adams tells us, was much affected, and answered with tremor. "Sir," he said, "the circumstances of this audience are so extraordinary, the language you have now held is so extremely proper, and the feelings you have discovered so justly adapted to the occasion, that I must say that I not only receive with pleasure the assurance of the friendly dispositions of the United States, but that I am very glad the choice has fallen upon you to be their minister. I wish you, sir, to believe and that it may be understood in America, that I have done nothing in the late contest but what I thought myself indispensably bound to do by the duty which I owe to my people. I will be very frank with you. I was the last to consent to the separation; but the separation having been made, and having become inevitable, I have always said, as I say now, that I would be the first to meet the friendship of the United States as an independent power. The moment I see such sentiments and language as yours prevail, and a disposition to give to this country the preference, that moment I shall say, let the circumstances of language, religion, and blood have their natural and full effect." The last sentence is not so good as the rest, but the King's emotion and his habitual want of command of language disarm strict criticism.

We can hardly doubt that Pitt shared the desire of Shelburne to restore family relations. On the other hand it seems not unlikely that Americans at the Court of St. James's sometimes put on a republican air. A rebuff administered by them to aristocracy and monarchy is recounted by the biographer with a smile. There were even causes for mistrust. Gouverneur Morris takes offence at the coldness with which he is received by a British minister.

1790. By his own avowal he had just been instigating the French government to form a hostile confederacy against Great Britain and make a war on her which she had done nothing to provoke. It is not unlikely that the British minister had an inkling of this; if he had his coldness was excusable. The British statesmen of that day, when we repine at what we think their folly in failing to clap their padlock on the American heart, are entitled to the benefit of later experience. ⟨ It seems that no harmony is so difficult to restore as that between two kindred nations which have once broken the tie. ⟩

Government showed its new force in grappling with a foe nearer home. In the procession at Philadelphia on the ratification of the constitution were seen a citizen and an Indian chief seated together in an open carriage and smoking the calumet to personify peace on the frontiers. It was easier to personify peace than to install it. ⟨ Washington had to deal with a formidable Indian war in the northwest. ⟩

1791. One of his generals, St. Clair, met with a defeat not less disastrous than that of Braddock, the disgrace of which is cast wholly on British officers and troops. But General Wayne restored the day, and by a great victory over the Indians practically closed the struggle with the tribes as a power, and the influence of that struggle on American history. Assimilation, however, never took place. The displacement of Indian tribes by advancing civilization continued, though mitigated by a system of reservations. The desultory conflict between the Indian and the frontiersman, with its savage features, steeping the frontier character in ferocity, continued in the far west, and is not extinct even at this day.

〈Washington had also to deal with the local renewal of the anarchy created by the civil war and by the absence of a national government in the interval between the war and the union. A part of Hamilton's financial policy was an excise. Against this an insurrection broke out among the restive population of Western Pennsylvania. By Washington's firmness and wisdom the revolt was put down and law was enforced without bloodshed.〉 1794.

〈Washington's re-election, like his election, was unanimous.〉 He might have wavered more between the call of public duty and his yearning for private happiness had he foreseen the storm that was to rage during his second term. The mine in France to which American revolt had set the match had now exploded and the French revolution had been launched on its mad career. At first all Americans hailed the dawn of French liberty. But when to the dawn of liberty a day of confusion, massacre, blasphemy, anarchy, and public lunacy succeeded, the educated, wealthy, and religious classes for the most part recoiled. The law-loving Englishman awoke in them and they began to sympathize with England as the power of ordered liberty against the frenzy of the Jacobins. Yet the sympathy of the masses remained with France and seemed to be intensified, instead of being diminished, by her extravagances and crimes. It rose to the pitch of delirium when France 1792.

1793. declared war against England.   A French envoy, Genet, was welcomed with transports of popular enthusiasm.   He was young, ardent, imbued with a piratical diplomacy of the philanthropic Republic.   He proceeded with Jacobin energy to treat the United States as a satrapy of revolutionary France, to use its territory as the base of a maritime war against England, to fit out in its ports privateers which, manned with American seamen, preyed upon British commerce, and even to set up courts of admiralty for the condemnation of his prizes.   By the privateers in conjunction with two French frigates fifty British vessels were captured, some of them in American waters.   He appealed to privileges which the United States had by treaty accorded to France, but which, even assuming that the regicide Republic was the heir of the monarchy, could not, any more, than treaty arrangements of the ordinary kind, override international obligations.   In all his outrages, Genet was wildly applauded by the Republican masses.   When his piratical

1793. frigate sailed into Philadelphia flaunting the English colours reversed with the French flag over them, the whole population of what was then the political capital of the Republic turned out to display its sympathy.   The 4th of July, we are told, seemed more like a French than an American demonstration.   Could Louis XVI have looked down in spirit upon the scene, he, who had saved the Americans from sure disaster, might have beheld a civic banquet given in honour of the regicide emissary and graced by the presence of the governor of an American State at which after singing " The Marseillaise " the head of a pig was handed round and stabbed by the knife of each of the guests in turn with appropriate maledictions. Those who blame the British statesmen of that day for

showing coldness towards the American Republic are bound
to remember that England received from an American
party, not on account of her misdeeds but on account of
her monarchical character, demonstrations not of coldness,
but of frenzied hatred.⟧ ⟨Washington, faithful to international duty, issued a proclamation of neutrality and enforced   1793.
it with vigour, as he alone could have done. Jefferson,
thoroughly sharing the popular feeling, no doubt winced
under the necessity of doing his duty as Secretary of State;
yet he did it⟩ His sagacity taught him that Genet's
extravagance would be ruinous to his cause in the end. So
it proved, when Genet, utterly losing his head, appealed
from Washington's government to the people. His recall
was then demanded and was granted the more readily as
in the swift phantasmagoria of the revolution the ascendancy of his faction had passed away. Washington had
also to restrain the sympathies of his own envoy at Paris,
Monroe, who, losing the ambassador in the enthusiast,
allowed himself to be publicly welcomed by the convention
as the representative of a revolutionary republic having a
common cause with Jacobin France, and to receive from
the President that hug of fraternity in which confiding
nations died. ⟨There can be no doubt that the crimes and
orgies of the revolution were hateful to Washington, who
was not only a political conservative, but believed, and in
his farewell address declared, that religion was the indispensable basis of public morality.⟩⟨But he restrained his
feelings and amidst the storm of party passion raging
around him kept morally as well as legally the path of
strict neutrality.⟩ The Jacobin press of America, including
the reputed organ of his own Secretary of State, assailed
him, especially when he had denounced the Jacobin clubs

which had been founded in the United States on the French model. He was stung sometimes to the heart, but his resolution was not moved.

⟨Washington's authority was put to the severest test by his treaty with Great Britain. Relations with that power were extremely strained. On both sides some of the articles of the treaty made at the close of the American revolution remained unfulfilled, and in addition there were questions touching liberty of commerce, the exercise of belligerent rights by Great Britain against the traders of America as a neutral power, and the impressment of 1794. British seamen found in American vessels.⟩ ⟨To effect a settlement and avertwar Washington determined to send an envoy to England and his choice fell upon the Chief Justice, John Jay, of whom Webster said, that the ermine — the English emblem still clinging to American imagination — touched nothing less pure than itself when it fell upon Jay.⟩ The envoy was no doubt English in mental frame and political sentiment, but there is not the slightest reason for believing that he failed in his mission to do his best for his country. His treaty, as it restored amity with England, was sure to displease the French party.⟩ Wash- 1796. ington kept it secret for some time. ⟨When it was disclosed a furious storm arose ; Jay was accused of having sold his country. It was doubtful whether the treaty would pass the Senate.⟩ The scale was turned in its favour by a speech which ranks among the masterpieces of American oratory from Fisher Ames, who, supposing himself to be in the last stage of disease, addressed the assembly with the pathetic force of a dying man. Ames said that there was little use in combating the particular objections to the treaty ; that whatever the terms might be no agreement with Great Britain would satisfy those who urged against the ambassador that he was not ardent enough in his hatred of her, who declared that no treaty ought to be made with an enemy of France, that England was a den of sea-robbers, that her people deserved to be extirpated, and that it would be well for mankind if she were sunk in the sea. He no doubt represented truly enough the feelings and language of the French party. The influence of the father of his country was tried to the utmost in the ratification of Jay's treaty, but it prevailed, and peace, if not friendship, was for the time secured.

Nothing would induce Washington to accept a third term. He was growing old and deaf. He longed for peace and his farm. The attacks of the *Aurora*, the fiercely democratic and anti-British journal of Duane, an Irish refugee, and other organs of the republican press, despicable as they were in themselves, being taken as the utterances of a large party sometimes drew from him passionate outbursts of grief, especially when the purity of his motives was impugned, and he, the most disinterested of men, was charged with designs against the liberty of his country. He retired, a genuine Cincinnatus, to Mount Vernon. At his departure he issued a farewell address, 1796 which ranks amongst the sacred documents of American history. In this he solemnly exhorted his fellow citizens to unity and love of their country, warning them against geographical divisions, against the excesses of party, and, most emphatically, against entanglements with European politics, and the indulgence of inveterate antipathies to particular nations and passionate attachments to others, which, as he said, made a nation a slave to its antipathies and attachments, and in both cases equally led it astray

from the path of its duties and its interests. Excellent
advice, loudly applauded and little observed! > The para-
graph dwelling on the value of religion as one of the
pillars of national prosperity and cautioning against the
supposition that without it morality could be maintained,
can hardly have failed to be construed as a thrust at the
Jacobins and at the free-thinking Jefferson. < Addresses of
profuse gratitude and veneration were voted by Congress. >
A few murmurs of dissent were heard. One notably from
Andrew Jackson, the Congressman from Tennessee, of
gaunt frame and grim aspect, with elf locks hanging over
his face and his hair tied behind in an eel skin, and so
hot in temper that when he tried to speak his utterance
was choked by passion. Nor could the *Aurora* and its
republican consorts in the press be silent. In the *Aurora*
appeared an article ascribed to a young pupil and favourite of Jefferson, who hailed the day of Washington's departure as the day of salvation, rejoiced that he who had
been the source of all the misfortunes of the country
was at length brought down to the level of his fellow
citizens, that he could no longer by his name give currency to political iniquity or afford support to suspicious
projects, and that the designs which he had formed
against the very existence of public liberty were now at
an end. "If ever a nation," said the *Aurora* editorially,
" was debauched by a man, the American nation has been
deceived by Washington. Let his conduct then be an
example to future ages. Let it serve to be a warning
that no man may be an idol. Let the history of the
federal government instruct mankind that the mask of
patriotism may be worn to conceal the foulest designs
against the liberty of the people." Rather let these words

serve as a warning against the blind frenzy of parti-
sanship and the inherent evils of party government.
Upon Washington's name were also poured the vials
of hatred by Thomas Paine, on whose behalf, when he
had become a French citizen, sat in the Convention, and
fallen into the fangs of the terrorists, Washington declined to interpose. In truth Washington did belong in
political and social sentiment to a departing age and to
a different sphere. His spirit, as well as the man himself,
was passing off the scene. What would be his feelings if
he could now see a presidential election?

Washington's renown is always present in the name of
the national capital, the site of which after its temporary
sojourn at Philadelphia was, in accordance with his wish,
finally fixed on the Potomac, where it might seem to link
the North and South together. Hamilton had induced
Jefferson to consent to the assumption of the State debts
by the Union on condition that the national capital should
be placed on the Potomac. This is the first case of log-
rolling in the history of Congress. It seems to have been
a complex case, the South consenting against its financial
interest to the assumption of the State debts on the tacit
understanding that Congress should turn a deaf ear to
petitions against slavery. Washington thought that the
city on the Potomac would become an important mart.
It never did; nor did it, till very recent times, become
anything but a political and administrative capital in the
wilderness, with but little of general society to temper the
roughness of the legislators and mitigate the violence of
party conflict. The presence of slavery was not conducive
either to good manners or to virtue. No wonder if politics
at Washington were somewhat rude, if affrays and duels

were not uncommon, if the dullness of senatorial boarding
houses was too often relieved by drinking or gambling,
and their lack of domestic happiness by connections to
which slavery everywhere opens the door. The error of
placing the seat of the legislature away from the social
centres has been repeated by almost all the States and by
the Canadian confederation.

Parties were by this time distinctly formed. Their machinery had been set on foot though not brought to modern
perfection. The weakness of the elective system, the in-
ability of electors unknown to each other to concur in a
choice, had been revealed, and the party ticket had taken
the place of a really popular election. Federal parties extended, as they ever have, to State politics, the party in
each State being a sort of donkey-engine to the great
federal machine. By Washington's retirement the controlling hand which suspended their conflict had been withdrawn. Of the Federalist party Hamilton was the soul
but not the head, its Achilles but not its Agamemnon.
Between John Adams, who had been Vice-President under
Washington, as the Federalist, and Jefferson, as the Republican candidate, the election for the Presidency lay.
1797. John Adams was elected. The voting betrayed the political division between North and South which Washington
might deplore but could not blot out, since its line was
traced by the hand of nature. There is nothing in a rational
republic to forbid the existence of great political houses,
and the family of Adams is the nearest approach to such a
house which the American republic has seen. John Adams
was a high Federalist and an admirer of the British constitution, on the purified principles of which he desired
that American institutions should repose. But he was

one of the sires of the revolution and, as an American,
thoroughly loyal to the republic. Moreover, as envoy to
St. James's he had come in contact with British society in
an unpropitious hour, and being personally sensitive was
far from friendly to Great Britain. By a recent American
historian he is described in familiar language as "a burly,
round-faced, bald-headed, irascible man with a tough fibre,
who was little understood by the people and to whom Congressional debates had been a sealed book." In integrity
he was an ancient Roman. He had more force than play
of character, and though his experience was wide, for he
had been ambassador as well as statesman, more knowledge
of books than of men. He was somewhat dogmatic, somewhat pedantic, and from his childhood too self-conscious
and too laboriously self-trained, as his methodical diary
shows. He had soon to deal, like his predecessor, with the
overbearing violence of revolutionary France, now flushed
with victory, governed by a Directory composed of the
unscrupulous and rapacious men who are thrown to the
top by revolution, and having for its foreign minister
Talleyrand, imbued, after a brief sojourn in the United
States, with a low notion of American power. Under
colour of belligerent rights the French preyed on American commerce in both hemispheres, two of their cruisers
being commanded by Barney, an American, while as the
price of forbearance and an amicable treaty they insisted
in effect that the United States should take part with
them as a vassal ally against Great Britain in the war.
Adams sent three envoys to Paris. Talleyrand, through
his reptile agents, gave them to understand that the
American Republic, if it would escape the displeasure of
the Directory and obtain a treaty, must, like other com-

Oct.
1797.

monwealths which France had taken to her bosom, pay her tribute and, in addition, a large sum as a bribe to the Directors and himself. His sagacity for once had failed him. The publication of the papers called the "X. Y. Z. Correspondence" because Talleyrand's agents were denoted by those ciphers, kindled in America a fierce flame of resentment, and for a moment hatred of England was lost in indignation at the insolent tyranny of France. Federalists were exultant, Republicans were downcast. Jefferson quaked and watched the storm with close-reefed sails. Popular feeling swelled high. French emblems disappeared. The black cockade of the American revolution replaced the tri-colour. "Hail Columbia" was composed to oust the "Marseillaise." "Millions for defence, but not a cent for tribute," was the cry. Talleyrand was burnt in effigy, and President Adams found himself the object of an enthusiasm which personally he could never have excited. Preparations for war were made by land and sea. Washington was called upon to take once more the command of the army and consented in words which showed his deep sense of French outrage. War had in fact commenced by sea, and a French frigate had been captured by an American, when the President, who had taken the strongest ground of national dignity, to the surprise and dismay of his party, appointed a minister plenipotentiary to France. By this time the battle of the Nile and the turn of fortune in Italy had tempered the pride of the Directory and a treaty was made. It cost Adams the attachment of the more vehement members of his party, but whether he was perfectly right or not in his treatment of his political friends, it cannot be doubted that he was right in avoiding war.

Apr. 1797.

1798.

〈On this occasion Adams did not consult his cabinet, a name given to the great heads of departments, the Secretary of State, or Minister of Foreign Affairs, the Secretaries of the Treasury, War, the Navy, and the Interior, the Post Master General, and the Attorney General, whom the President usually takes into his counsel, though their offices strictly speaking are merely departmental and they exercise no collective function, like that exercised by the British Cabinet, of initiating and controlling legislation.〉

〈The Federalists still had the upper hand, but they threw away their advantage by using it to excess.〉They passed two acts called the Alien and Sedition Acts, menacing to liberty. The United States were full of political refugees from Europe, most of them revolutionists, some of them agitators by profession, who had got the political press largely into their hands. Against these was pointed the Alien Act giving the government power of expulsion. The Sedition Act, even in the form in which it passed and which was milder than the original Bill, did not well observe the line between lawful criticism or constitutional resistance and sedition.〉 A violent revulsion of public feeling ensued. Jefferson welcomed the rising gale. He was indeed carried out of his usual prudence and reserve. He drew up a manifesto for the use of his party in Kentucky designating the Union as a compact among States, claiming for the States severally the right of resisting any breach of the compact, and pronouncing that for a legislative encroachment on the part of the federal government the remedy of a State was nullification. This doctrine took no effect at the time, but it did not die. 〈With the Alien and Sedition Acts was passed a Naturalization Act, increasing the term of necessary residence from five to

1798.

1798.

fourteen years. > This measure betrayed the alarm of
native Americans caused by the influx of a motley tide
of immigrants, including a number of Irishmen, most of
whom were exiles through discontent and infected with
revolutionary fever.< The Act was repealed a few years
afterwards and the old term of five years was restored in
1802. > In those days anything like a closing of the door of
the universal asylum seemed impolitic as well as inhospi-
table, whatever national interest may prescribe now.

These political struggles, over which no baton of impartial command was waved any more, enhanced the intensity
and bitterness of party. Right-minded men deplored the
effect on social relations. The party press grew in volume,
the number of political journals mounting from forty to a
hundred, in power since each party journal had the minds
of its readers to itself, and at the same time in slanderous
virulence. Callender, a vagabond whose pen Jefferson
had stooped to employ, and who afterwards turned against
him and libelled him, was a type of the class. Attacks
were made on the personal characters of statesmen, and
Hamilton, assailed with a baseless charge of corruption,
was compelled in his defence to confess that he had been
guilty of an adulterous amour. Congress saw its halls
profaned by a brutal affray between two of its members.
The State politics of New York and in a less degree those
of Pennsylvania, full of cabal and corruption from the
beginning, mingled with the current of federal politics
and deepened the darkness of its tide.

< In the choice of candidates at the next Presidential
election there was on the side of the Federalists a good
deal of intrigue, scope for which at that time was given
by the mode of election, each elector voting for two men

as President or Vice-President, without saying which of
the two he preferred for the Presidency, so that the ultimate choice was left to the House of Representatives.
John Adams, the natural candidate of the Federalists,
received an ugly thrust from Hamilton, whom he had
incensed by his conduct in the affair with France.
Hamilton himself soon after fell in a quarrel arising out
of New York politics by the pistol of Aaron Burr, a local
Catiline whose unscrupulous ambition he had crossed,
falling a victim to a false code of honour which survived
when other relics of feudalism had passed away, His
work, or as much of it as was practicable, was done. To
keep the Republic out of the hands of the democracy and
in the hands of the chosen few was impossible, but Hamilton had succeeded in making it national, and in giving it
a strong central government. In this his policy received
the powerful and timely aid of Marshall, the great Chief
Justice of the United States, who by a series of judgments
on constitutional questions upheld and enlarged the power
of the federal government.   The clause of the constitution
authorizing Congress to make all laws which should be
necessary and proper for carrying into execution its
enumerated powers afforded scope for a liberal interpretation of which the Chief Justice took full advantage.
His decision in favour of the creation of a federal bank
was a notable instance.   It is allowed that he might with
equal reason have decided the other way.

The result was that the seed which Jefferson had for
years been assiduously sowing bore its fruit. He became
President and with power to give his policy full effect.   In
him the Republican party completely triumphed, while the
Federalist party sank to rise again no more in that form or

July 1804.

1801.

under that name. Adams, stung to the heart by the election of Jefferson, refused to witness the hateful spectacle
of his successor's inauguration. He spent his last hours in
filling up vacancies to place patronage out of Jefferson's
reach; then he departed, the old order in his person giving
place with a frown and a shudder to the new. Adams
did not hate monarchy, he thought that for England it
was good. In the eyes of Jefferson monarchy was the
incarnate spirit of evil and to. rid mankind of it by
example was the mission of the American Republic. >
< Every vestige of the half monarchical state which
Washington had retained was now banished from the
President's mansion and life. > No more coaches-and-six,
no more court dress, no more levées. Although Jefferson
did not, as legend says, ride to his inauguration and tie
his horse to the fence, he was inaugurated with as little
ceremony as possible. He received an ambassador in
slippers down at the heel, and in the arrangement of his
dinner parties was so defiant of the rules of etiquette as to
breed trouble in the diplomatic circle. Yet with all his
outward simplicity the Virginian magnate and man of
letters, though he might be a Republican, could not in
himself be a true embodiment of democracy. < He was the
friend of the people, but not one of them. > From him to
the rough warrior of Tennessee, the hard-cider drinking
pioneer of Ohio, and the rail-splitter of Illinois, there was
still a long road to be travelled. Nor had Jefferson anything in common with Jacobins who guillotined Lavoisier
saying that the Republic had no need of chemists; for
among the cherished objects of his government was the
encouragement of science.

The desired day had come when the philosopher was to

govern. The words of the address which Jefferson, unlike
the demagogic sons of thunder in the present day, read in
a very low voice, are the expression by its great master and
archetype of the republican idea which has hitherto reigned
supreme in the mind of the American people. These words
are monumental, 'Equal and exact justice to all men, of
whatever state or persuasion, religious or political ; peace,
commerce, and honest friendship with all nations, entangling
alliances with none ; the support of the State governments
in all their rights, as the most competent administrations
for our domestic concerns and the surest bulwarks against
anti-republican tendencies, the preservation of the general
government in its whole constitutional vigour, as the
sheet-anchor of our peace at home and safety abroad ; a
jealous care of the right of election by the People ; a
mild and safe correction of abuses which are lopped by the
sword of revolution where peaceable remedies are unprovided ; absolute acquiescence in the decisions of the
majority, the vital principle of republics, from which
there is no appeal but to force, the vital principle and
immediate parent of despotism ; a well-disciplined militia,
our best reliance in peace and for the first movements
in war, till regulars may relieve them : the supremacy of
the civil over the military authority ; economy in the
public expense, that labour may be lightly burdened ; the
honest payment of our debts, and sacred preservation of
the public faith ; encouragement of agriculture, and of
commerce as its handmaid, the diffusion of information,
and arraignment of all abuses at the bar of public reason ;
freedom of religion, freedom of the press, and freedom of
person under the protection of the *habeas corpus*, and trial
by jurors impartially selected ; — these principles form the

bright constellation which has gone before us and guided our steps through an age of revolution and reformation."

Jefferson's wand was the pen. Yet he is strangely apt to fall into mixed metaphors and even into platitudes. This address has not escaped criticism. A constellation goes before the people and guides their steps. In the sequel the constellation becomes a creed, a text, a touchstone, and should the people wander from the "touchstone," they are conjured to "retrace their steps and regain the road." In the genius of a man who made so vast an impression on such a nation we must believe, yet it is sometimes an exercise of faith to believe in the genius of Jefferson for anything but party management and personal fascination.

Politicians out of power are apt to be opposed to strong government; in power, they feel that a reasonably strong government is necessary to the execution of beneficent designs. There are few more illustrious cases of inconsistency than that of Jefferson, the austere champion of strict construction, when he nobly stretched or rather broke the constitution to enlarge his country's heritage by 1803. the purchase of Louisiana. It was a principal aim of Bonaparte's policy to give France a colonial empire; he had wrested from the weakness of Spain the retrocession of Louisiana, but after the brief and hollow peace of Amiens war again impending with the power which remained mistress of the seas, as he saw that his transatlantic prize must infallibly be lost, he resolved to put it beyond the grasp of Great Britain and replenish his military chest at the same time by selling Louisiana to the United States; privately promising himself, we can hardly doubt, to enforce another retrocession when he was left master of the world. The constitution clearly gave the government no power of acquiring foreign territory, and had Washington or Adams been President, Jefferson would have denounced the assumption of such power as usurpation and as evidence of monarchical designs.) Being himself President, he over-rode the law, looking for indemnity to a national authority, the existence of which it would have been hard for him to reconcile with the doctrine of the compact of the States promulgated by him in the Kentucky manifesto.< Thus a vast and fruitful territory with the mouth of the Mississippi was added to the domain of the United States. A population alien in race, language, character, and religion, was at the same time incorporated.> But the digestive power of the American Republic proved sufficient for political assimilation, and of French Louisiana there presently remained only traces prized by the lover of the social picturesque. <A large section of the new world was thus liberated from the control of the old world and annexed to the realm of the American experiment. Unhappily there was also a great extension of the realm of slavery.)

The example of Bonaparte in its turn fired American 1805–7. fancy. Aaron Burr, the assassin of Hamilton, a true scion of New York politics as they then were, a showy and restless adventurer with revolutionary morals and a gift of misleading youth, and by grace of factious cabal Vice-President of the United States, formed a design of severing Louisiana from the Republic and carving out for himself a Napoleonic empire in central America. But his plot, after creating some noise and confusion, ended in a farcical catastrophe.

< Jefferson's first term was benign and prosperous.>/It 1801–4. was an era of financial success, reduction of debt, public

frugality, expansion of trade and manufactures, sound progress, general prosperity and contentment, a felicity which
it owed to the firm government, unlike Jefferson's ideal,
by which it had been preceded.   The accession of Louisiana made it even glorious.❭ It could disappoint only those
whom Jefferson's jeremiads over the encroachments and
corruptions of monocracy under the first two Presidents,
had led to expect a new heaven and a new earth. ❬On his
advent to power the President had proclaimed that there
was to be no more party; all were Republicans, all were
Federalists.❭ The pledge implied in these loving words he
qualified by removing some Federalist office holders and
putting Republicans in their places, and he has been
branded as the author of the spoils system.   But his
removals were not wholesale nor very numerous, and he
did not cease to pay homage to the better principle : he
had an excuse in the natural claims of his friends, whom
he found up to that time totally excluded from the public
service, and a less respectable excuse in the importunities
of partisans, for politics had now become a trade and office
seekers began to swarm.   His apology, however, raised a
laugh.   "If a due participation of office," he said, "is a
matter of right, how are the vacancies to be obtained?
Those by death are few, by resignation none.   Can any
other method than that of removal be proposed?"

Jefferson was disposed, as some other popular leaders
have been, to show jealousy of the judiciary, as a power
independent of the people and its chiefs.   Under his
administration the Circuit Court Act, extending the
action of the supreme judiciary and the number of judges
802. appointed for life was summarily repealed.   On the power
of the Supreme Court, then filled with judges appointed

by the opposite party, he could not fail to look with a
jealous eye. The impeachment of Justice Chase for par-   1803.
tisanship on the bench had, no doubt, his sympathy, though
he was too cautious to show his hand. The collapse of
the impeachment left the Supreme Court more independent than ever. But in the Union generally, from the tendency to make the judges elective and their tenure not
during good behaviour but for a term of years, the depression of the judiciary in the period succeeding this was the
rule.

< In Jefferson's second term fate was unkind to him.   The   1805-9.
philanthropist was called upon to deal with a question of
peace or war between his government and those of France
and Great Britain.> Europe had become the scene of a
vast and mortal struggle between the Napoleonic empire
and the independence of nations, in which at length the
British navy remained the sole stay of independence.
Napoleon's only law was his will. His will was that
there should be no neutrals. It was declared in his Berlin
and Milan decrees, and was carried into effect by the ruthless confiscation of American ships and goods. Great
Britain on her side exercised with a high hand against
neutral trade belligerent rights which the policy of nations
has since discarded. As the French Emperor treated her
islands so she treated the French Empire as in a state of
legal blockade, and intercepted American commerce with
its members. The situation, regarded even from our point
of view, was highly complicated, and allowance must be
made for the difficulties of those who had to deal with it
on either side. <The Americans might claim the right of
neutral trade.>But in this case the right could not be
exercised without practically taking part in the war, since

Great Britain, the land being entirely in the power of the enemy, had nothing left her but to press him by sea, which she could do only by cutting off his trade. To British apprehension the neutral trade was war in disguise. It was carrying supplies to a place besieged. John Randolph of Virginia, no Anglomaniac, painted the character of the trade with eccentric frankness. Supposing the choice of a British statesman to lie between the two evils, it might have been hard to say which was worse, open war with the United States, or the aid which their neutral trade would lend to France. You may have a right to traffic on a battle-field; but you will have difficulty in exercising it, especially if the battle-field is one in which nations are fighting for their lives. By keeping off the scene of conflict while the conflict raged, at the same time closing her own ports against combatants, America might have avoided collision; she could hardly avoid it in any other way.

With Great Britain there was another cause of quarrel, the impressment of British seamen found on board American vessels. Here Great Britain was clearly in the wrong. She ought to have kept her seamen by increasing their pay and putting an end to the grievances which 1797. produced the mutiny of the Nore. In heartlessly neglecting to render the service just to the common sailor, and at the same time making a brutal use of impressment, aristocratic government showed its dark side. It is true that impressment was conscription in a coarse form, and that the extreme notion of indefeasible allegiance still prevailed. But the practice, however lawful, was intolerable, and its offensiveness was sure to be aggravated by the conduct of British commanders full of the naval pride of their nation and perhaps irritated by the loss of their crews ; (for it is not denied that many British seamen were seduced from the service and that the American marine, both mercantile and national, was largely manned in this way.) We hear of a British captain having his whole crew spirited away without redress, and of a dozen British ships detained at once by loss of hands.⟨ The attack of the British ish *Leopard* on the American *Chesapeake* for the purpose 1807. of enforcing impressment was a flagrant outrage, and though apology was made and satisfaction was tendered by the British government, this was not done in a way to pluck the thorn out of the American bosom. It was unfortunate that England's foreign minister was at this time the surpassingly brilliant but not so wise, too often sarcastic, and sometimes insolent Canning.⟩ Feeling was embittered by the disclosure of a pretended plot on the part of the British government to sow dissension among 1809 the American States through Henry, a low adventurer, 1812. with whom Sir James Craik, the Governor of Canada, had been betrayed into imprudent relations, and who to ground a claim on the government for money had been tampering with malcontents in New England. What might have been done by courteous explanations and friendly appeals to avert the quarrel was unhappily not done.

Meantime the neutral trade in spite of all obstructions and aggressions was very gainful, commerce adjusted itself to the risks, British cruisers protected American merchantmen against French and Spanish privateers. The American merchants though they grumbled were willing to submit ; not from them came the demand for war. ⟩

"Our passion," said Jefferson, "is peace." He not only recoiled as a philanthropist from bloodshed, but as a

politician he with reason dreaded military propensities
and sabre sway. Such preparations for war as he could
be induced to make were scrupulously defensive, and his
fleet of gun-boats for the protection of the coast to be
launched when the invader should appear excited a smile.
Alone among all statesmen he tried to make war without
bloodshed by means of an embargo on trade. American
vessels were forbidden to leave port, foreign vessels were
obliged to sail in ballast, and coasting vessels were prohibited from landing their cargo at any but American
ports. ⟨ Total denial of trade would, Jefferson thought,
bring the belligerents, especially commercial England, to
reason.⟩ By his great majority in Congress and his personal
ascendancy he was enabled to carry this extraordinary
measure and to enforce observance with a high hand and
in language towards recalcitrants almost autocratic.⟩ An
extraordinary measure it was and more easily defensible
perhaps as an exercise of the war powers of the central
government than as an exercise of the power given it by
the constitution to regulate commerce, since total prohibition, whatever the courts of law might say, could hardly be
called regulation. On the part of Jefferson such a stretch
of authority was startling; but he had left his anarchical
theories on the steps of power, and had begun to boast of
the strength of republican government.⟨ Commerce ceased.⟩
The ships lay idle at the wharves, and the seafaring population lost its employment. ⟨The people suffered greatly
by the withdrawal of the profitable though hazardous trade.⟩
The measure of their loss was given by the crowd of vessels which, when the embargo was lifted, put to sea. New
England was to some extent indemnified by the development of her manufactures under the stringent protection

afforded by the embargo. ⟨ But on Virginia the effect was ruinous.⟩ Yet the respect of the people for the central authority was on the whole to a wonderful extent displayed by their submission to the law. At this the spirit of Alexander Hamilton might have rejoiced. But Jefferson's government became the object of hatred and his vast popularity waned. England remained obdurate; her situation was too desperate, her passions too highly inflamed for concession; her strong aristocratic government was not easily to be turned from its purpose by the sufferings of trade or industry, while her shipping interest gained by relief from American competition. After resorting to measures of enforcement which on the part of a monocrat he would have deemed flagrant tyranny, Jefferson was at last compelled to give up the embargo. Weariness and despondency overcame him. He let fall the reins of government before the term of his Presidency had expired, and he went into philosophic retirement at Monticello whence he returned no more. It is not the highest of his titles to fame in the eyes of his countrymen, but it may be not the lowest in the court of humanity, that he sacrificed his popularity in the attempt to find a bloodless substitute for war. His memory recovered from the shock and his reign over American opinion endured.

⟨ Jefferson's successor was his shield-bearer, Madison, another of the Virginians whom wealth and leisure enabled 1809. to devote themselves to politics and to supply the young Republic with statesmen.⟩⟨He had been at first a Federalist and a fellow worker of Hamilton and Jay, but he had been afterwards attracted to Jefferson and had perhaps recognized in Republican principles the passport to power.⟩ By American writers he is invested with the highest mental gifts. Yet the impression which he makes on the ordinary reader is rather that of a cultivated and somewhat prim mediocrity, though combined with a clear understanding, a scientific knowledge of politics, statesmanlike training, and a surefooted ambition. At his right hand was Gallatin, a Swiss, a man whose standing was, owing to his foreign origin, below his ability, once revolutionary enough to bear an equivocal part in the Whiskey Insurrection, now grown more moderate and the great financier of the Republic.

The event of Madison's Presidency is the war with England. Few things are more repulsive or less profitable than the study of the diplomatic embroilment in which the government of the United States was for years involved with those of England and France and which issued in a disastrous war. It is scarcely disputed by American historians that the injuries received by American commerce at the hands of France were fully as great as those received at the hands of England. Napoleon had confiscated American shipping and goods to an immense amount and coolly reckoned on the fruits of his violence as revenue. He seized a hundred and fifty ships in one year alone. His Rambouillet decree was a barefaced proclamation of rapine to which effect was at once given by a sweeping confiscation of American vessels. Not only was his will his sole law, but he pretended submission to no other, whereas England at all events recognized international law, and held herself ready to atone for a breach of it. But England was hated, France was not, and as an American historian says, insults and injuries which, coming from Great Britain, would have set the whole country on fire, were submitted to with patience and even with the

1812 to 1814.

pleasure with which a lover sometimes allows himself to
be trampled on and plundered by an imperious and profligate mistress.   Napoleon, it is true, did his best by false-
hood and subterfuge to lead the American government to
believe that he had withdrawn his decrees and that the
British Orders in Council alone stood in the way of the
recognition of neutral rights.   But the American government was, to say the least, not unwilling to be deceived.〉

A new influence, making for war, had come upon the
scene of American politics.   Settlement having now
crossed the whole line of the Alleghanies, the West, fast
becoming the great West, was added, and the union from
being an Atlantic was becoming a continental confederation.   In Kentucky, the population drawn mainly from
the slave States, was a picturesque but formidable mixture
of the slave owner and the pioneer.   The character of the
Kentuckian was that of the hunter and the frontiersman
with an imported strain of the slave owner, and he was
always engaged in murderous war with Indians.   His food
was salt pork without vegetables; whiskey he drank from
morning till night.   That he should be quarrelsome naturally followed.   His amusements were horse-racing, cock-
fighting, betting, and gambling, to the last of which he
was much given.   He was always fighting, and in fighting
he kicked, tore, bit, and gouged.   In all his proceedings
he showed a lawless vigour which might prove the wild
stock of civilized virtue.   In the financial field he presently distinguished himself by wild-cat banking, by the
delirium of paper money, and consequent repudiation.
Removed from the sea, he and the western people generally had not, like New England, a commerce to be ruined
by war, and of the English tradition and sentiment which
still lingered at Boston he was utterly devoid.

As were the people, so were the leaders of their choice, and of these the foremost was Henry Clay, a highly refined Kentuckian, yet a Kentuckian, as his taste for gambling, among other characteristics, showed. Clay put himself at the head of a set of young politicians who were bent on forcing the government into war. Calhoun, from South Carolina, the future champion of the slave power, was of the same set. But Clay was the most fiery, as well as the most fascinating. Not only did he want a war with England, but he looked forward to a series of wars to be carried on till one of the nations should be crushed, and the war of 1812 was among the achievements which he wished to be inscribed on his tomb. The President did not want war, but he wanted re-election, and he was made to feel that to be re-elected he must declare war. The fact is recorded without disguise. We have come down from Washington to Madison. When Napoleon, to turn the scale against England, feigned a withdrawal of his decrees, Madison affected to believe him; it seems not certain that he did.

1812 to 1814. England had given no special provocation at this juncture. On the contrary she was showing a disposition to make concessions. In fact the Orders in Council which stood first among the ostensible causes of quarrel had been withdrawn when war was declared. Clay then said that war must be waged against impressment, though he afterwards, as a commissioner treating for peace, was content to let that issue drop, and he was so far from being inflexible as to the principle concerned that, as Secretary of State at an after day, he offered Great Britain to surrender deserters from her military and naval service and from her mercantile marine, if she would surrender fugitive slaves who had taken refuge under her flag. For what cause he cared little; war he would have. The fingers of the Kentuckian were twined in the locks of hated England and would not let go because the special ground of quarrel happened to be withdrawn. England was sorely pressed in the struggle with Napoleon. Of her allies none were left but the Spanish people and Russia, which Napoleon was preparing to invade. The opportunity for striking her was tempting, and Canada seemed an easy prey. The prospect of sharing Napoleon's victories would also have its attraction, nor is there anything in the violence of a brilliant tyranny uncongenial to the violence of such democracy as that of young Clay. These probably were the real motives of the war which was made by Kentucky and the slave owners, and against which New England protested from the outset, not on commercial grounds alone, though on her commerce the heaviest blows were sure to fall, but because it would bring the Republic into unnatural alliance with the universal tyrant against the independence of nations and the rights of man. On the independence of nations and the rights of man Kentucky and the slave owners probably set little store. But had Napoleon won, the turn of America would have come. Nothing seems more certain than that he would have stretched his arm across the Atlantic, reduced the United States to vassalage, and enforced the retrocession of Louisiana. Of all things, what he hated most was a republic. That the conquest was practicable, the events of the war with England proved. It was unlucky that Erskine, the young British envoy at Washington, in his eagerness to preserve peace, promised concessions which exceeded his instructions and was disowned by the evil genius of Canning in a manner which inflamed the quarrel. The war was not national; it was made by the war-hawks, as Clay and his party were called. ⟨ In the House of Representatives, the great organ of popular sentiment, the declaration received a majority of only thirty votes, far less than the normal majority of the Democratic party, fifteen Republicans voting in the minority, and it passed the Senate with difficulty and only by the close vote of nineteen to thirteen, six Republicans voting against war. ⟩ The division was geographical, the North being in a majority of two to one against the war. At Baltimore the mob seconded the party of violence by riot and massacre.

⟨ The war of 1812 while it rekindled the fires of unnatural hatred, and renewed the schism of the Anglo-Saxon race, was to both combatants barren of profit and honour. ⟩ Only the "war-hawk" politicians who did not shed their own blood gained in political advancement, and perhaps by the exercise of war patronage. ⟨ Clay and Calhoun had confidently promised the Americans the conquest of Canada. The militia of Kentucky, Clay said, would of itself suffice for the achievement. Instead of this, the forces the Republic put forth in the invasion were repelled by a small body of British troops aided, not as appears at the outset zealously, by the local militia, and Michigan was lost. ⟩ As the war went on the Americans learned discipline, were better led, and were more successful, but Clay's boast remained unfulfilled. ⟨ The French Canadians were kept true to Great Britain by the same influences as before, and helped to gain more than one brilliant victory in her cause. ⟩ At sea the Americans had better fortune. The British, confident in their naval prowess, not considering that the Americans were as good seamen as themselves, better shipbuilders, and more expert as gunners forgetting, too, the exploits of

Paul Jones, ventured on frigate duels with inferior armaments and lost three frigates, one of which was carried into an American port. The shock was far greater than the loss, and was but half counteracted by a victory in a duel on equal terms between the *Shannon* and the *Chesa-* 1813. *peake*. On the other hand five thousand British regulars under Ross, landing on the American coast, paraded the country at their ease, scattered before them the militia which was drawn out to meet them at Bladensburg and 1814. took Washington, giving thereby one more proof of the ascendancy of discipline in war. ⟨The public buildings at Washington were burned, an act of folly and vandalism which no plea of retaliation for American ravages in Canada could warrant. The object of war is a good peace, and the fewer thorns are left in the heart of the enemy the better the peace will be. ⟩

⟨ Kentucky, Tennessee, and the Southern fire-eaters were hot for the war, but elsewhere there was luke-warmness or worse. The ranks of the army were unfilled, the finances were exhausted, specie payments were suspended, the military administration had disgracefully broken down.⟩ ⟨Roused by the loss of the three frigates, Great Britain put forth her naval power, and the American ports underwent strict blockade.⟩ Privateering, though destructive, was unremunerative and even cried out for government bounties to keep it on foot. In New England discontent approached the point of secession, and a convention of New England States at Hartford not only protested against the war but demanded an organic change in confederation.⟩ Meantime the fortunes of Napoleon sank at Moscow, at Leipsic, at Vittoria.⟨ England's fleets and armies, released from the struggle with him, were set free for action in America.⟩

⟨The war party then gave way and envoys were sent to
Ghent to treat for peace. It was a peace which showed
that there ought to have been no war, for no question was
settled, nor was anything surrendered on either side. The
questions of belligerent rights and of impressment, about
which America had ostensibly gone to war, were simply
allowed to drop. Mr. Clay was one of the American
envoys. He did his best to make the negotiations mis-
carry, but at last he set his hand to the treaty. There
were those in England who desired that she should continue the war, bringing her full force, now at liberty, to
bear, and send Wellington to America. But if the result
had been an extension of her American territories with a
deeper entanglement in American affairs, the gain would
have been a loss. That there was no real object to be attained was Wellington's own judgment. Peace was welcome to all except the farmers on the northern frontier of
the United States who had been growing rich by selling
supplies to the British troops.⟩

⟨There was no ocean cable in those days. Peace had
already been made at Ghent, when at New Orleans General
Pakenham, possessed apparently with the same blind confidence which had been shown by the British commander
1815. at Bunker's Hill, led his troops to the attack of the impreg-
nable and almost unapproachable breastworks with which
the city had been protected by the skill and energy of
General Andrew Jackson, who appearing on the scene at
a decisive moment, showed his extraordinary powers of
command. The British soldiers, formed by the pedantry
of their commander in close column and unable to reach
their enemy, fell helplessly under the fire poured upon
them in perfect security by the riflemen who swarmed be-

hind the breastworks. The death of the British Commander-in-Chief, by causing confusion, enhanced the
disaster. At the single point where the veterans did
encounter their enemy, he, as Jackson himself frankly said,
fled before them. The American loss in killed and wounded
was thirteen. Such was the battle of New Orleans. It
would have been almost as much of a battle and a victory
had the British army been overwhelmed by the Mississippi.
But the affair had important results, for it made General
Jackson the idol of the American people, and the autocratic President of the United States.⟩

The war is sometimes justified on account of its supposed effect in consolidating American union. To make
war for such a purpose would surely be a satanic policy.
⟨Instead of consolidation, the war nearly produced secession, to the very verge of which it drove New England.⟩
⟨The true instruments of consolidation were, not the
war, but the improved means of intercommunication, the
national roads, the canals, the steamships, the railways, to
which the period following the war gave birth, as well as
the growing activity of the press, and the other intellectual
agencies which overcome geographical distance. The fruit
of moral or political effort is not to be won by violence.⟩
A second war of independence the war of 1812 has been
called, but how could America be made politically more
independent of the mother country, and how could war
sever the historical bond or weaken the influences which
a mother country will always exercise over a colony, let
the political relation be what it will? Mental independence was promoted, not by the war, but by migration
westward which left old world ideas and sentiments
behind. Violent antipathies like passionate attachments,

as Washington said, do not emancipate but enslave. The schism in the Anglo-Saxon race had been renewed, and Canada, instead of being annexed, had been estranged. On industry and commerce and the wealth of the nation the effects of war are always the same. Such is the debt of gratitude due to the " war-hawks." It will not be much increased if to the material results of the conflict we add an inflation of military pride which there was nothing in the balance of victory and defeat to warrant, but which nevertheless ensued.

Twenty years afterwards the eyes of American politicians desirous of aggrandizement were once more turned toward the British dominions in North America by a Canadian rebellion which stretched out its arms for aid to the republicanism of the United States. But national ambition was not aroused. Sympathy was confined to filibustering along the border. A bubble of war which the burning of the *Caroline*, an American armed vessel, by Canadians had blown, burst after an international altercation without harm. There still remained between Great Britain and America dangerous questions about boundaries in Maine and Oregon. The Oregon question at one time assumed an angry form, and in the United States democratic mobs and " war-hawks " were shouting " fifty-four forty or fight," while their British counterparts, such as Palmerston, were or affected to be not less eager for the fray. But diplomacy, under the auspices of such statesmen as Peel and Webster, brought about a peaceful settlement. Canada perhaps receiving in both cases less than her due, but as much as could be expected by a dependency which leaned upon the arm of the Imperial country, itself contributing nothing to the armaments of the empire. The settlement was made

1837.

easier by the indifference of the southern fire-eaters to ex-
tensions of territory in the north which would turn the
political balance in favour of freedom. War and serious
danger of war being at an end, American hatred of England
might have subsided had not Irish immigrants brought
with them their inveterate feud and imposed their sentiment on the politicians and press of the United States.

<After Madison came Monroe, the last of the Virginian 1817.
line, who was elected with ease and re-elected virtually by
acclamation.> Since the day of his Jacobin accolade he
had become a sober and commonplace statesman. <Wash-
ington was his model, and something like the state of the
Washington period reigned again at the White House.>
<Monroe's title to renown is the doctrine, stamped with
his name, which proclaims the new world independent of
the old.><The American dependencies of Spain had now
risen in revolt against the Imperial country, while in Spain
herself the Holy Alliance dominating over Europe had by
the hand of the restored Bourbons of France crushed
parliamentary government and reinstalled absolute monarchy. There was reason to fear that the Alliance meant
to extend its policy of reaction to South America and
perhaps to place a Bourbon on the throne of a South
American Empire. It was to close the door against anything of this kind that Monroe put forth his manifesto,
which warns the European powers that the western hemisphere is no longer a field either for their colonization or
for their political interference. Any attempt on the part
of a European power to control the destiny of an American community the American President declares will
be viewed as a manifestation of an unfriendly disposition towards the United States; implying thereby, be it

observed, that the United States are the guardian power of the hemisphere. It may be that Monroe was not the sole or the first promulgator of the doctrine. But by him it was propounded most clearly and at a juncture which gave it practical force. Great Britain and the United States were now acting in union. For Great Britain, whose function it has always been to preserve the balance of tendencies as well as of power in Europe, was opposed to the domination of the Holy Alliance as she had been to that of Napoleon, and Canning, as her foreign minister, was beginning to show his liberal side. ⟩

Clay's ardent spirit would have led him at once to give the embrace of fraternity to the new-born Republics of South America. More cautious counsels prevailed and confined the action of the government to the promulgation of the Monroe doctrine and a prompt recognition of South American independence. It soon appeared even to Clay himself what sort of embrace that of the South American Republics would have been. He had been transported with the glorious spectacle of eighteen millions of people struggling to burst their chains and be free. He soon had reason to confess that the result of bursting chains, in the case of those who are unfit for freedom, is not freedom but a change of chain. Webster may have meant to cap Clay as well as to show his cultivated feeling for the parent of literature and art when in a grand oration he proposed to send a commissioner as an envoy of sympathy to insurgent Greece. Here the Washingtonian tradition of non-interference in European affairs prevailed. ⟨ Indeed if the Monroe doctrine was to be respected and Europe was to keep her hands off America, it was necessary that America should keep her hands off Europe. ⟩

CHAPTER IV.

DEMOCRACY AND SLAVERY.

THE eight years of Monroe's Presidency were a halcyon
period after the storm of war; they were years of revived commerce, of return to specie payments, of renewed
immigration, of the continued expansion westward which
was not only enlarging the area of equalized wealth and
the field of the great political experiment, but shifting
the centre of power from New England and Virginia
towards the west. There was a general absence, during
these years, of great party questions and a lull in party
strife which caused Monroe's Presidency to be called the
era of good feeling. The calm, however, was broken by
one blast which, though it died away for the time, was the
premonitory gust of a tremendous storm. Free and slave
States had so far been admitted to the Union in pairs, one
slave State and one free, so that the political balance
between the two interests was preserved, not in the House
of Representatives, where the representation was by population, but in the Senate, where each State, large or small,
had two members. The demand of Missouri, a part of the
Louisiana purchase, over which slavery prevailed, to be
admitted as a State, threatened to upset the balance, and
awakened the dormant but mortal antagonism between
slavery and freedom. Conscience, indeed, though drugged

by policy had never entirely slumbered. Among the Quakers of Pennsylvania it had remained awake. ⟨The opponents of slavery moved for its exclusion from Missouri as a condition of her admission to the Union. The struggle between them and the friends of slavery was long and angry.⟩ It brought the national House into collision with the federal Senate. When apparently composed, it broke out again in a new form. ⟨But at length fear for the stability of the Union, which by this time had become an object of general worship, prevailed, and a compromise was effected by which all north of the latitude thirty-six, thirty, saving territory included in Missouri, was secured for freedom, and all south of that line was given up to slavery.⟩ 1820. ⟨The political balance was preserved by the simultaneous admission of Maine⟩ The truce thus obtained lasted, so far as the national parties were concerned, for twenty years, proving by its duration the paramount importance attached by the American people to their Union. ⟨But three ominous results of the struggle still remained. In the first place the geographical line had been drawn between the domain, social and political, of slavery and that of freedom. In the second place it had been shown that whatever pains might be taken to designate slavery as a purely domestic institution over which the national government had no jurisdiction, and with which the national conscience was unconcerned, the fact was that the question was national and one with which the national government would in the end be compelled to deal. In the third place slavery had shown itself no longer as a vanishing relic of the past, but as a permanent interest and power. Whitney's invention of the cotton gin had enormously increased the production of cotton, and with it the value of slave labour and the addiction of the South to the system.⟩

The lull of party was no lull of personal ambition or of personal contests for the Presidency. Now we see in full force the Presidential fever and its effects on the character and conduct of public men. Soon in place of the Congressional caucus, through which the politicians of each party had hitherto nominated candidates for the Presidency, comes the popular convention, at first local and then national, with the grand campaign of party with its sinister accessories such as we have it at the present day. Now culminates the reign of the "machine," with its retinue of office-seeking workers, first perfected in New York by DeWitt Clinton and Van Buren, with their Albany Regency and their "Bucktails." Foremost in the arena were Henry Clay the Kentuckian, Daniel Webster the New Englander, and John C. Calhoun of South Carolina. Clay was perhaps the first consummate party leader of the Congressional and platform type, Jefferson having worked, not on the platform, but in the closet and through the press. He was a paragon of the personal fascination now styled magnetism. Magnetic, indeed, his manner and voice must have been if they could make the speeches that he has left us pass for the most cogent reasoning and the highest eloquence. Yet multitudes came from distances, in those days immense, to hear him. A cynical critic said that Clay could get more people to listen to him and fewer people to vote for him than any other man in the Union. He however did get many votes though never quite enough. His power of winning the hearts of men was unique. When at last he missed his prize by losing the election for the Presidency his partisans wept like children; one of them is said to have died of grief. He was ardently patriotic, after the war-hawk fashion, but the Presidency was always in his thoughts and its attraction accounts for the perturbations of his political orbit. He said that he would rather be right than be President; but it has been too truly remarked that even at the moment of that memorable utterance he was thinking more of being President than of being right. His policy and sentiments were intensely American and by the cosmopolitans would now be designated as jingo. He was a protectionist on what he deemed patriotic grounds, and the chief author of a system to which Hamilton had only moderately inclined. He was for national expenditure on public works, for national grants of money to the States, for everything that could magnify the nation. The Union, as the palladium of national greatness, was his idol, and his proudest achievements as a statesman were compromises by which the Union was saved for a time when it had been imperilled by collision between the slave States and the free. Over each of these compromises he drew the brilliant rainbow of complacent eloquence, which, however, proved no guarantee against the flood. A native of the great slave State of Virginia, settled in Kentucky where slavery existed though it did not predominate, he seems at least to have felt the evils of the system, and he had done himself credit by opposition to it in his earlier days. But the highest and the absorbing object of his affection was national greatness embodied in the Union.

As Henry Clay was a genuine, though adopted, son of Kentucky, so Daniel Webster was a genuine son of New England. His character was cast in the Puritan mould, and formed by the New England school system under which he had been a teacher as well as a pupil. He was grave, staid, and in the cast of his character moral and

devout.   In his later years he was given to running carelessly into debt and like many other men of his day too
fond of wine.   As an orator of reason he has no superior
if he has an equal in the English language.   It is difficult
at least to say what political speech can vie in logical force
and impressiveness with his speech defending the Union
in reply to the southern separatist Hayne, or what forensic
speech excels in the same qualities his speech for the prose-
cution in the murder case of White.   By the speech in 1830.
reply to Hayne he produced a great and permanent effect
on the political sentiment of the American people. —
"While the union lasts, we have high, exciting, gratifying
prospects spread out before us, for us and our children.
Beyond that I seek not to penetrate the veil.   God grant
that, in my day at least, that curtain may not rise.   God
grant that on my vision never may be opened what lies
behind.   When my eyes shall be turned to behold for the
last time the sun in heaven, may I not see him shining on
the broken and dishonoured fragments of a once glorious
union; on States dissevered, discordant, belligerent; on a
land rent with civil feuds, or drenched it may be in fraternal blood!   Let their last feeble and lingering glance
rather behold the gorgeous ensign of the Republic, now
known and honoured throughout the earth, still full high
advanced, its arms and trophies streaming in their original
lustre, not a stripe erased or polluted, not a single star
obscured, bearing for its motto no such miserable interroga-
tory as What is all this worth? nor those other words of
delusion and folly Liberty first, and Union afterwards, but
everywhere spread all over in characters of living light
blazing in all its ample folds as they float over the sea and
over the land and in every wind under the whole heavens

that other sentiment dear to every true American heart —
Liberty and Union, now and forever, one and inseparable."
These words thrilled through all American hearts at the
time, remained engraved in all American hearts forever.
We must bear in mind their influence and the force of the
sentiment to which they appealed when we find the American people wavering between morality and the Union.
Webster's economical and financial speeches are also first
rate of their kind. His style has been compared to the
strokes of a trip hammer, which his sentences resembled in
measured force but not in monotony. The majesty of
intellect sat on his beetling brow and he had the look and
port of Jove. He was and felt himself a king. It is told
of him that when one of his notes had fallen due, he majes-
tically waved his hand and said " Let it be paid." All men
bowed down to him; all men crowded to hear him. He
swayed the opinions of all men; but he did not, like Clay,
win their hearts. He never was a great party leader, nor
was he ever a hopeful candidate for the Presidency. It
must be added that his moral strength was not equal to
his power of mind. In regard to the great moral question
of slavery, his desire of the Presidency at last overcame
his principle. In his general sentiments and opinions he
was a descendant of the old Federalist party, a republican
without being a democrat, a believer in property as a qualification for political power, an upholder both in his State
and in the federation of the conservative parts of the constitution, as well as devoutly loyal to the Union. 〉
〈 A figure in some respects more striking than that of
either Clay or Webster, and one to which a melancholy
interest attaches, is that of John C. Calhoun of South
Carolina. Calhoun was a man of Scotch-Irish origin, with

the fervent but sombre energy characteristic of that race.⟩
By temper he was a political Calvinist, while South Carolina gave him for a creed slavery, of which she was the
centre and the soul. ⟨As a speaker he impressed, not by
anything that appealed to the imagination, but by intense
earnestness and logical force.⟩ On his face and character
there was a shade of sadness which deepened as his career
took a more tragic turn. ⟨No one questioned his purity or
sincerity, yet in his course also the effect of the Presidential fever may be traced.✗He set out with Clay as one of
the war party of 1812, devoted to national greatness.✗He
walked at first in the trodden path of ambition; was
Vice-President, was Secretary of State, and had the Presidency in view. But a cloud came over his prospects and
he was gradually led to fall back on slavery as his peculiar
platform, to identify himself with the institution, to become not only its defender but its propagator, and, in its
interest, the upholder of State right.✗He was the first
statesman who, discarding not only the philosophic condemnation of slavery fashionable among the old republicans of the South but the apologies of its moderate upholders, proclaimed that slavery was a positive good, that it
was the only relation possible between the white and black
races, and even that the system of society based on it was
the best and alone stable, while the system based on freedom and equality was unstable and anarchic.⟩ "Many in
the South," he said, "had once believed that slavery was a
moral and political evil. But that folly and delusion are
gone. We see it now in its true light and regard it as
the most safe and stable basis for free institutions in the
world." He was even ready to maintain that it gave the
labourer more than was given him by free labour, while it

exempted society from the disorders and dangers arising
out of the conflict between labour and capital. ⟨Calhoun
became the idol and the guiding star of the slave-owning
aristocracy, above all of the hot Southern youth. ⟩When he
died there was laid over his grave at Charleston, a great
slab of marble inscribed with the single word " Calhoun "
as the sufficient epitaph of his greatness. ⟨He was one of
the men who are born to bring questions to an issue.⟩⟨He
distinctly saw that on the two sides of the geographical
line which separated freedom from slavery there were two
communities opposed to each other in social and political
structure, in character, sentiment, and interest, which
though yoked together by the union were not united. His
proposal of two Presidents, one for the free States, the
other for the slave States, each with a veto on all national
legislation, was impracticable and grotesque, but it pointed
true to the nature of the problem.⟩

Oratory and orators ruled the hour. The chief scene of
the great debates of this period was the Senate, always
attractive of the highest ability. Its number was less than
fifty, but the audience, though small, was of the choicest,
and on grand occasions the galleries were crowded by
people not only from Washington but from distant cities.
⟨Of the struggle between freedom and slavery the Senate
was the natural arena, because there, representation being
by States, the forces were evenly balanced, whereas in
the House of Representatives, the population of the free
States, increasing faster than that of the slave States, had
a great preponderance notwithstanding the constitutional
compromise which gave slavery two votes for every three
slaves.⟩Thus, in regard to the two groups of States, the
Senate was the safeguard of the federal against the national

principle.⟩ Nor were Clay, Webster, and Calhoun the only Senators of mark. Not far beneath them was Benton from Missouri, which was a western and semi-slave State, apt to breed statesmen neutral or wavering on the question of slavery and caring most for the Union. Benton was for thirty years a Senator. He was of coarse mould compared with the other three, but of great power, gigantic industry, and possessed of an extensive knowledge of politics, which he sometimes grotesquely displayed; perhaps the first thorough specimen of a politician, with a virtue genuine but not adamantine, and a patriotism which yielded only to the strong exigencies of party, it might be in the sincere belief that the party was the country. Hardly to be named with these men was John Randolph, a Virginian of high family, with more than the arrogance of his class, who used to come into the Senate in his hunting dress with his hunting whip in his hand, and behave as if he were in his kennel; a man of natural ability, without good sense or power of self-control, firmly attached to no party or even opinion, keen and reckless in invective, the terror of those at whom his lean finger was pointed in debate, at last a political wreck and almost a maniac. Randolph sometimes told wholesome truths in a pungent way.

⟨ Apart from slavery the great question was the tariff. Before the war New England had been commercial, and as such in favour of free trade. The war, suspending her commerce turned her to manufactures to which it afforded strict protection. Peace bringing an influx of British goods made New England manufacturers crave for a protective tariff. Clay on patriotic grounds was the ardent advocate of what he styled the American system.

though he was reminded by Webster that the system, by
his own showing, had not been American but European. 7
" This favourite American policy, sir," said Webster, " is
what America has never tried, and this odious foreign
policy is what we are told foreign States have never pursued.   Sir, that is the truest American policy which shall
most usefully employ American capital and American
labour, and best sustain the whole population.   With me
it is a fundamental axiom that is interwoven with all my
opinions that the great interests of the country are united
and inseparable, that agriculture, commerce, and manufactures will prosper together or languish together, and
that all legislation is dangerous which proposes to benefit
one of these without looking to consequences which may
fall on the others." ⟨Webster at first opposed protection,
and upheld with admirable breadth, clearness, and cogency
the doctrine of Adam Smith.⟩ There is nothing better
on the side of free trade than his speeches.   He crushed
the fallacy of the balance of trade, showing by a familiar
example that if the excess in value of imports over ex-
ports proved the trader to be a loser, the fruits of the most
gainful voyage might be set down as a loss.   He ex-
pounded the true nature of commerce as being not a
gambling among nations for a stake, to be won by some
and lost by others, not tending to impoverish one of the
parties to it while it enriched the other, but making all
parties gain, all parties alike profit, all parties grow rich.
He showed that in buying foreign articles we do not encourage foreign labour to the prejudice of our own, since
every such article, being earned by our own labour, is as
much the product of our own labour as if we had manu-
factured it ourselves.   " I know," he said, " it would be

very easy to promote manufactures, at least for a time, but probably only for a short time. If we might act in disregard of other interests we could cause a sudden transfer of capital and a violent change in the pursuits of men. We could exceedingly benefit some classes by these means; what then would become of the interests of others?" If Adam Smith had been before him in all this, he gave it new force by his eloquence and put on it the stamp of practical statesmanship. Webster's arguments have lost none of their weight though he afterwards showed his want of moral stability by striking his flag to protection and rather lamely defending his inconsistency on the plea that, though his principles remained unchanged, protection having then become the established system, there was nothing for him but to accept it and look to the interests of his own constituents. The great speech of Clay on American industry is a declamation based throughout on the assumption that protection is patriotic, as though any economical measure could be patriotic which was not productive of wealth to the whole nation. Clay's knowledge of economical history and of history in general may be measured by his reference to Spain as a nation which had declined owing to her lack of a protectionist system. His clearness of economic vision may be measured by his dictum, uttered in defence of protectionism, that "the great desideratum in political economy is the same as in private pursuits; that is, what is the best application of the aggregate industry of a nation that can be made honestly to produce the largest sum of national wealth?" He could not have stated more clearly the main argument of his opponents. With more reason might Clay point to the practice of other nations and notably to that of England

which still had and was destined for many years longer to
have her corn laws and Navigation Act. It must also be
remembered in justice to Clay and others who were trying
to force manufactures that the evils of the factory system
had not then been seen on a large scale. Further it
must be said that Clay regarded protection as temporary,
and perhaps could hardly have been expected to foresee
that what was granted as temporary would, by the combined force of the favoured interests, be made eternal.
Some demurred, apparently with reason, to the assumption by Congress of a power of imposing taxes for any
purpose but that of revenue. ⟨The constitution gave Congress power to regulate commerce, but not to regulate
industry or to force the people to leave one industry for
another.⟩ The vices of protectionism soon appeared. In
1828 a conjunction of sinister interests carried by log-
rolling for their own benefit a tariff which was justly styled
the tariff of abominations. We are told that members
of Congress voted for the bill at the bidding of their constituents while they were opposed to its objects, foreseeing the abuses which it entailed, and that it offered the
means of wide-spread bribery in the elections. We see
incidentally that the elective system had disclosed another
of its fatal liabilities, and that the representative instead
of being a man of superior lights, picked out for the great
work of legislation, was becoming a mere delegate and the
mouth-piece of his constituency without free judgment or
conscience of his own.

With reference to this tariff of 1828 Benton in his
history of the Senate says, "tariff bills each exceeding
the other in its degree of protection have become a regular
appendage of our Presidential elections, coming round in

every cycle of four years with that returning event."
McDuffie, from South Carolina, raised with an apocalyp-
tic vehemence the veil of the future. "Sir, when I consider that by a single Act like the present from five to
ten millions of dollars may be transferred annually from
one part of the community to another, when I consider
the disguise of disinterested patriotism under which the
basest and most profligate ambition may perpetrate such
an act of injustice and political prostitution, I cannot hesitate for a moment to pronounce this very system of indirect bounties the most stupendous instrument of corruption
ever placed in the hands of public functionaries. It brings
ambition and avarice and wealth into a combination which
it is fearful to contemplate, because it is almost impossible
to resist. Do we not perceive at this very moment the
extraordinary and melancholy spectacle of less than one
hundred thousand capitalists by means of this unhallowed
combination exercising an absolute and despotic control
over the opinions of eight millions of free citizens and the
fortunes and destinies of ten millions? Sir, I will not
anticipate or forbode evil. I will not permit myself to
believe that the Presidency of the United States will ever
be bought and sold by this system of bounties and pro-
hibitions; but I must say that there are certain quarters
of this Union in which, if a candidate for the Presidency
were to come forward with the Harrisburg tariff in his
hand, nothing could resist his pretensions if his adversary
were opposed to this unjust system of oppression. Yes,
sir, that bill would be a talisman which could give a
charmed existence to the candidate who would pledge himself to support it; and although he were covered with all
the ' multiplying villanies of nature,' the 'most immaculate

patriot and profound statesman in the nation could hold
no competition with him if he should refuse to grant this
new species of imperial donative." Mr. McDuffie, coming
from the South which exported and did not manufacture,
was perhaps enlightened, as his opponents were blinded,
by local interest. In the economical firmament it was still
early dawn. To Clay and his friends the policy of fostering native industries till they were able to stand alone
might well seem wise. Experience had not yet shown
that the protection once given would never be willingly
resigned, and that a combination of privileged interests
log-rolling for each other would be sure to prevail over
the public good. But it may surely be said that for a
nation so active, so intelligent, so inventive, perfect industrial liberty would always have been best.

Not unconnected with the question between free trade
and protection was that of the sale of public lands. Should
they be regarded as a national property out of which profit
was to be made by the federal government, or should they
be thrown open freely to the settler? The protectionists
generally leant to the former, free traders to the latter and
more liberal side. The effect of throwing freely open all
the lands of the west to settlement was to diminish the
value of the lands in the east and by drawing away labour
westwards to enhance its price to the eastern employer.
After a temporary obstruction of settlement and some
gambling and speculation in public lands the higher
interest prevailed.

National expenditure on improvements, such as the
great Cumberland road, was an issue on which those who
championed a strong nationality and a liberal interpretation of the constitution in favour of the central government

were pitted against the jealous upholders of strict right and strict construction. In this case also the opponents of the policy might have pointed to the dangers of corruption.

For the succession to Monroe there were four com- 1824. petitors: John Quincy Adams, son of the President; Henry Clay; Crawford, a powerful and crafty politician, who showed the tenacity of the Presidential fever by re- maining a candidate when he had been stricken with paralysis; and Andrew Jackson, whose blood-red star was now rising above the political horizon and threatening with extinction those of the politicians who had evoked the war spirit for the purposes of their own ambition. Jackson had ninety electoral votes, Adams eighty-four, Crawford forty-one, and Clay thirty-seven. No one hav- ing a clear majority the election was thrown by the article of the constitution providing for the case into the House of Representatives, while the decision was thrown into the hands of Clay, who though out of the pale of election himself, as the choice of the House was confined to the . three having the highest number of votes, commanded followers enough to turn the scale. Clay decided in favour of Adams. The Jacksonians contended that their man having the largest number of votes was the choice of the people, whose fiat the House ought to have registered. To which the answer was, first, that there was nothing to show that in a contest between Jackson and Adams by themselves Jackson would have had the majority, and in the second place that to make a plurality decisive would be to abrogate an article of the constitution. Clay, per- haps too conscious of rectitude, ventured to accept the Secretaryship of State from the man whom his influence had made President. The Jacksonians cried out that he had been bought and the calumny systematically and unscrupulously worked by his enemies pursued him to his grave.

1825. ⟨Monroe was the last President of the Virginian line, John Quincy Adams the last from New England⟩⟨The centre of power was passing from the east to the west. Adams was a genuine New Englander of the Puritan stock, austerely moral, from his boyhood laboriously self-trained, not only staid but solemn in his teens, intensely self-conscious, ever engaged in self-examination, the punctual keeper of a voluminous diary, an invariably early riser, a daily reader of the Bible even in the White House, scrupulously methodical and strictly upright in all his ways; but testy, unconciliatory, unsympathetic, absolutely destitute of all the arts by which popularity is won. His election does the highest credit to the respect of the electors for public virtue unadorned.⟩ The peculiar features of his father's character were so intensified in him that he may be deemed the typical figure rather than his father. In opinions he was a Federalist who having broken with his party on the question of foreign relations and the embargo had been put out of its pale but had retained its general mould. ⟨As he was about the last President chosen for merit not for availability, so he was about the last whose only rule was not party but the public service.⟩ So strictly did he observe the principle of permanency and purity in the Civil Service, that he refused to dismiss from office a Postmaster-General whom he knew to be intriguing against him. The demagogic era had come but he would not recognize its coming. He absolutely refused to go on the stump, to conciliate the press, to do anything for the purpose of courting popularity and making himself a party. His obstinacy was fatal to his ambition but is not dishonourable to his memory.

⟨Adams was a candidate for the usual second term. But he stood no chance against Jackson whose candidacy had commenced on the morrow of the last election.⟩Nobody stands much chance against a successful soldier in a country where military glory is rare. In the United States there have been, if we include Washington, five distinct soldier Presidents, while a military record has contributed to other elections and nominations.⟩In England, an old war power, but one man can be said to have been made prime minister by glory in war, and the Duke of Wellington was not merely a soldier, since besides having been in Parliament as a young man and Irish Secretary, he was almost the chief political adviser of monarchical and aristocratic Europe.⟩ Military glory moreover is outside the pale of ordinary rivalries and escapes the envy which in all democracies has great force. ⟨Jackson, though he had once been in Congress, as we have seen, and had vented his jealous spleen on Washington, was a fighter, with an iron will and great powers of command, ill educated, destitute of the knowledge and the habits of a statesman, with an uncontrolled temper and almost as much swayed by passion as any Indian chief, though, like many an Indian chief, he could bear himself when he pleased with dignity and even with grace.⟩⟨That he had beaten the British at New Orleans was his title to the headship of the nation, and he had not lessened his popularity by the lawless execution of two Englishmen, Ambrister and Arbuthnot, or by some acts of equally lawless aggression on Spanish territory⟩ outrages against which a moral minority in Congress had protested in vain,

1828

while John Quincy Adams, swayed probably by his dislike
of England, had for once deviated from his moral course
and helped to whitewash the man who was destined to
oust him from the Presidential chair. But a greater force
even than that of military renown was bearing on Andrew
Jackson to the Presidency. Hitherto the Republic had
not been democratic. The common people had been content with their votes and had left government to an aristocracy of intellect drawn largely from the bar. But now
they desired to govern. They were beginning to suspect
that they were fooled by intellect and to wish to see one
of themselves in power. Andrew Jackson was one of
themselves; he was not only the old hero but "Old Hickory," a plain honest man who would govern by a good
homely rule, sweep away abuses, and see that no more
tricks were played by superior cunning upon the people.
To rule, a multitude must be incarnate in a man, and the
American multitude was incarnate in Andrew Jackson.
The old hero's transcendent availability drew around his
standard a host of machine politicians, office-seekers, and
journalists, to blow his trumpet and organize the campaign in his favour. Jackson Committees were formed
all over the country to carry on the crusade, and were
aided by a partisan press inspired from a centre. This
was perhaps the first regularly organized campaign.
Feeling was red hot and calumny was rife. Adams was
charged with monarchism, with aristocracy, with corruption, with libel, with odious wealth, with insolvency, with
greediness of public money, with being wrong in his public
accounts, with charging for fictitious journeys, with using
government servants to electioneer for him, with corrupting the civil service, with employing the federal patronage

to influence elections, with charging the public for a
billiard table which he put in the White House, with
patronizing duelling (while Jackson was a desperate
duellist), with having quarrelled with his father, with
acting as procurer to the Emperor of Russia, with having
married an Englishwoman. On the other hand aspersions
were cast on Jackson's somewhat irregular marriage, which
goaded him to fury. The result was that Jackson got 178
electoral votes to 83 for Adams. The difference in the
popular vote was not so large, Adams having 508,064
to Jackson's 648,273. >

Jackson, and "triumphant democracy" in his train, 1829.
made their victorious entry into Washington with an
enormous crowd largely composed of office-seekers who
had worked for them in the campaign. An eye-witness
has described the sight as very like the inundation of
Rome by the northern barbarians, except that in this case
the tumultuous tide, instead of coming from the north,
came from the west and the south. "Strange faces," says
the same narrator, "filled every public place, and every
face seemed to bear defiance on its brow." The city as
well as the lobby swarmed with Jacksonian editors. On
the morning of the inauguration the neighbourhood of the
capitol was an agitated sea of heads, and it was necessary
to repress the surging crowd by stretching a ship's cable
across the flight of steps. After the inauguration came
a reception. There was orange punch by the barrelful,
but as the waiters opened the door a rush was made, the
glasses were broken, the pails of liquor were upset and
the semblance of order could be restored only by carrying
tubs of punch into the garden to draw off the crowd from
the rooms. Men stood in muddy boots on the damask

covered chairs to get a sight of the President. "The
reign of King Mob seemed triumphant," says Judge Story,
who was glad to escape from the scene.

The seat of government having been stormed by General Jackson and his train was at once given up to pillage.
" To the victors belong the spoils," was the saying of
Marcy, a New York manager, not of Jackson ; but the
sequel of Jackson's victory was its first memorable illustration. A ruthless proscription swept the Civil Service to
make places for Jackson's political soldiery. Jefferson,
not without excuse, made removals by tens ; Jackson made
them by hundreds and without excuse since he followed a
President who in his dealings with the Civil Service was
not pure only but a purist. Webster tells that the number of dismissals was reckoned at not less than 2,000.
There was a reign of terror in Washington, no civil servant feeling sure for a day of his head ; a whisper killed,
and perfidy was sometimes added to the cruelty of turning
an innocent official, perhaps in advanced age, upon the
street. No merit or record would save you. Major Mel-
ville was a veteran of the revolution and had been one of
the Boston Tea-Party, yet he was turned out of a place in
the Custom House which he had held for many years.
Those who could get access to Jackson had a chance of
escaping by appeals to his vanity. One official is said to
have saved his head by begging for the old hero's old pipe.
Thus was inaugurated the spoils system together with
the trade of place-hunting by a President who came
probably with a sincere desire of clearing government
from corruption and of making simple honesty the rule,
and of whom it must in justice be said that his own hands
were perfectly clean.

The new court was soon convulsed by a court quarrel. Eaton, a member of Jackson's Cabinet, had married a widow who before her marriage had lived in Washington as Peggy O'Neil, and whose reputation under her maiden name had been doubtful. The wives of other cabinet ministers and the great ladies of Washington refused to visit Mrs. Eaton. Jackson made it a personal quarrel and threw himself into it with his usual fury. He is supposed to have been fired by the recollection of the aspersions cast at the time of the election on his own marriage to a wife to whom he was tenderly attached. Mr. Van Buren, being a widower and having no female fastidiousness to combat, was able to call on Mrs. Eaton and thereby to establish himself firmly in Jackson's favour. But other ministers failed to overcome the virtuous pride of their ladies and a Cabinet crisis was the result. The Dutch ambassador was threatened with a demand for his recall, because his wife had refused to sit by the side of Mrs. Eaton. Whatever may have been Mrs. Eaton's real character, and whether the scruples of those who declined her society were overstrained or not, thanks may be due to the Washington ladies who in the catastrophe of public principle stood out for the purity of domestic life.

Van Buren, a sagacious, smooth, and wily manager of New York politics, was the chief of Jackson's regular counsellors and no doubt knew how to play upon his temper. But to his regular counsellors Jackson preferred a set of familiars who were called his Kitchen Cabinet. These men, experts in wire-pulling, used their arts to keep alive the sentiment which had carried their chief to power, inspired his partisan press, and traduced his enemies through its organs.

⟨Jackson regarded himself as the only direct and genuine
representative of the people. The authority of Congress
and of the Supreme Court he seemed to think unaccred-
ited by the popular will and almost usurped. He trampled on the Senate, the dignity of which made it the
special object of his aversion; he flouted the judiciary,
and would have trampled on it if he had dared.⟩Congenial
to his policy was the doctrine that members of Congress
were delegates, bound to deliver the mandate of the people
whose opinions and passions the autocrat could control.
Whatever was eminent and independent was, in the eyes of
Jackson, as in those of other demagogic despots, an offence,
and his instinctive tendency was to level it to the ground.
This feeling probably entered largely into the war which
he waged against the National Bank.⟨The Bank, created
by Hamilton in the interest of central government as well
as in that of finance, had been abolished by the Jeffersonian
party whose motive likewise was probably political.✗But
another Bank had been founded to meet the financial
difficulties entailed by the war and restore the soundness
of the paper currency⟩ The time for the renewal of the
charter was now not far off, and no opposition was ex-
pected⟨The Bank had given the nation a sound currency,
it had been honourably managed and enjoyed the confidence of commerce.⟩ A Congressional Committee of
enquiry reported that the government deposits were safe
in its keeping.⟨ Nor does the National Bank appear to
have meddled with politics, while it seems certain that the
private banks did.⟩ But the suspicion that its political
influence had been used on the wrong side was breathed
by its enemies into Jackson's ear, and he, who was totally
ignorant of finance, inserted words of threatening import

into a message to Congress. Clay, now in fierce opposition, unwisely took up the gauntlet in the name of the Bank and made the renewal of the charter a political issue. In doing this he stood himself on weak ground since in his fervidly democratic youth he had taken part in the abolition of the former Bank. Jackson welcomed the war, which was waged with the utmost fury on both sides. He and his staff denounced the Bank as a monopoly, as a money power, as a political engine of the enemies of the people, as an ally of the rich against the poor. By this time he had no doubt talked himself into a belief that all this was true. At length the President directed his Secretary of the Treasury, Duane, to remove the government deposits from the Bank, probably against the law; and when that minister refused, he was dismissed, and Taney, more compliant and afterwards notorious in another way, was put in his room. The renewal of the charter 1832. was vetoed by the President, and Clay's party not having a two-thirds' majority in the Senate to carry the Bill over the veto, the Bank fell. The government deposits were distributed, not of course without political favouritism, amongst State Banks, where they furnished the means and stimulus for reckless speculation, notably in the public lands. Wild-cat banks multiplied, especially in the adventurous West, and flooded the country with their delusive paper. Alarmed at the inflation Jackson put forth an edict that nothing but gold or silver should be taken in payment of taxes or other debts to government. The suddenness of the check brought on a crash, and there followed the tremendous financial crisis of 1837, with the universal suspension of cash payments, and general wreck of commerce and industry; the suffering falling chiefly, as it always does, on those poorer classes whose champion against the plutocratic tyranny of the Bank Jackson averred and no doubt believed himself to be. By the mouths of Clay and Webster reason, sound finance, and justice protested in vain. The popularity of the old hero swept away all opposition. His ignorance of finance was taken by his masses as a pledge of his probity and good sense. On his freedom from personal corruption they might with justice rely. Nor was it difficult for him to raise a mob against a corporation which could be denounced as a political and social organ of the money power, though as a matter of fact a large proportion of the stock was held by people of small incomes or by charitable institutions.

In the course of the struggle Jackson's autocratic notions were fully developed. He laid it down that in the interpretation of the constitution, including those articles of it which defined the extent of his own powers, his guide was to be his own conscience, an assumption which would have put him above law. When the Senate passed a resolution of censure on his dictatorial proceedings he took them sharply to task for presuming to arraign his conduct, which he said they had no right to do except in the form of impeachment. Nor was his revenge slaked till his party having ultimately gained a majority in the Senate under his henchman and successor in the Presidency, he made that hated assembly taste the cup of humiliation to the dregs by the erasure of the resolution from their journal, in manifest defiance of the article in the constitution which requires a record of proceedings to be kept. His fury in this battle was inflamed by his personal hatred of Clay and Calhoun; of Clay, who had deprived, and as he swore, cor-

ruptly defrauded him of the Presidency on the occasion
when Adams was elected; of Calhoun, who, as Jackson
learned from a malicious informant, had as a member of
Adams' Cabinet condemned his outrages in Florida and
his execution of Ambrister and Arbuthnot.

⟨With Calhoun as the representative of South Carolina
and her unhappy interests Jackson was brought into collision in a better cause, and one in which his force of characte
served the Republic well.   The protectionist tariff while it
enriched or was supposed to enrich the manufacturing cities
of New England, impoverished the South, which manufac-
tured nothing, and being, like all slave-owning communities, poor in the midst of apparent wealth, could ill bear
the addition of fiscal burdens.⟩ South Carolina, the land
of slavery Hotspurs, rose against the tariff, planted her
feet on State right, assumed a menacing attitude, and proceeded to carry into effect the doctrine laid down by
Jefferson in his draft of the Kentucky resolutions by a
nullification of the federal law. ⟨Secession and civil war
seemed imminent, but Jackson proclaimed in tones of
thunder that the Union must be preserved, and at once
prepared, if the law was resisted by South Carolina, to
execute it by arms.⟩ He is said even to have threatened
to hang Calhoun, though he would have found the summary execution of a United States senator under the
shadow of the Capitol a more dangerous operation than
the summary execution of two helpless Englishmen on a
lonely strand.   The sages of the Senate, with Clay at
their head, in the end brought about one of those compromises of which Clay was the grand artificer. ⟨A Force Bill,
which empowered the President to put down resistance in
South Carolina by arms was coupled in its passage with a

Bill reducing the obnoxious tariff.⟩ It is doubtful whether
South Carolina, having extorted this concession, did not
really come out victorious after all.   Webster and others
thought that she did, and were for bringing her to her
knees before any concession was made.⟨ Jackson's heart
was with slavery, as on other occasions he plainly showed,
though above all things he was for the Union.⟩ In the case
of Georgia and the Creek Indians, where the State, in the
process of improving the Indians off the face of the earth,
had set at nought a treaty made with them by the federal
government, Jackson failed to assert the authority of the
nation.   But he probably regarded a treaty with the
Indians and the claims of the weaker race to justice as
things of small account.

The force which never failed Jackson was again shown
with honour and advantage to his country in exacting from
France the indemnity due for former aggressions on American commerce which the French Chambers were unwilling
to pay.   A private hint which the French government gave
him to strengthen its hand in dealing with the Chambers,
by the use of a little energetic language was taken, as it
was sure to be, with a vengeance.   But neither this service
nor any firmness which Jackson may have shown in uphold-
ing the Union against nullification, could make up for the
terrible and lasting mischief done to public life and character by the ascendancy of such a man, by the spoils system
which he introduced, by the practices and examples of the
agents whom he brought forward, by the personal press
and the machinery of slander which were employed in his
interests, by the venom which he infused into party contests, and by his contempt of constitutional right.   His
equestrian statue, prancing in front of the White House,

seems to beat down the constitution under its hoofs. ⟨Not
the least among the evils of his reign was the systematic
corruption of the press. ⟩It degraded, as Webster said, the
press and the government at once.   Fifty or sixty editors
of leading journals, if Webster may be believed, were appointed to offices, and the propagation of opinions favourable to the government through the press had, according
to the same grave authority, become the main administrative duty. ⟨From Jackson and his circle a spirit of violence seemed to have gone out over the whole land.⟩
⟨Rowdyism, rioting, duelling, and lynch law were never so
rife.⟩ Outrages were committed in the streets of Washington and if the victim was Jackson's political opponent protection was sought in vain.   Fraud and violence became
common in elections.   A race in which courage is not
rare, which has proved its valour in many scenes, surely
does itself wrong by worshipping mere courage, even when
allied with strength of will, in such a character as Andrew
Jackson.

⟨The Jacksonian era was naturally the era of people-
worship, and of application to the multitude of language
applied in the Bible to the Almighty⟩ as though ignorance
and passion millions of times multiplied could be divine ;
as though the will of any man or of any number of men,
apart from reason and conscience, could constitute right or
absolve from guilt those who in bowing to it did wrong.
Jefferson had gone far in this direction, but he had still
been loyal to public reason, or what he took for it, and had
not paid slavish homage to mere will.   "Mr. President," 1832.
said Webster in his speech on the message sent down by
Jackson with his veto on the chartering of the Bank, "we
have arrived at a new epoch.   We are entering on experi-

ments with the government and the constitution of the
country hitherto untried and of fearful and appalling
aspect. This message calls us to the contemplation of a
future which little resembles the past. Its principles are
at war with all that public opinion has sustained and all
which the experience of the government has sanctioned.
It denies first principles; it contradicts truths hitherto
received as indisputable. It denies to the judiciary the
interpretation of law and demands to divide with Congress
the origination of statutes. It extends the grasp of executive pretension over every power of the government. But
this is not all. It presents the chief magistrate of the
Union in the attitude of arguing away the powers of that
government over which he had been chosen to preside,
and adopting for this purpose modes of reasoning which
even under the influence of all proper feeling towards high
official station, it is difficult to regard as respectable. It
appeals to every prejudice which may betray men into a
mistaken view of their own interests, and to every passion
which may lead them to disobey the impulses of their
understanding. It urges all the specious topics of State
rights and national encroachment against that which a
great majority of the States have affirmed to be rightful
and in which all of them have acquiesced. It sows, in an
unsparing manner, the seeds of jealousy and ill-will against
that government of which its author is the official head.
It raises a cry that liberty is in danger at the very moment
when it puts forth claims to powers heretofore unknown
or unheard of. It affects alarm for the public freedom when
nothing endangers that freedom so much as its own unpar-
alleled pretences. This even is not all. It manifestly seeks
to inflame the poor against the rich, it wantonly attacks

whole classes of the people for the purpose of turning
against them the prejudices and resentments of other
classes.   It is a State paper which finds no topic too exciting for its use, no passion too inflammable for its address
and its solicitation.   Such is this message.   It remains
now for the people of the United States to choose between
the principles here avowed and their Government.   These
cannot subsist together.   The one or the other must be
rejected.   If the sentiments of the message shall receive
general approbation the constitution will have perished
even earlier than the moment which its enemies originally allowed for the termination of its existence.   It will
not have survived to its fiftieth year."   In a community so
full of political life and of self-preserving power as the
American Republic no man can seriously meditate usurpation.   But if any man could meditate usurpation he would
act as Jackson acted; he would stretch his power under
pretence of asserting popular right; he would give himself
out as the embodiment of the popular will; he would de-
grade constitutional assemblies and the judiciary; he would
ostentatiously appeal from their judgment to that of the
people; he would corrupt the public press; and he would
stir up the hatred of the poor against the rich.

(Andrew Jackson, however, was able to do what no other
President has done, he was able to bequeath the succession.)
His devisee was his faithful lieutenant Martin Van Buren.
Van Buren was presiding over the Senate when Clay
thundered out an awful warning to the usurping executive and rhetorically charged Van Buren to repeat it to
Jackson.   Van Buren listened with an air of simplicity,   1834.
as though he were treasuring up every word for repetition
to the President, and when Clay had finished, left the

chair, crossed over to the orator, and asked him for a pinch of his famous snuff. This incident depicts the man. Van Buren was arch-engineer of the political machine in his own State, the secret of which he had brought with him to Jackson's councils. He was a man of great tact and address, and had early recognized in the political sky the star of Andrew Jackson. Except under the stress of party he was patriotic as well as sagacious, nor was he a bad President. But on his head fell the consequences of his master's dealings with the Bank and the deposits. He was overwhelmed by the financial crisis of 1837, when commercial ruin and repudiation filled the land; and though the President showed no want of coolness or resource, nothing could avert the effects of public calamity on the reputation of the government and the party in power.

Party lines had now been drawn again. On one side was the Democratic party, of which Jackson had been the head and which partook of the character of its chief. On the other side was the party which by this time had assumed the name of Whig, having for its head Clay, holding with him for protectionism, expenditure of national money on internal improvements, a broad construction of the constitution in favour of the central government, and a national bank, at the same time maintaining the constitutional authority of Congress and the judiciary against stretches of the executive power such as Jackson had essayed. The Democrats were for strict construction, State right, and economy. The spirit of the old Federalists had migrated into the Whig party, that of the Jeffersonian Republicans into its rival. The Whigs, like the Federalists, were stronger in the North than elsewhere,

they had the men of intellect and the most substantial
farmers on their side, while the Democrats had the
populace of the great cities. On both sides the politicians, whose religion was the Union, would fain have
kept the question of slavery out of sight, but though
it might not be made a party issue, to keep it out of
sight was impossible. State right, the old Democratic
doctrine, served a new purpose as the bulwark of slavery against the nation, and "dough faces" or Northern men with Southern principles became eligible as
candidates.

A curious current had for a time been running across
the main stream of party. The catastrophe of a Free-
mason, named Morgan, who after betraying his intention
of revealing the secrets of the order had disappeared and
was supposed to have been murdered, produced an outbreak of popular fear and wrath against Freemasonry,
which spreading over a great part of the Union, gave birth
to the ephemeral party of Anti-Masons. This irregular 1832.
movement, while it lasted, rent the webs and perplexed
the souls of the regular politicians, but having its origin
in a panic it could not last long.

Van Buren's term at an end, the natural candidate of 1840.
the Whigs for President was Clay, the head, the author,
and the pride of their party. But Jackson's success had
taught the wire-pullers the value of availability. They
cunningly burked Clay's candidature, while they looked
around for an available man. An available man they
found and a counter-charm in all respects to the "Old
Hero" and "Old Hickory" in "Old Tippecanoe," the
name which most happily for electioneering purposes they
gave to William Harrison, a worthy old country gentle-

man in Ohio, who in a combat at Tippecanoe gained a victory over the Indians.   Harrison was presented to the people as equal or superior to Jackson in homeliness and simplicity, living in a log cabin garnished with coon skins and drinking hard cider.   For him the wire-pullers, in their own phrase, "set the ball rolling," and gloriously it rolled.   There ensued a campaign of enthusiasm, almost of delirium.   Railroads, now extending over the country, gave facilities for large gatherings.   The whole population was excited and set in motion.   Men laid aside their occupations.   Monster meetings were held.   At a meeting in Ohio where Harrison appeared it was said that a hundred thousand people were present.   Processions five miles long chanted "Tippecanoe and Tyler too," Tyler being the candidate for the Vice-Presidency.   The ball which had been set rolling and the emblems of Harrison's bucolic virtue, the log cabin and the coon skins, were everywhere displayed.   Men of intellect like Webster stooped to exert their eloquence in a coon skin campaign and to drink the health of the Presidential candidate with forced enthusiasm in hard cider.   The results were a complete victory of the Whigs and the ascendancy of availability over other qualifications and claims in the choice of candidates for the Presidency.   It is probable however that availability would in any case have ultimately prevailed.   What the Harrisonian frenzy denotes in its relation to American character it is not easy to say.   Had the American people traversed in half a century the whole distance between the phlegmatic Englishman and the wild shouter for Tippecanoe, or was this strange outburst of political poetry a recoil from a too prosaic life?

"Tippecanoe" vacated life and the Presidency a month 1841.
after his inauguration. The cause of his death seems to
have been the buzzing swarm of office seekers which had
followed him to Washington as much as an accidental
malady. Tyler his Vice-President stepped into his place.
Tyler had been put on the ticket to propitiate the Southern
wing. By his conduct as President he read his party a
lesson which Americans have hardly yet laid to heart on
the expediency of being careful in the selection of a candidate for the second place, and not using that nomination
as a sop. He turned against his party ; vetoed their pet
measure, the erection of a national bank ; and tried to form
a party of his own with a view to re-election, of which
however he had no chance. His excommunication by the
party could not deprive him of his veto power. It only
illustrated the difference between British and American
forms of government. Had Tyler been a British Prime
Minister deserted by his party he must have at once fallen.
A more serious question than that of the Bank soon loomed
up. Houston, an American filibuster and an old comrade
of Jackson, with a body of intrusive Americans had planted
himself in Texas, which belonged to the Republic of
Mexico, and when the Mexicans took arms to put him
down and recover their province, had defeated them at the
battle of San Jacinto. He now, probably in pursuance of 1841.
a scheme preconcerted with Jackson, threw himself into
the arms of the American Republic, which could not
receive him without going to war with Mexico, whose
accession to the sisterhood of freedom had recently been
the subject of jubilation. The South was for the annexation, which opened a vast vista of extension for slavery
ever hungering not only for new political domains but for

fresh fields to till, since slave culture, especially the culture of tobacco, was exhausting to the soil. The Northern spirit was opposed to annexation for the same reasons. Tyler entered with alacrity into the intrigue; he was ready for the annexation of Texas or for anything which could gain him re-election. When the time came he was contemptuously swept aside, but he had opened the question on which the election turned and which proved fatal to the chief of his enemies.

1844. ⟨ Annexation of Texas with slavery behind it was the decisive issue in the next Presidential campaign between the Whigs whose candidate was the brilliant Clay and the Democrats whose candidate was the far from brilliant but highly available J. K. Polk.⟩ Van Buren, to his credit, had been laid aside on account of his unwillingness to embrace annexation. Each party had still a southern as well as a northern wing, but the strength of the Whigs lay in the north, that of the Democrats in the south, and their respective affinities to freedom and slavery were seen through the veil which the politicians laboured to keep spread. ⟨The Democrats taxed the Whigs with anti-slavery leanings, and the Whigs could not retort the reproach. ⟨ Clay, striving to balance himself between annexation and opposition to annexation, that he might hold his southern without losing his northern wing, fell as the political acrobat is apt to fall. His great achievements as a statesman were compromises. But as a candidate he found a compromise between opposite policies too much for his address. A letter in which dallying with annexation he used an expression plainer than he intended, set him fatally at odds with a third party which would listen to no compromise, and which though small was large enough

to turn the scale. This was the Anti-slavery party, or the
Liberty party, as the political section of the abolitionists
styled itself, now coming as an organized force upon the
scene. Naturally these men would have preferred Clay,
who was half with them, to Polk, who was entirely against
them; but exasperated at Clay's trimming letter, which
seemed to them a wound received in the house of a friend,
they left his side and threw away their votes on Birney a
candidate of their own. Clay thus lost New York and
the election. Loud were the lamentations which arose
from all his followers. Even the victors were almost
ashamed of their victory. The wail has been prolonged
in history. Unquestionably the election of Polk against
Clay was the preference of mediocrity to distinction. But
such is the law of democracies, and after all Clay was a
dazzling and fascinating but artful politician who owed his
fall to a false step in the practice of his own art. Nor was
his fate unretributive. As the chief of the war-hawks
he had called forth that military spirit which, embodied in
Jackson, crossed and ruined his own career.

Polk as President did that which he had been elected to   1845.
do. He pushed the quarrel with Mexico, which formed as
striking an illustration as history can furnish of the quarrel
between the wolf and the lamb, and which no American
historian of character mentions without pain. To add the
disgrace of private covetousness to that of public rapine it
seems that some of the chief promoters of the aggression
were speculators in Texan securities. The use of the
phrase re-annexation instead of annexation, having no
warrant in fact, did not cover the wrong. Mexico was at
last pressed and goaded into doing what by a hypocritical
fiction was pronounced an act of war, and was invaded by

an American army. The Mexicans, poorly armed and ill commanded as well as people of a weaker race, notwithstanding their numbers were as sheep to the butcher. They were defeated by Generals Taylor and Scott in a series of engagements, and the invader marched into their capital. That they fought as well as they could against over-mastering wrong must always be recorded to their honour. It forms a bright spot in the dark and sordid

1845. pages of their history. The immense expanse of Texas was ceded to the conqueror, annexed to the United States and re-annexed to slavery, which had been abolished under the Mexican constitution. Nor did annexation end there,

1850. but was extended to New Mexico and Arizona. At the same time the golden California was seized against the will of its few inhabitants on the pretext, for which there was not the slightest foundation, that Great Britain had designs upon it. All this was done, be it remembered, by the slave power then dominant and its political retainers. Northern morality protested, as the readers of the " Biglow Papers " know.

1849. The next President could be no other than Taylor, the victorious general of the war, although Taylor neither was nor pretended to be anything of a statesman. A tolerably shrewd candidate he was, and in this respect Clay might have envied his tact. During the canvass he received a letter from a planter running thus: — " Sir, I have worked hard and been frugal all my life, and the results of my industry have mainly taken the form of slaves, of whom I own about a hundred. Before I vote for President I want to see that the candidate I support will not so act as to divest me of my property." The general replied: " Sir, I have the honour to inform you that I too have been all my life in-

dustrious and frugal, and that the fruits thereof are mainly
in slaves, of whom I own three hundred." Taylor turned
out a plain, honest man, not a bigot or henchman of
slavery, in spite of his three hundred slaves, and showed
no tendency to play Jackson. He died in the White House
and his place was taken by Vice-President Fillmore, who 1850.
left no mark. The election that followed was the last
chance of Daniel Webster's ambition, and his desperate
attempt to grasp it was a sad example of the influence
of that dazzling prize upon the characters of public men.
He who had been the stately champion of freedom, of
liberty of opinion, and of right, now, to attract southern votes, stood forth as the defender of slavery, of the
fugitive slave law, and the gag. He derided the anti-slavery
doctrine as a ghostly abstraction, and descended almost to
buffoonery in ridiculing the idea of a law higher than that
which ordained the hunting down of fugitive bondsmen.
His character, to which friends of freedom in the North had
long looked up, fell with a crash like that of a mighty tree,
of a lofty pillar, of a rock that for ages had breasted the
waves. Some minds willing to be misled he still drew
after him, but the best of his friends turned from him
and his life ended in gloom.

Mexico was avenged on her spoiler, for the acquisition of
Texas re-opened the fatal controversy between slavery and
freedom which the Missouri compromise had put to sleep in
Congress for thirty years. Texas being large enough to
make four States, the North was threatened with a formidable extension of the slave power. A proviso was moved
by Wilmot excluding slavery from Texas. Thereupon a
desperate struggle began in Congress. Webster and Clay,
the statesmen and the hierophants of Union, appeared with

a parting splendour on the scene of their achievements, and Calhoun, a dying man, sat in the Senate while a colleague read his last speech. Passion was so fiercely excited that a revolver was drawn in the hall of the serene Senate. Not Texas only but New Mexico and Arizona which went with Texas, and California into which there had been a rush of gold-seekers and which urgently demanded political organization, seemed to be breaking out, when Clay once more came forward as an angel of mediation with a compromise in his hand. Texas was consigned to slavery but was left a single State. New Mexico and Arizona were also consigned to slavery against which however they were practically guarded by nature, being unsuited for slave labour. California was admitted as a free State. At the same time a fugitive slave law of a more stringent kind was passed, a concession vital and fatal to the South. How conscience in passing this law struggled with policy was seen when thirty-three Northern members paired, stayed away, or dodged the vote. This was the third and the last compromise.

The Whig party which had striven to keep the slavery question out of the political arena and to build its platform of such planks as a protective tariff, a national bank, internal improvements, the cultivation of national spirit, and devotion to the Union, combined with the opposition to Jacksonian violence and encroachment, lost the foundation of its existence : in fact it was buried in the grave of Clay, to whom in a great measure it owed its life. It faded away like a dissolving view, while in its place appeared the lineaments, first of a Free Soil, then of a National Republican, or in brief, a Republican party formed on the grand issue and destined to try with slavery, first at the ballot and afterwards on the battlefield, the inevitable question whether the country was to be wholly slave or wholly free.

⟨ Slavery was confident and aggressive⟩ After Polk it made Pierce, another of its satellites, President. Under Pierce it planned the annexation of Cuba to which it feared emancipation, now triumphant in Great Britain and Europe, might be extended. Three American ambassadors to European Courts, Buchanan, Mason, and Soulé, met at Ostend and put forth a manifesto the effrontery of which startled Europe, intimating that Spain must be compelled to sell or give up Cuba to the United States. Lopez, a filibuster, made an attempt, with the sympathy of the South, to seize the island, but perished with his band. Walker, another filibuster, also with the sympathy of the South, invaded Nicaragua, made himself dictator, and was preparing to introduce negro slavery, when he also met his doom. A revival even of the African slave trade was in the air; a contraband trade in African negroes went on upon a large scale with the connivance even of the Federal authorities at the South.⟨ As Great Britain was now leading a crusade against slavery she became the object of diplomatic enmity to the slave-owners who were in power at Washington and whose discourtesies, set down to the account of the whole American nation, had a bad effect upon British opinion at a later day.⟩

1853.

1854.

The last act of the struggle between the Jacksonian Democrats and the Whigs was complicated by the commencement of another sudden tornado of opinion sweeping like the Anti-Masonism, from an independent quarter across the field of the regular parties, and for the moment confusing their lines. This was the movement of the American party, or as it was nicknamed, the party of the Knowno-

things. That they "knew of nothing illegal or disloyal"
being the regular answer with which they parried curious
inquiry. The American party was called into transitory existence by dislike and dread of the foreign element, now increasing in volume and influence, and especially of the Irish
Roman Catholics. The Irish Roman Catholics, always to
be distinguished from the Scotch-Irish of the Protestant
North, were now pouring from their famine-stricken country
into the United States and were fast becoming that dread
power, the Irish vote, henceforth a serious factor in American politics, though perhaps from a nervous sense of the
present situation even historians seem to shrink from the
mention of its name. These people of a hapless land and a
sad history, ignorant, superstitious, priest-ridden, nurtured
in squalid poverty, untrained in constitutional government,
trained only in conspiracy and insurrection, were a useful
addition to the labour of their adopted country ; of its politics they could only be the bane. Clannish still in their
instincts, herding clannishly together in the great cities and
blindly following leaders whom they accepted as chiefs, and
in choosing whom they were led more by blatant energy than
by merit, they were soon trained to the pursuit of political
spoils and filled elections with turbulence, fraud, and corruption. Through the connivance of a judiciary elected largely
by their own votes they were permitted to set the naturalization law at defiance, and fresh from the seat of their native
wretchedness to assume and misuse the powers of American
citizens. Their numbers and cohesion soon enabled them to
influence the balance of parties. But as a body they went
into the Democratic party and there remained, attracted at
first perhaps by its name and confirmed in their adherence to
it as the party of slavery, which it ultimately became, by their

bitter antipathy to the negro, who might compete with them
in the labour market and whose degradation alone saved
them from being at the bottom of the social scale. Their
influence could not fail thenceforth to intensify the Anti-
British sentiment in American politics, and to envenom all
disputes between America and the mother country. Knownothingism presently passed away, its object being lost in
the more pressing issue. But the cause of it did not pass
away.

⟨Meantime in ways more important than politics, and in
spite of political factions, the country had been advancing
with mighty strides.⟩⟨Since the Union the number of the
States had more than doubled.⟩⟨Population had rapidly
multiplied and had been swollen by a great immigration,
not Irish only but German and Scandinavian which sought
happier homes and brighter prospects than those of the
peasantry in the old countries of Europe.⟩ At the time of
the Union settlements still clung to the Atlantic seaboard.
It had now passed the Alleghanies in force, entered the
valley of the Mississippi, and was turning what had once
been merely a mental horizon and afterwards a boundary-
line into a central waterway. At last to the Atlantic the
Pacific coast, with its sunny shores and half tropical wealth,
had been added. Humanity had staked out the vast field on
which the great experiment of democracy was to be tried.
Intercommunication had been vastly improved by enterprise and invention. The great Cumberland Road had
opened a broad highway for civilization from Maryland
across the Alleghanies. Clinton had turned from the factions and corrupt politics of New York to the construction
of the Erie Canal, which in its magnitude rivals and by
its utility shames the works of the Pharaohs. Steam had

begun to open a new era. Steamboats plied on the water-
ways and the railway took the place of the crawling stage.
⟨ A railway from the Atlantic to the Pacific was already
planned. Thus not only were the States of the Union
bound together and one mind diffused through the whole
frame, but the appliances of agriculture and civilization were brought, with the march of settlement, into the
virgin wilderness. ⟩The mineral resources of the country
were being opened.⟩ Spinning-jennies and power-looms, the
inventions of Hargreaves and Arkwright, were imported.
Manufactures on a large scale had grown up in the North-
eastern States and had superseded the spinning-wheel.
Civilization moving westward had a ragged edge of roving
and lawless adventure, at least where it moved from the
quarter of slavery. With the commercial expansion attendant on the rapid development of new resources inevitably
went gambling speculation with its wild-cat banks, frauds,
bankruptcy, and crashes, the effect however of which was
limited and transient, commerce like industry rising elastic
from its fall and wealth with all its accompaniments, moral
and social as well as material, advancing by leaps and bounds.
Nor had the distribution of wealth yet ceased to be equal, at
all events in comparison with its distribution in the old world.
⟨ The last church establishment, that of Connecticut, had
fallen, and religious equality everywhere reigned.⟩ The
people were still religious; Christianity generally, and in
all cases theism, remained the basis and sanction of their
morality. ⟨ But orthodoxy was giving way and philosophy
was gaining ground. Emerson had come out of the church
and was teaching morality without a creed. Religion without a creed found an eloquent preacher in Theodore Parker. ⟩
In the ferment of progress utopian schemes of society be-

gan to abound.   Some of the social utopias, as that of the
Shakers and that of the Perfectionists, took a religious
form, and Revivalism made its wild protest in favour of
the spiritual interests of man.

Intelligence was mainly engrossed by the pursuit of
wealth, practical science and invention were active, while of
literature there was as yet but little, and that little was not
native in character but European.   Denial of copyright to
English writers, by causing their works to be pirated and
sold in cheap editions, discouraged American authorship
and thus kept American intellect in thraldom to Europe.
An international copyright law would have done more to
emancipate from British influence than any war with Great
Britain.

Oratory, both political and forensic, on the other hand
had been carried to a high point, and if in the hot and ex-
citable youth of the nation it was often bombastic, sometimes, as in Webster and Choate, it was not.   The national
debates on slavery and other momentous questions stimulated eloquence among the leaders and habits of political thought among the people.   The political press drew
to it a large share of ability and had become a great
power ; with power, irresponsible so long as the circulation
can be sustained, came the inherent danger of abuse.

⟨ Political democracy was now full grown in the Northern
States and at Washington, so far as the Northern spirit prevailed there ; all officers were elective, all office-holders were
in the fullest sense servants of the people, every man's
tenure was precarious and dependent on popular favour,
rotation in office was the rule.⟩   Even the judiciary had
become elective in most of the States.   To the people and
its will everybody had bowed, as once everybody had bowed

to royalty and to the will of kings. Property qualification
for the franchise had generally disappeared. Manhood suffrage was the rule. With the good of the system came its
inevitable evil, the machinery of party and electioneering,
demagogic arts and strategy, factions, passion, and vituperation, the reign of the caucus and the boss, and where the
foreign element, especially the Irish, prevailed, ballot-stuff-
ing, repeating, rioting, and corruption. Only in the slave-
owning South oligarchy still held power. Social democracy
also was in outward forms and manners complete; in substance it was much more advanced than it was in the old
world, though nothing could efface the social lines drawn by
wealth and personal superiority. Labour and lowly birth
instead of being a disparagement were a boast and a title
to political preferment. A nation which had been at school
and which read paid a homage to intellect perhaps greater
than that which it paid to commercial success.

CHAPTER V.

RUPTURE AND RECONSTRUCTION.

THE question of slavery, in spite of all the attempts to elbow it out of politics and prevent it from breaking the beloved Union, had now forced itself to the front, and the "irrepressible conflict" was at hand.⟩ ⟨ Slavery is dead, and the Southerners would not revive it if they could. They have wisely accepted its abolition, as they have magnanimously accepted defeat by the greater power. ⟩ Denouncing it now seems like trampling on a grave. ⟨ It was the offspring of soil and climate rather than of character, though morally it was more alien to republican and Puritan New England than to Anglican and monarchical Virginia, while by the Quaker of Philadelphia it was always condemned. ⟩ But its extinction was entirely to be desired. Ancient slavery may have been a step forward in evolution. In the age of tribal wars it was an improvement on extermination. ⟨ It ended in emancipation, and ultimately in the fusion of the races.⟩ But American slavery was not a step forward in evolution; it was a long step backwards; ⟩ it was a winter fallen into the lap of spring. ⟨ Its sole source was the desire of Europeans in a languid climate to have the work done for them instead of doing it themselves. ⟩ Fusion in the case of negro slavery was fatally precluded by colour. There could be no intermingling except that which arose from the abuse of the negro woman by her white master. ⟨Emancipation was greatly discouraged.⟩ The emancipated slave was a suspected pariah. He was trampled on more than a slave, because in him the race of the bondsman seemed to pretend to equality. To talk of the system as gradually elevating the negro was idle when permanent marriage and domestic ties, the first elements of moral civilization, were denied him, when it was penal to teach him to read and write, when the chance of raising himself above the coarsest manual labour, even by petty trades, was withheld. Not less idle was the pretence of making him a Christian, which the Southern clergy, religious henchmen of the system, were fain to put forward. How make a man a Christian without the domestic morality and affections essential to the formation of a Christian character, and when Christianity in his master was always presenting itself to him as a religion of wrong? Calhoun brought himself to believe that the Southern family was superior to the Northern family as having a third relation, that of master and slave, in addition to those of husband and wife, parent and child. But what became of the family of the negro? Household slavery, no doubt, was often, perhaps generally, mild: but the cruelty of plantation slavery, at least on the large plantations, is too well proved. The negro there was abandoned to the driver, a man of a low and generally disreputable class, whose sole object was to raise the largest crop of cotton, and who used up the slave like a beast of burden. Not only was the plantation slave overworked and tortured with the lash, he was sometimes murdered, and with impunity, as negro evidence was not admitted against whites. If the slave was happy, why those fetters, those bloodhounds, that hideous slave code? If he was contented, why those laws forbidding him to hold meetings, to move freely about, rendering him liable to summary arrest and to scourging if he was found wandering without a master? Why was Southern legislation a code of terror? The Southerners and their wives lived in constant dread of slave insurrection. They took every alarm as an announcement of it. At Charleston, though summer evenings were sweet, the city was shut up early and handed over to the patrol. This is the answer to Calhoun's boast that slavery excluded angry and dangerous questions between the employer and the employed. Most revolting, if not most cruel of all, were the auction, at which husband and wife, parent and child, were sold apart, the sight of droves of human cattle on their way to it, and the advertisements of human flesh, especially of girls nearly white. Negro quarters on a plantation were hovels; the negro's clothes were rags; his food was coarse; his life was foul. That he was happier than he would have been in his African hamlet was more easily asserted than proved. His happiness at best was that of swine. In his African hamlet, too, he had the chance, if he had any capacity, of one day rising in the scale of civilization. Against the negro in America the gate of the future was inexorably barred. The general effect upon the character of the slave-owner could not be doubtful. Brave, frank, hospitable, free-handed, courteous to his equals, a first-rate rider and sportsman he might be: his wife might be soft, elegant, and charming, though there was an element in her character of a different kind, which civil war disclosed; but it is not in the exercise of

domestic despotism, with passion and language unre-
strained, amidst whips, manacles, and blood hounds, that
the character of a true gentleman can be formed. The
temper of the boys was spoiled and their minds were
tainted by familiarity with slaves. With slavery always
goes lust. The number of half-breeds was large. White
fathers might even sell their half-breed children as slaves,
and a Southern lady was heard to complain that she was
but the head of a harem. If, as some desperate advocates
of slavery contended, the negro was not a man, what were
all those half-breeds to be called? The great planters
were prodigal, many of them were in debt, and in their
mansions luxury and ostentation, rather than comfort,
reigned. The table was profusely spread; there was a
number of servants in livery, but broken windows remained unmended, and doors would not shut. The number, however, of the owners of many slaves was small, that
of the owners of any slaves not very large, compared
with that of the "mean whites," who, disdaining industry
as the lot of the slave, and full of insensate pride of colour,
though the very negroes despised them, lived a half vagabond life as parasites of the slave system, farming but
little and very poorly, slave-driving, slave-hunting, loung-
ing and drinking, sponging on the great planters, whose
dependents, socially and politically, they were. ⟨ Nothing
is better attested than the inferiority of Southern to Northern life in comfort, thrift, cleanliness, and all the elements
of civilization. ⟩ Slavery at Athens and Rome had supported
an intellectual community. In the slave States of America
there was no literature or science. ⟨ Culture was confined
to a few of the richest men ⟩ ⟨ There was not mechanical invention. The inventor of the cotton-gin himself was

a native of Massachusetts. Poor were the universities,
and the schools were poorer still.⟩ Young Southern gentlemen were sent to the universities of the North. Some
jurists were produced by the practical need of law. The
clergy were not only inferior in education but degraded
by the necessity of cringing to slavery, and of perverting
Scripture and paltering with conscience in that interest.
What sort of pastor was that Methodist clergyman of
Tennessee, who, when a negro had been burned alive,
defended the act in print as one of necessary self-defence,
avowed that he should have been glad to take part, and
expressed his wish that, instead of being merely burned,
the victim had been torn with red-hot pincers and his
limbs cut off one by one? Politics were an oligarchy of
planters, the single aim of whose statesmanship was extension and perpetuation of slavery. ⟨Nor was the economical
aspect of the system better than the rest. Slave labour was
unwilling, stupid, and sluggish : it lacked intelligence for
variety of production and unvaried crops exhausted the soil.⟩
In Virginia, old tobacco fields were covered by forests
of pine. ⟨Larger crops of cotton have been raised by free
labour under all the disadvantages of recent emancipation.⟩
The slave, having no interest in thrift, was wasteful.⟩
The ownership of infancy and decrepitude was unprofit-
able. High industries, being socially and politically antagonistic, as well as economically alien to the system,
could flourish only in a few of the larger cities. On the eve
of Secession, Mr. Olmsted, a very fair-minded inquirer, made
a tour of observation through the South. His "Cotton
Kingdom" depicts general barbarism thinly veiled and
barely relieved by a few seats of commerce or mansions of
private wealth. In the house of civilization are many man-

sions, and very peculiar institutions may serve humanity
in their way, but in no way could humanity be served by
American slavery. On the other hand, American slavery
threatened humanity with aggression. Hunger of land
as well as craving for political power and the needed bar-
riers against the advance of emancipation drove it on.
It had shown its tendencies in buccaneering attacks on
South American republics and on Cuba, as well as in the
conquest of Texas. It had its eye on the West Indies
and Hayti. It was looking to the reopening of the slave
trade, which would have brought it into collision with
Great Britain as an emancipating power. In the absence
of the slave trade, the demand for more negroes, bred by
the increasing value of cotton, was met by the conversion of Virginia, which had exhausted much of its
own land, into a breeding State, a shameful end for
the mother of Presidents and the Old Dominion. The
plea put into the mouth of a good slave owner no doubt
has force; he might feel that he was doing his duty to
his slaves; he might complacently contrast his peaceful
household with the labour wars of the North, his gentle
wife and daughters with its female agitators, his political calm with its democratic turmoil. But for the system,
the only valid apology was the supreme difficulty of saying in what relation other than slavery the two races
brought together under an evil star, and, as it seemed,
radically unequal in capacity, could be placed towards
each other. That problem has hardly yet been solved.

Could that knot have been untied instead of being cut
by the sword of civil war? Only, it would seem, by
peaceful separation. Compensated emancipation, like that
which freed the slaves in the West Indies, would have

cost but a fraction of the price which in the end was paid. But the slave-owner, even if he would have sold his slaves, would hardly have sold his pride or his power. Nor, the white dominating at the South, and swaying by his compact force the policy of the Union, would there have been strong security against the practical re-enslavement of the negro. Such changes can hardly be brought about peacefully by anything but superior power, such as that of the British Parliament, which emancipated the slaves in the West Indies, or that of an autocracy such as emancipated the serfs in Russia. We cannot say what might have happened had the colonies not parted violently from the mother country. They might have gone with her in emancipation. They might have fallen into two groups, one free, the other slave; and in that case freedom, by its moral and industrial superiority might have ultimately prevailed.

The philosophic abolitionism of Jefferson and his compeers had long since died out. It grew faint after the invention of the cotton-gin, which made cotton the immensely profitable staple of the South, and it received its death stroke in the slave insurrection of 1832. Nothing was left of it but a colonization society for transporting free negroes to Africa, and there forming them into a community to be the germ of a negro civilization. But this was at best a plan for ladling out the sea, and was suspected by abolitionists of being a scheme for getting rid of black citizens. Slavery was now dominant in the United States. It elected the Presidents, it filled the offices, it swayed the Senate, it cowed the House of Representatives and the nation generally by threats of breaking up the Union, the idol of an American heart. Its leaders in

Congress were in their way statesmen, holding their seats, unlike the representatives of popular constituencies, by a sure tenure, devoted through life to politics, accustomed to command. It held the Northern merchants by the bonds of a vast commercial interest and a great debt due to them as providers of its capital. A New York trader would tell abolitionists plainly that he knew as well as they did that slavery was wrong, but New York commerce was bound up with it, and abolitionists must be put down. Over the mercantile society of the North, especially over its wealthy chiefs, the South threw the unfailing spell of aristocracy. The Irishman was the faithful liegeman of the political power which enabled him to keep his foot on the neck of the negro, and O'Connell's denunciations of slavery were forgotten or disregarded. The genius of Roman Catholicism and of High Church Anglicanism, was, to say the least, not intolerant of slavery. The Protestant churches were fearful of a rupture with their Southern wings. Their clergy, moreover, had commercial pewholders and trustees. All, or almost all of them, in proclaiming the wrath of heaven against sins, left out one fashionable sin ; all, or almost all of them, preached submission to the law. Submission to the law, in fact, seemed a paramount duty to the mass of a law-abiding people ; the people were in their consciences persuaded that they were indefeasibly bound by the covenant made with slavery in the constitution. Popular literature bowed to the yoke, and even missionary works were expurgated in deference to slavery. Foreign lights of freedom and philanthropy, brought into this atmosphere, burned dim. Kossuth, when he visited the United States, excused himself from touching the question as it was not one of national independence, and Father

Mathew could not remember that he had signed an anti-slavery manifesto.   The slave owner was master of opinion as well as of Congress.

Still there were protests.   There were political protests against the aggrandizement of the slave power.   Opposition had been made on that ground to the acquisition of Texas, and a compromise had been enforced. ⟨There had been a series of petitions for the abolition of slavery in the federal District of Columbia, over which Congress had undoubted power.⟩ The Southerners in Congress had tried to impose the gag by decreeing that no petition relating to slavery should be received.   This called forth a doughty champion of the right of petition in the person of Quincy Adams, who when he had failed at the election for the Presidency, instead of returning to ex-presidential nullity, went into the House of Representatives, and there, without avowing himself an abolitionist, waged a long and memorable war against the gag.   One day the old man announced that he held in his hand a petition signed by slaves.   A tornado of Southern wrath ensued.   Waiting till it was spent Adams announced that the petition was in favour of slavery.   Seward's brilliant star now glittered in the anti-slavery quarter above the political horizon.   By him were uttered the fateful words, "irrepressible conflict."   Sumner, a senator from Massachusetts, stood forth as an open and passionate enemy not only of slavery, but of the slave-owners.   Chase, Hamilton Fish, Wade, and Foot were strenuous on the same side.   The slave trade in Columbia at least had been stopped, and the droves no longer passed by the portals of the Capitol of liberty.

Nor were morality and religion mute though their voices were low.   Emerson assailed slavery with philosophy, the

author of the " Biglow Papers " with ridicule. Channing
pronounced on it a condemnation measured and wary,
going, however, so far as to say that, rather than give up
Texas to it he would see the Union repealed. Theodore
Parker denounced it more fearlessly, and his sermon on the
death of Webster, the great apostate, is the flower of anti-
slavery eloquence. Even in the orthodox churches there
were searchings of heart and as to the lawfulness of slave-
holding, which in one case brought on schism between the
Northern and Southern wings. Nor could the Christian
doctrine of brotherhood be preached without pricking conscience on the forbidden theme. ⟨ Mrs. Beecher Stowe by
her " Uncle Tom's Cabin," which swept Europe as well as
America, did as much for the anti-slavery cause as could be
done for any cause by a work of fiction, which everybody
reads with a feeling of its unreality. ⟩ But slavery had more
ardent and uncompromising foes. Lundy, a mechanic, who
had lived on one of the highways of the home slave trade,
and had seen the coffles go by, went forth on a humble crusade, lecturing even in a Southern State, where his gentle-
ness seems to have been his protection, and afterwards
publishing a little anti-slavery journal. He was presently
joined by William Lloyd Garrison, a young journalist of
promise, who devoted his life to the cause. At Baltimore,
a port of the slave trade, Garrison denounced in his journal
a New England merchant who, false to New England principle, was lending his ship to the trade. He was convicted
of libel and suffered imprisonment, which he underwent
with a light heart, drawing from it fresh devotion. In
face of an adverse world he brought out *The Liberator*, an
anti-slavery journal on the humblest scale, at Boston, printing as well as writing it with his own hands, and living in

apostolic poverty, in the meanest lodging on the scantiest fare. ⟨For thirty-five years he continued this work. It brought him no money but it brought him disciples. His doctrine was thorough-going. He denounced slavery not only as an evil but as a crime and the sum of all crimes. He was for nothing less than immediate, unconditional, and uncompensated abolition, so that between him and the slave-owner there was internecine war.⟩ At the North, if there was not slavery, there was prejudice of colour the most intense. The negro was worse than servile, he was unclean. No white would eat with him, share a public conveyance with him, kneel beside him in church. Fellowship with him would have been social ruin, intermarriage as bad as incest. ⟨The slightest taint of negro blood was hopeless degradation.⟩ On this prejudice Garrison trampled, openly consorting with blacks, and carrying about with him as his fellow crusader, the eloquent Douglas. Frankly acknowledging that the constitution established slavery, he blasphemed that idol, calling it an agreement with hell and a covenant with death, and at last publicly burned it before a multitude on the fourth of July. ⟨One stormy night, in a back street of Boston where negroes dwelt, Garrison, with eleven friends, founded the first anti-slavery society, which presently became the mother of hundreds, the cause finding its way to the hearts of simple people who did not hold Southern securities and were not politicians.⟩ Wendell Phillips, a scion of Boston aristocracy, the finest platform speaker of his day, joined the movement and became the most fiery of its champions. His language, that of *The Liberator*, and of the abolitionists generally, was cutting, not unfrequently too cutting, and was fiercely resented. The South boiled with fury, threatened the agitators with

personal vengeance, rifled the mails which contained their
tracts. Commercial interest, political timidity, and colour
feeling at the North, responded to the angry call of the
South. ⟨Abolitionists were mobbed and insulted, they were
dragged before magistrates who knew no justice, their
meetings were broken up, one of their halls was burned,
one of them, defending himself and his party, was slain.⟩
A school which a lady had opened for negro girls was
broken up, and she was driven away with insult; and this
in moral and orderly Connecticut. ⟨Garrison himself was
assailed at Boston by a mob of "highly respectable citizens," dragged through the streets with a rope round him,
and found shelter from worse violence only in a gaol.⟩
Public exasperation had been inflamed to the utmost by
the importation of Thompson, a famous anti-slavery lecturer from England, whose country was unbeloved, and
whose interference was taken as an affront to the nation.
⟨Abolition societies nevertheless multiplied.⟩ They multiplied notwithstanding divisions in their camp, contests for
leadership, the extravagances of wild enthusiasts who had
fastened themselves on the cause, and the identification
of the movement by its leader with other movements of
which an era teeming with change was full, but to which
it had no relation, such as opposition to bibliolatry or Sab-
batarianism, and theories of government, or rather of spiritual emancipation from temporal government, which, in the
world as it was, must have led to despotism or anarchy.
⟨Garrison's sole aim was to awaken the conscience of the
people.⟩ Political action and even the use of the suffrage
he renounced, dreading nothing so much as that his crusade should become a political party with party ambition
and venality. There was another abolitionist movement

led by Birney, a man of admirable character, a slave owner
who had freed his own slaves, and underwent much persecution for the cause. This movement was political. It
sought, hopelessly enough, the abolition of slavery by constitutional action, and its vote in a New York election had
taken the Presidency from the waverer Clay.

The North generally, though not true to morality on the
subject of slavery, remained true to the principles of a
republican constitution. It resented the interference with
the right of petition, it resented the aggression on the
freedom of speech and of the press. The Southern slave
was far away; his wail hardly reached the Northern ear.
But when, under the new fugitive slave law, the Northern
people saw with their own eyes the slave-hunter plying his
trade in their cities, and beheld innocent men and women
dragged from their asylum and borne off to chains, when
they witnessed tragic, and sometimes murderous struggles
between the negro and his captor, their hearts were moved.
When the negro Anthony Burns was carried off from
Boston, the hearth of freedom, there was an uprising of
the citizens. A life was lost in the fray. It was necessary
to call out troops, and the slave was led away with great
military parade amidst the execrations of the multitude
and along streets hung with black. The love of excitement blending with philanthropy, an " underground railway " was organized to forward slaves to Canada where
they were safe under the British flag. Some of the States
passed Liberty Bills, giving those claimed as slaves securities for justice which the fugitive slave law denied them :
and these were treated by the South, not without some
reason, as breaches of the constitution and acts of disunion. To the mine thus charged, the match was applied

by Stephen Douglas, a Western politician, and the type of
his class.   He was about the first notable instance of the
power of voice in politics, which the increasing size of
audiences has enhanced, and is still enhancing.   His force
as a speaker contrasted with the smallness of his stature
caused him to be nicknamed "The Little Giant."   His
eloquence was of the most Boanergic kind.   In the midst
of his thundering, says an eye-witness, to save himself from
choking, he stripped off and cast away his cravat, unbut-
toned his waistcoat, and had the air and aspect of a half-
naked pugilist.   He was able, prompt, and unscrupulous
in debate.   It occurred to him that the quiver of the Democratic party, to which he belonged, was spent.   To replenish
it he invented or revived the doctrine of squatter sovereignty, according to which the settlers in any Territory
were to decide for themselves in framing their constitution
whether they would admit slavery or not.   This upset the
Missouri compromise, geographical compromise altogether,
and its tendency was to make slavery national instead of sec-
tional. The principle of squatter sovereignty was presently
applied on the motion of Douglas by the Kansas-Nebraska
1854. Act to the Territory of Kansas, a portion of the Louisiana purchase. As if in concert with Douglas's move,
Taney, who had been rewarded for his service to Andrew
Jackson in the destruction of the bank, with the chief jus-
ticeship of the Supreme Court, went out of his way in the
1857. case of a claim to liberty on the part of a negro, Dred
Scott, which came before him, to rule that Congress had no
right to prohibit slavery in the Territories, and that the
Missouri compromise was unconstitutional. At the same
time, he laid it down that the negro was not included by
the framers of the constitution in the designation of " man "

or as having any rights against the white, though it appeared
that at the time when the constitution was framed, some
freed negroes were enjoying civil rights in Massachusetts,
and had been in arms for colonial freedom.   The Chief Justice did not say whether if the negro had no rights against
the white man, the white man had any rights against the
negro, or whether the negro was morally at liberty to kill
or rob the white man.   By this presentation of the iniquity, naked and in its most repulsive form, Taney did no
small harm to the party which he intended to aid.   It has
been said that slavery plucked ruin on its own head by its
aggressive violence.   It could not help showing its native
temper, nor could it help feeding its hunger of land,
insisting on the restoration of its runaways, or demanding
a foreign policy such as would fend off the approach of
emancipation.   But Taney's judgment was a gratuitous
aggression and an insult to humanity at the same time, for
which, supposing that the Southern leaders inspired it,
they paid dear.   If the slave was mere property, his owner
might be entitled to take him anywhere, and thus slavery
might be made national.   The boast of a daring partisan
of slavery might be fulfilled, that the day would come
when men might be bought and sold in Boston as freely
as any other goods.   The issue, which all the politicians
had striven to keep out of sight, was presented in its most
startling and shocking form.

The Kansas-Nebraska Act having passed, Kansas became the prize and theatre of a struggle between slavery
and the Free Soilers, which was the prelude of civil war.
From the adjoining slave State of Missouri, the vanguard
of slavery came in to occupy the ground; but it was soon
encountered by Free Soil men, who poured in from the

Northern States under the auspices of the abolition societies, and well armed by them with Sharp's rifles, even the
clergy being carried away by the moral movement and
going so far as to open their churches to meetings for the
purpose. In the not unbloody conflict which followed,
the use of the rifle, the bowie-knife, and the torch, was
curiously combined with that of political trickery under constitutional forms, the American citizen preserving in the
hurly of the fight his formal respect for public law. The
slavery men outran their opponents in fraudulently framing a constitution with slavery, called the Lecompton
constitution, the acceptance of which was pressed on Congress by a pro-slavery President. The Free Soilers framed
a constitution without slavery at Topeka. Victory in the
end remained with the Free Soilers, while the slavery men
from Missouri were mere raiders. Nature, too, through
the soil and climate, had laid her ban upon slavery in
Kansas.

In Congress meantime the heat was extreme : debate
was always on the verge of violence. Members went to
the Capitol armed. Sumner having made a speech somewhat more than scathing and extremely personal, on what
he called the crime against Kansas, Brooks, a Southern
fire-eater, was so stung that under the sacred roof of the
Senate he fell on Sumner and beat him within an inch of
his life. The North thrilled with indignation. The
South applauded, and presented Brooks with a complimentary cane.

The political hosts, the Free Soil, or as it presently called
itself, the Republican party on one side, and that of
slavery and its friends, styled Democratic, on the other,
were now drawn out for battle. The Democrats still

bore on their banner the old Jeffersonian motto of State
right, opposed to federal centralization. But State right
had now come to mean the safeguard of slavery against
national interference. In the period of flux during the
process of formation, the Knownothing party acquired a
momentary accession of strength by giving refuge to old
Whigs who shrank from abolition. But this was soon
over, and Knownothingism left the scene. At the next
presidential election, the Republicans put up Fremont,
who was available as the Path Finder, having distinguished himself in California as an adventurous explorer
and a pioneer. They were beaten, and Buchanan, one of   1856.
the framers of the Ostend manifesto, became the last
slavery President. But the Republicans showed a strength
which was an earnest of future victory.

John Brown, a zealot of the Covenanting or Crom-
wellian stamp, had fought against slavery in Kansas ruthlessly, perhaps more than ruthlessly, though some Mis-
sourian ruffians instead of shooting, he forced at the point
of the rifle for the first time probably in their lives, to
kneel and pray. One of Brown's sons was shot by a clerical champion of slavery from Missouri. Exalted by his
anti-slavery enthusiasm almost to the pitch of madness, he
afterwards entered Virginia with two sons and a small
band, seized Harper's Ferry, where there was a Federal   1859.
arsenal, and called the slaves to freedom. No slaves
answered his call. He was soon surrounded, with his
party; his two sons were shot, and he, fighting with
the coolest intrepidity, was wounded and overpowered. He
was hanged with military parade and met his fate with
more than martyr calmness and courage. His bearing
impressed his enemies. The consolations of religion ten-

dered him by a pro-slavery clergyman, he declined, remembering perhaps the clerical filibuster in Kansas. Virginia was filled with panic and rage. At the North there was much sympathy for John Brown, disguising itself under faint disapprobation. In the war which ensued, his figure was glorified, and his soul, marching on in the battle hymn, led the hosts of emancipation against the slave power.

⟨ In 1861 came the catastrophe. By this time the spirit of secession was rife among the leaders of the South.⟩ On the nomination of Presidential candidates the Democratic party split. The thorough-going adherents of slavery nominated Breckinridge, the party of the union with slavery including the majority of the Northern Democrats, nominated Stephen Douglas. A third section, styling itself Constitutional, and vainly hoping to shut out the question of slavery and save the constitution, nominated Bell for President and for Vice-President Everett, the model orator, who at this crisis essayed to pour oil on the raging waters by going round and lecturing on the character of Washington.

The Republican convention was held at Chicago, and moral as was the cause in which it met, there was the usual display of electioneering arts, the usual bargaining, and the usual uproar. Seward was the most eminent man of the party and its natural candidate. For that very reason he was set aside, eminence being always dogged by rivalries and jealousies. ⟨The choice fell on Abraham Lincoln, a man whose eminence was not yet such as to give umbrage, a citizen of the powerful State in which the convention was held, and available as a rail-splitter.⟩ Rails said to have been made by him were carried about the convention. ⟨ Abraham Lincoln is

assuredly one of the marvels of history.⟩⟨No land but
America has produced his like.⟩This destined chief of
a nation in its most perilous hour was the son of a thriftless and wandering settler, bred in the most sordid poverty.
He had received only the rudiments of education, and
though he afterwards read eagerly such works as were
within his reach, it is wonderful that he should have
attained as a speaker and writer a mastery of language,
and a pure as well as effective style. He could look back
smiling on the day when his long shanks appeared bare
below the shrunken leather breeches which were his only
nether garment. His frame was gaunt and grotesque but
mighty.⟩ He stood six feet four, and was said to have
lifted a cask full of beer and to have drunk out of the
bunghole. This made him a hero with the Clary Grove
boys. He had a strong and eminently fair understanding,
with great powers of patient thought which he cultivated
by the study of Euclid. In all his views there was a
simplicity which had its source in the simplicity of his
character.⟨His local popularity was due largely to his
humour, and the stock of good stories, always pointed,
though not always delicate, which through life it was his
delight to collect and repeat. At the same time he was
melancholy, touched with the pathos of human life, fond
of mournful poetry, religious though not orthodox, with a
strong sense of an overruling Providence which when he
was out of spirits sometimes took the shape of fatalism.⟩
His melancholy was probably deepened by his gloomy
surroundings and by misadventures in love.⟨ Like his
father he was without habits of settled industry. He tried
boating, he tried store-keeping, he tried surveying, he
tried soldiering in an Indian war, though he never came

under fire. At last he became a lawyer, or rather an advocate. This suited him better and he pleaded successfully in rude courts. But for his roving spirit politics was the trade. Those who knew him best thought him intensely ambitious, and he was probably the more disposed to public life, when his domestic happiness had been marred by marriage with a woman, his love of whom was so doubtful that he once shirked the wedding, after losing by death a woman whom he certainly loved. He was elected, one of a group called "the long nine," to the Legislature of his State. As a politician he played the game; he jumped out of window to break a quorum, and conspired in wrecking a hostile journal by the furtive insertion of a ruinous editorial. Still his character was at bottom thoroughly sound. Both as an advocate and as a politician he was "honest Abe." As an advocate he would throw up his brief when he knew that his case was bad. He equipped himself for politics by a careful study of constitutional law, while from his early life he drew an inestimable knowledge of the minds and hearts of those whom he called the plain people. The sight of slavery in his early wanderings, and still more perhaps the natural love of justice which was strong in him, had made him a Free Soiler. But his abolitionism was temperate. In opposing slavery he never reviled the slave-owners, nor was he blind to the inferiority of the negro. He held the negro to be the white man's equal only in certain inalienable rights, in the right, above all, to eat the bread which his own hands had earned. He had been made known to fame by a series of platform tournaments with the redoubtable Stephen Douglas, in which his powers of reasoning fairly as well as closely, and of telling statement, were displayed. In one of his speeches he had uttered words not less memorable than Seward's "irrepressible conflict." "A house," he said, "divided against itself cannot stand. I believe this government cannot endure permanently half slave and half free. I do not expect the Union to be dissolved; I do not expect the house to fall; but I do expect it will cease to be divided. It will become all one thing or all the other." Either the opponents of slavery will arrest the further spread of it, and place it where the public mind shall rest in the belief that it is in course of ultimate extinction, or its advocates will push it forward till it shall become alike lawful in all the States, old as well as new, North as well as South." After his campaign in Illinois, he had been brought to speak at New York, and, in spite of his ungainly figure and quaint costume, had made a deep impression. But it was mainly to cabal against Seward that Lincoln owed the Republican nomination. He was elected President after a campaign of intense excitement, commerce struggling hard to escape from the yawning gulf by the election of Douglas as a conservative. But the votes cast for him fell short by a million of those cast for Douglas, Breckinridge, and Bell together, and his support came almost entirely from the North.

There could be no mistake about the significance of the election by Northern votes of a President who looked forward to seeing slavery "put where the people would be satisfied that it was in course of ultimate extinction." As a Southern Senator said, Republicans did not mean to cut down the tree of slavery, but they meant to gird it about and make it die. Southern fire-eaters welcomed the event. From South Carolina, the centre of slavery, went up the signal rocket of Secession amidst transports of enthusiasm,

1860.

Dec. 20, 1860.

which the women frantically shared, unconscious of the
coming doom. ✕ It was answered in rapid succession by the
1861. other States of the group, Mississippi, Alabama, Louisiana,
Texas, and Georgia, though in Georgia not without a
strong spasm of reluctance.   Afterwards followed the
more Northern group, North Carolina, Tennessee, and
Virginia.〉 The Old Dominion was conservative, and, as
the slave-breeding State, had no interest in the renewal of
the slave trade.   Unionism made a stand in East Tennessee, Western Virginia, and the uplands of North Carolina,
hill districts from which nature had repelled slavery. 〈The
border States, Maryland, Kentucky, and Missouri, in
which slavery existed but was not dominant, wavered and
remained debatable, the two last nearly to the end, though
all three were kept formally in the Union. ✕ Otherwise
secession swept the South, though more or less of violence
no doubt was everywhere used to crush dissent or hesita-
tion, and the revolution was the work of a thorough-going
minority, as revolutions usually are. ✕ The ordinances by
which the States had severally entered the Union were
repealed, a congress was held, and a Southern confederacy
was formed, with a constitution modelled in general after
that of the United States, but distinctly recognizing State
sovereignty and proclaiming negro-slavery as the foundation of the new commonwealth. ✕ Changes of detail, perhaps improvements, were made, such as the lengthening
of the Presidential term, with the abolition of the power of
re-election, and the admission of ministers of state to Congress; but it is needless to dwell on them, as they were
still-born.〉 Alexander Stephens, the Vice-President, said,
" The negro, by nature and by the curse against Canaan,
is fitted for the condition he occupies in our system.   An

architect, in the construction of buildings, lays the foundation with the proper material, the granite; then comes the brick or the marble. The substratum of our society is made of the material fitted by nature for it, and by experience we know that it is the best not only for the superior, but for the inferior, race that it should be so. It is, indeed, in conformity with the Creator. It is not for us to inquire into the wisdom of His ordinances, or to question them. For His own purposes He has made one race to differ from another as He has made one 'star to differ from another star in glory.' The great objects of humanity are best attained when conformed to His laws, in the constitution of governments as well as in all things else. Our confederacy is founded upon a strict conformity with these laws. The stone which was rejected by the first builders is become the chief stone of the corner in our new edifice." After such an avowal, and in face of the fact that the line of political cleavage exactly coincided with that of slavery, following its windings both generally and in the exceptional cases of Tennessee, Virginia, and North Carolina, while the border States, which were half slave, remained politically waverers, who could doubt that slavery was the cause of secession? The question between free trade and protection, which the emissaries of the South in free trade England sought to present as the real cause, had, indeed, always divided the agricultural South from the manufacturing North, and had in Calhoun's time given rise to Nullification. But it was derivative, and its influence was secondary. The Confederacy was in its essence a slave-power, and as such boldly flaunted its banner in the face of humanity. Jefferson Davis, a man after the Southern heart, able, impetuous, and overbearing, was elected President. His government was recognized and obeyed over a compact territory larger than France, Spain, Portugal, and the British Islands put together, with a population greater than that of the old thirteen colonies, and with many times their wealth. A new flag, or rather the old flag with a secessionist variation, was unfurled, and the slave power took its place for four years among the nations. Richmond, a new capital, confronted Washington. Under whatever constitutional forms the Confederate government might be set up, the South, when the war had commenced, had no constitution but that of a beleaguered city. Its President became a commandant; its Congress sat in secret, mutely registering his decrees; all safeguards for personal liberty were suspended; the government assumed absolute mastery not only of the property but also of the persons of all citizens for the purposes of the war: the press became a sounding-board. The revolution which had given birth to such liberties could not fail to provoke the mockery of the North, but it was invasion which made the government of the South despotic, and laws must sleep when a nation is struggling for its life. It was true, however, that the spirit of the slave-owner ruled at Richmond, and showed its pitiless and masterful temper beyond even the necessities of war.

As the States seceded, their representatives withdrew from Congress with farewells more or less defiant. Had Jackson been President, instead of being suffered to depart, they might have been laid by the heels, and their plot might have been disconcerted for the time. But Buchanan, besides being the nominee of the slave-owners, was a weak man, and his position was weaker still. He was

an outgoing President, about to be replaced by a President-
elect of the opposite party.   These intervals, during which
government is severed from power, are a weak point in the
American constitution, and are one of the proofs that its
framers failed to foresee the ascendancy of party, and the
situations which would thereby be created.   Buchanan
first, in a double-faced manifesto, pronounced that secession was unconstitutional, but coercion was illegal.   Afterwards, Southerners having left his Cabinet, and being
replaced by Unionist Democrats, he somewhat altered
his tone, while one of his ministers, General Dix,
sent the telegram, "If any man attempts to haul down
the American flag, shoot him on the spot"; to which
the spirit of the North gave a response which might
have been a warning to the South.   But Buchanan's sole
desire was to be gone, and cast the burden on his successor.
His conduct could not be less resolute and brave than that
of Congress, which, in truth, was an ominous lesson on the
character of the politician trained in the caucus and upon
the platform.⟨ Congress, finding that disunion, beneath
the threat of which it had long cowered, had really come,
fell on its knees, and offered the slave owners boundless
concessions.   It was ready to give slavery new guarantees
and extension, to sharpen still more the fugitive slave
law, to deprive the negro claimed as a slave of the last
shred of legal protection, to call upon the States to repeal
all their personal liberty bills, to extend the Missouri compromise line to the Pacific, and admit New Mexico, including Arizona, with a slave code, to satisfy the prejudice of
race by disqualifying all men of negro blood for civil
office.   It even offered to place slavery beyond the reach
of constitutional amendment, and make it, so far as law

could make it, eternal. A resolution to this effect passed the House by a vote of 133 to 65, and the Senate by 24 to 12, just the requisite two-thirds. It would, as Mr. Blaine says, "have entrenched slavery securely in the organic law of the land, and elevated the privilege of the slave-owner beyond that of the owner of any other species of property." This resolution received the vote of a large number of prominent Republicans, and if the Southern members of Congress would have stooped to vote instead of seceding they might have riveted their political yoke on the neck of the American nation forever. Even pronounced enemies of slavery, such as Mr. Seward and Mr. Sumner, seem to have trembled in silence. Nor did Congress much misrepresent its constituents. In spite of all the signs in the political sky, nobody had believed that the deluge was coming; everybody had trusted the providence which watched over the American Union. When the crisis arrived a cold shudder ran through the nation. Local elections began to go against the Republicans. The Republican party, Mr. Blaine says, was utterly demoralized. Its great organ in New York conceded the right of withdrawing from the Union, declared against all coercive measures, and even said that the South had as good a right to secede from the Union as the colonies had to secede from Great Britain. Democratic organs went further, and declared the election of Lincoln a greater provocation than that which the American colonies had received from the mother country. Those who spoke of secession as rebellion were met with cries of dissent. Abolitionist orators and lecturers were refused a hearing. Wendell Phillips, after reviling Lincoln as a trimmer, would himself have yielded to secession. "Here," he said, "are a series of States, girding the Gulf, who think that their peculiar institutions require a separate government. They have a right to settle that question without appealing to you or me." General Scott, the head of the Federal army, was so far carried away by the tide of panic as to propose the division of the Union into four separate confederations. Men clung to the hope that the trouble would blow over, and commerce prayed for peace at any price.

It need not, however, be assumed that because the North did not take arms against slavery, nor was entitled to the sympathy of the world on that account, it had no motive for making war except the vulgar desire of territorial aggrandizement. Northern men might, and no doubt did, believe that they were fighting for a violated constitution, for a compact which had been faithlessly broken, for the vindication of law, reverence for which had been deeply planted in their hearts, and even for the political fortunes of humanity, which, according to American belief, were embarked in the ship of the Union.

Had the Confederates played their game warily, had they spoken the North fair, pleaded the hopeless incompatibility of the two systems, and promised friendship and fidelity to commercial engagements, they might have been let part in peace. But wariness was not Southern. Seeing the North thus cling to the Union, the Southern gentlemen thought that the "greasy mechanic" would not fight, and they dared him to smell Southern powder and taste Southern steel. They were fatally mistaken. The greasy mechanic was of their own race, and though he clung to the Union, he would fight.

There is little use in renewing the bottomless contro-

versy about the State sovereignty and the right of secession. The constitution was on this point a Delphic oracle.
Its framers had blinked the question of State sovereignty,
as they had compromised on that of slavery. They could
not have ventured to avow that the States were disclaim-
ing their sovereignty in accepting the constitution. They
trusted to time, and had slavery been out of the way, time
would have done the work. ⟨ In sentiment, the allegiance
of the Northern heart was to the Union⟩ The Northern
people were imbued with Webster's sentiment. Moreover,
the new States, which now outnumbered the old thirteen,
were the offspring of the nation, and of their people many
were immigrants from Europe, strangers to any original
compact. Thus California, on the far Pacific Coast, being
a child of the nation, stood steadily by the cause of the
Union. The allegiance of the Southerner, more home-
keeping than the man of the North, and with a narrower
range of vision, was to his State, which, moreover, he
regarded with reason as the bulwark of his peculiar institution. ⟨ Many people of the South, who had no personal
interest in slavery, and were opposed to secession, thought
it was their duty to go with their State, and their sense of
their duty grew stronger when their State was invaded by
Northern arms.⟩ Lincoln himself had said, " Any people
anywhere, being inclined and having the power, have the
right to rise up and shake off the existing government, and
form a new one that suits them better. This is a most
valuable, a most sacred right, a right which we hope and
believe is to liberate the world. Nor is this right confined
to cases in which the whole people of an existing government may choose to exercise it. Any portion of such
people, that can, may revolutionize and make their own of

so much of the territory as they inhabit." So had thought
the American people, and, therefore, they had sympathized
with revolt all over the world. Southern revolution
could not have asked for a clearer sanction. But it was
not necessary to invoke formally the right of revolution.
Wendell Phillips hit the mark. Two communities, radically differing in social structure, and, therefore, in political requirements, had been clamped together in ill-assorted,
uneasy, contentious and immoral union. At length, in the
course of nature, they fell asunder and formed two separate nations, the stronger of which proceeded to attack,
conquer, and reannex the weaker. This was the simple
fact. It was natural that the mind of the North should
be possessed by the ideas of union and the constitution;
that it should regard secession as treason and rebellion.
But those names were really out of place, as the North
itself was fain practically to confess. Not for a moment,
or in a single instance, did it treat the Southerners as
traitors or rebels. From the very outset it treated them
as combatants in a regular war, and accepted the same
treatment at their hands. The threat of dealing with the
crew of a Confederate privateer as pirates, being met by a
threat of reprisal, was instantly withdrawn. Foreign
powers saw this, and with good reason at once recognized
the South as a belligerent. Even the term civil war is
hardly correct, since this was not a struggle between two
parties for the same land, like that between the League
and the Huguenots in France, or that between the Cavaliers and Roundheads in England, but between two communities, territorially separate, for the land of one of them
which the other had taken arms to reannex. Only in the
border States, in each of which two parties were struggling
for ascendancy, could it be strictly called a civil war.

⧸ Lincoln stole by night into the capital. His life had
been threatened on his journey by that same mob at
Baltimore, the Plug-uglies as they were called, which
had risen and massacred in favour of the war of 1812.
When he reached Washington, and had been inaugurated
under military protection, his situation was one which
might well have made his heart sink. Before him was
secession. Behind him were fear and fainting of hearts.
Around him was treachery. He was a minority President.
That he had been raised to power by a party, not by the
nation, he was reminded by the swarm of partisan office-
seekers, which surrounded and distracted him even in this
supreme hour. He had hardly a good adviser, for even
Seward, the Secretary of State, had for the time lost his
head, and talked wildly about sinking the slavery question
in a spirited foreign policy, and challenging the powers of
Europe to war. His greatest encouragement came, perhaps,
from Stephen Douglas, who, though an advocate of squatter sovereignty and slavery, was a patriot and true to the
Union. Those who had manœuvred the rail-splitter into
the nomination, and had voted him into the Presidency,
must have quaked. But they had chosen much better
than they knew. ⟨Lincoln stood firmly on his own feet,
and faced the peril with a calmness and a wisdom drawn
largely from his moral character and his trust in Providence; for fear is generally selfish, and Lincoln could
have no selfish fears.⟩ He presented himself as the servant
and guardian of the constitution, naturally failing to see
that nature had torn up that compromise. ⟨He disavowed
any purpose of interfering directly or indirectly with
slavery in the States where it existed, declaring that he
had neither the right nor the inclination so to do; " not

to save slavery or any minor matter" would he permit "the wreck of government, country, and constitution.") The preservation of the Union, with or without slavery, he proclaimed as his paramount duty. (The Union, he maintained, was perpetual, a government, not a mere association of the States, and all resolves and ordinances to the contrary were invalid. He announced his intention of holding all the property, exercising the authority, and performing the functions of government in the Southern States, but of doing this without violence or bloodshed, unless they were forced upon him by the South.) "In your hands, my dissatisfied fellow country-men," he said, "is the momentous issue of civil war. The government will not assail you. You can have no conflict without being yourselves the aggressors." He appealed to the principle of government by majorities, arguing that if it was to be disregarded the end would be anarchy. He appealed to fraternal affection, and challenged the malcontents to point out an instance in which the constitution had been plainly violated. Their answer would have been that the constitution was a com-pact, to which the election of a President holding that slavery was to be placed where the people would know that it was in the course of ultimate extinction, had morally put an end. But Lincoln thus kept the weather gage of opinion, and his language, moderate, calm, and conciliatory, presented a favourable contrast to the violent and somewhat blustering manifestos of his Confederate rival. His repeated disavowals of any intention of inter-fering with slavery inevitably estranged thorough-going abolitionists. Commissioners from the South, coming to treat in the name of an independent power, he refused to receive, though Seward was inclined to dally with their overtures. His caution kept him in touch with general opinion. Horace Greeley goes so far as to assert, reckoning by the votes cast in the Presidential election, that three-fifths of the entire American people, exclusive of the blacks, "sympathized with rebellion in so far as its animating purpose was the fortification, diffusion, and aggrandizement of slavery." To be kept in touch with general opinion was Lincoln's statesmanship. His special object, in his dealing with the slavery question, was the retention in the Union of the border States, Maryland, Kentucky, and Missouri, the scenes of a fierce struggle between the Unionist and Disunionist parties, which were preserved probably in great measure by Lincoln's policy from secession. It was to propitiate these States that, even when the war was far advanced, he put forth a plan for abolition with compensation. He had also to consider the military men, without whom an army could not be formed, and who for the most part inclined to the side of slavery. He at the same time necessarily renounced his claim to the sympathy of foreign nations, especially of England, who could not be expected to regard the invasion of the South by the North as a crusade against slavery when the President declared it was nothing of the kind. The Southern Confederacy was avowedly founded with slavery as its corner-stone. It was, therefore, under the ban of humanity. This was the reason for desiring its fall, whatever might be the motives of its assailant. For the unity and aggrandizement of the American Republic many men in England and other nations cared, because they looked with hope to the great experiment of American democracy; but nobody was morally bound to

care. The South had been politic enough to pay homage
to the opinion of the world, especially of the British
people, and perhaps, at the same time, to propitiate the
slave-breeding State, by inserting into its constitution
a renunciation of the African slave trade, though it was
pretty certain that had the slave power triumphed this
article would have had little effect.

⟨War broke out in the natural quarter, at Charleston, the
fiery heart of slavery, the memorial shrine of Calhoun.
Fort Sumter, in Charleston harbour, was held by its commander for the Union. The government at Washington
proceeded to revictual it, thereby perhaps committing, as
the South contended, the first formal act of war. The April
Confederates bombarded and took the fort. The effect was 1861.
magical. At the outrage on the flag the North, of late so
cold and quaking, burst into a general flame of patriotic
wrath. Lincoln's call for volunteers was answered with
enthusiasm, and the "irrepressible conflict" began. The
second shot was fired in the streets of Baltimore where the
Plug-uglies rose for slavery, and attacked volunteers on
their march to Washington.⟩

⟨The Northern whites outnumbered Southern whites by
three to one, but the Southern whites had their negroes to
feed them.⟩The military qualities of the race on both
sides were the same, or rather the Northern and Western
farmer, when brought under discipline, was superior in
steady valour to the "poor white" of the South, though
his onset was not so furious as that of the "Louisiana
Tigers," nor his yell so loud. Both sides were untrained
to war; but the rough life of the poor white had been the
better preparation for the camp, and he was more accustomed to the endurance of hardship, as well as a rifleman

well fitted for forest war, and he marched well. The
Southern gentleman was a horseman, while the people at
the North used not the saddle-horse but the buggy. Not
that cavalry were much used for battle in this war; the
country was too tangled for their charges and even for their
formation; they were used chiefly for reconnaisances and
raids. The South also had over the North at first the
advantage which the Cavaliers had over the Roundheads;
the gentry were accustomed to command, and the common
people to obey. It took time to make the Northern Democrat submit to discipline. Lincoln, when he went out with
a corps against the Indians, had heard the first word of
command given by an officer to a private answered with an
oath. Discipline, however, came in time and was then
combined with greater intelligence. In intelligence no
army. except perhaps the Athenian, can have ever equalled
or approached that of the North. Most of the soldiers
carried books and writing materials in their knapsacks, and
mail bags heavily weighted with letters were sent from
every cantonment. Such privates would sometimes reason
instead of obeying, and they would see errors of their commanders to which they had better have been blind. But
on the whole, in a war in which much was thrown upon the
individual soldier, intelligence was likely to prevail. In
wealth, in the means of providing the weapons and ammu-
nitions of war, the North had an immense advantage, which,
combined with that of numbers, could not fail, if, to use
Lincoln's homely phrase, it "pegged away," to tell in the
end. It was also vastly superior in mechanical invention,
which was destined to play a great part, and in mechanical
skill; almost every Yankee regiment was full of mechanics,
some of whom could devise as well as execute. In artillery

and engineering the North took the lead from the first, having many civil engineers, whose conversion into military civil engineers was easy. The South, to begin with, had the contents of Federal arsenals and armouries, which had been well stocked by the provident treason of Buchanan's Minister of War. The Federal navy yard at Norfolk, with twelve ships, also fell into its hands. But when these resources were exhausted, replacement was difficult, the blockade having been established, though extraordinary efforts in the way of military manufacture were made. To the wealthy North, besides its own factories, were opened the markets of England and the world. Of the small regular army the Confederacy had carried off a share, with nearly half the regular officers. The South had the advantage of the defensive, which, with long-range muskets and in a difficult country, was reckoned in battle as five to two. The South had the superiority of the unity, force, and secrecy which autocracy lends to the operations of war. On the side of the North these were comparatively wanting. Party divisions continued, the war being openly opposed, and sympathy with secession almost openly avowed by the Copperheads. as they were called, from a reptile which waits on the rattlesnake, the rattlesnake being emblematic of the South. The North, on the other hand, had the advantage of the unforced efforts and sacrifice which free patriotism makes ; and, as the struggle went on, power was spontaneously entrusted to the government, which received during the greater part of the conflict the hearty and almost unquestioning support of a majority in Congress so large as to produce practical unity of counsels. Among its supporters were many of the Democratic party, who under the name of War Democrats followed the patriotic example of Stephen Douglas. ⟨ The evils of political influence were felt in the choice of generals and in the conduct of the war, but perhaps not more than those of favouritism on the other side. The press, if it gave trouble to the government, did not, like the slave press of the South, mislead the people by publishing, at the bidding of the war office, false news of successes which exalted for the moment, but led to depression when the truth was known. ⟩

⟨ At the North the supply of volunteers was at first abundant and from all classes, patriotic enthusiasm being general. After experience of the grim reality volunteering declined, and desertion, if the Comte de Paris may be trusted, became immense. ⟩⟨ It was necessary to resort to bounties, which led to bounty-jumping, that is desertion and re-enlistment for the purpose of getting the bounty paid over again, and at last to the draft with the paying of substitutes, in whose persons, as the jesters said, a man might leave his bones on the field of honour, and think of it with patriotic pride as he sipped his wine at home. Under the bounty, draft, and substitute system the quality of the enlistments could not fail to fall off, while recruiting agents would pick up all the waifs, native or foreign, whom they could find. But the bulk of the army to the end was native, though it included many Germans, British, and Irish, who had been naturalized, or who had settled in the United States, and could not fairly be set down as mercenaries. ⟩⟨ The South, almost from the first, resorted to conscription, ruthlessly enforced with the severest penalties for evasion or desertion, from which Northern democracy shrank. ⟩ Guards pressed men in the streets, and conscripts were seen going to Lee's army in chains. It

was complained that the slave-owners by various subter-
fuges escaped while they thrust the poor under fire.

The finance of the South in like manner soon became
requisition and confiscation, the inconvertible bank bills
which it issued in vast volumes having speedily lost all
value, so that its soldiers waived the farce of being paid
in them. It found purchasers for its bonds among its
European friends, who sacrificed to their sympathy with
its cause At the North a war taxation, heavy and search-
ing, was cheerfully borne. To meet further demands
bonds were issued, and an immense debt was contracted.
The North also unhappily resorted to the issue of an
inconvertible paper currency which in effect was a forced
loan, raised in a manner which impaired the faith of contracts, and disturbed industry and trade. The Supreme
Court, for reasons which must be deemed rather political
than judicial, afterwards sanctioned the exercise of a power
not given to the Federal Government by the constitution,
and denied, apparently for a reason universally applica-
ble, to the States. A depreciation of sixty per cent was
the result.

The South looked for help from England where it
believed that cotton was king. The free-trade argument,
early and skilfully urged, prevailed at Liverpool where
cotton indeed was king, and in other commercial centres
where the same interest prevailed. Politically Great
Britain was divided like the United States themselves.
On the side of the South was the aristocratic party, which
had always been taught to believe that the success of the
American Republic would be its doom. The journals
of that party, eminent as well as violent, poured the
gall of insult into the American heart in the hour of

peril and adversity when feelings are most keen. American hatred of England, and the former attitude of the Washington government, had left their sting. For the attitude of the Washington government the slave-owners, who had long held power, were chiefly to blame, but of this the English people were not conscious. English friends of the Republic not a few deprecated the war, thinking that it would be wiser to part in peace, and were unjustly confounded by the North with enemies. ⟨ But as soon as it was discovered, that, in spite of the disclaimers of the American Congress and President, the struggle was practically one between freedom and slavery, the hearts of the mass of the English people were with the North⟩ ⟨ Nor did the partisans of the slave power in the British Parliament ever venture on a serious movement in its favour.⟩⟨The dearth of cotton, though severely felt, was borne. The government throughout observed neutrality, refusing to recognize the Confederacy, or receive its ambassadors, even when victory seemed to have assured to it a place among the nations.⟩ Steady refusal met the overtures of the French emperor who, always striving to tread in the footsteps of the first Napoleon, and seeking to re-establish for France a colonial empire in America, urged a joint intervention which when the fortunes of the North were low could scarcely have failed to have been decisive. ⟨ For a moment it seemed that the power of Great Britain would, in her own despite, be thrown into the Southern Nov. scale by the rash act of the American Captain Wilkes, 1861. who, having confused his mind with the study of international law, took the Confederate envoys. Mason and Slidell, out of a British ship. The act being at first approved by the American Secretary for the Navy, and applauded

by the people, the British demand for redress was peremptory.⟩ Perhaps the temper of Lord Palmerston, who was
given to bluster, made it even more peremptory than was
needful. ⟨ But wisdom prevailed and the envoys were
given up. Among the British people, kinsmen of the
Americans and speaking the same language, as well as
connected by commerce, the war was a home question,
and the excitement was intense⟩ ⟨By the other nations of
Europe far less interest was shown. To them the American Republic was entirely foreign⟩ and the idea that
upon its success or failure hung the fate of democracy and
of human progress had not found place in their minds.
Even in France, while the government was scheming,
the people were almost indifferent. Russia, while with the
rest of the powers she recognized the belligerency of the
of the South, assumed a politic attitude of benevolent
neutrality towards the North. The spheres of Russia and
the United States were wide apart, the difference between
the governments in character was too extreme for political
jealousy; perhaps even as extremes they met and at that
time they had a common hatred.

⟨The strategical objects at which Northern invasion aimed
were the Mississippi, by regaining the mastery of which
Louisiana, Arkansas, Texas, and whatever the South had
of Missouri, would be cut off; Chattanooga, and other
positions in Tennessee, which commanded the lines of railway binding the Confederate territory together from east
to west, together with the entrance into the heart of the
confederation; and the coast, by blockading which the
South was to be debarred from the sale of its cotton, on
which its finance depended, and from receiving supplies
from Europe⟩ ⟨The political object was Richmond, in

choosing which for their capital, placed as it was on the northern edge of their territory, and near the centre of the enemy's force, the Confederates had propitiated Virginia at the expense of their military strength, though they no doubt hoped that Richmond in the end would not be a border city, since their territory would in the end embrace Missouri and Kentucky. The section of country between the two capitals, traversed by the Potomac, the Rappahannock, Rapidan, North Anna, and Pamunkey Rivers, thus became the grand scene of war. Above all, the object was to beat and destroy the armies of the South which gathered round Richmond. There went on a struggle, generally of the guerrilla kind, for Kentucky and Missouri. The South began by striking at Washington, the fall of which, though not a military, would have been a political, blow, and might have had an effect upon Europe. From the vast fortress in which it was beleaguered, its armies at times sallied forth to grasp the border States, to sweep off supplies, of which its need was always increasing, to turn opinion at the North, and make the assailant loosen his hold. Otherwise, it waged only a defensive war.

"On to Richmond" was the cry of the North. On, in spite of military warnings, the raw militia with a handful of regulars went. At the stream of Bull Run they met the Confederates under Beauregard. A confused engagement, the counterpart of Edgehill, ensued. A fresh Confederate force, coming up by rail, decided the day. Obstruction at a bridge turned panic flight into a rout, and the Confederates, had they pursued, might have entered Washington. But the victors were in little better plight than the vanquished. Aristocratic journals in Europe scoffed and jeered. Yet the list of killed and wounded on both sides

July 1861.

was an earnest of a bloody war, and in the midst of the panic Connecticut artisans had proved the pith of their order by the steadiness with which they bore off their guns. ⟨The South crowed loudly, but the North, instead of being discouraged, was spurred to effort and measured its task.⟩With their native versatility, the American people turned from the works of peace to those of war, took to drilling and learning to ride, to the manufacture of cannon and rifles, to the building of ships, or the conversion of merchantmen and ferryboats into vessels of war, to the organization of the commissariat and transport. for which hotel-keeping and railway-managing had well fitted them; or of the medical department, for the service of which steamboats and railway carriages were turned into field-hospitals.⟩ Politicians changed the sphere of their ambition from the Senate to the camp, not with much success, for no civilian commander attained more than a secondary reputation. ⟨There was a general rush to arms, a general outpouring of patriotic gifts and tender of patriotic services.⟩Congress voted men and money without stint, and the call for troops was promptly answered by the States. The force of spontaneous zeal in contrast to the iron despotism which grasped the resources of the South was seen, and the only question was whether it would last.⟩

⟨ In the west, the Federals had gained some advantages by which the public eye was turned on General McClellan, whom national fancy now exalted into a young Napoleon, and called to the command of the army with the amplest powers and the most lavish supplies. He proved to be an organizer rather than a general.⟩ It was said of him by a railway president, who had employed him as a civil engineer, that he would build the best of bridges, but would never go on it himself. ⟨A great organizer he was.⟩ He drilled to perfection an army of 150,000 men, yet having drilled it, he did not advance, but lay in his camp near Washington, still drilling and reviewing while weeks of good weather went by. His policy seems to have been to create an overwhelming force, bind the Confederate armies to the stake at Richmond, destroy them there, and thus end secession at a blow, perhaps without prejudice to slavery, to which, as a Democrat, he was no enemy⟩ In the controversy which ensued between him and Lincoln, the President wrote always with temper and forbearance, while McClellan was sometimes arrogant; but the presumption is against a civilian who meddles with war, and Lincoln's excessive fear for the safety of the capital is allowed to have led him into dictating at least one false move. That he felt political jealousy of McClellan as a Democrat, or a possible rival for the Presidency, is not to be believed, whatever may have been the feelings of party politicians around him.⟨At last McClellan moved on Richmond. He saw the spires of the Confederate capital, but his movements were tentative and irresolute, while his tone was always despondent.⟩ After a series of blind and bloody engagements, in a wooded and swampy country, he led back an army not conquered, though severely handled, in the field and decimated by malaria and straggling as well as by the bullet. ⟨It had been the good fortune of the Confederates to find at once a great general in Robert E. Lee, a Virginian aristocrat, and an officer of the regular army, who, though a Unionist, when his State left the Union felt bound to go with his State⟩ He had been joined by Jackson, nicknamed from his steadfastness on

April 1862.

, field of general panic Stonewall, a striking figure, a
Calvinist of the Scotch-Irish breed, deeply religious, a
believer in the destiny of the children of Ham, and a
soldier of extraordinary energy, valour, daring, and activity, the idol of his men.   Lee was henceforth the head,
Jackson the right arm, of Confederate war.⟩
⟨ McClellan having lost the confidence of his government
though not of his men was replaced by Pope who put
forth a gasconading manifesto, was outgeneralled by Lee
and Jackson, and defeated in a great battle.⟩ Emboldened
by victory the Confederate generals sallied into Maryland
in the hope of her rising, which though her heart was
with them she disappointed. She waited for the guarantee
of victory, perhaps also she shrank from her tattered and
squalid deliverers. A secondary object of the movement
was need of supplies.⟨No armies were ever so lavishly
supplied as those of the North. The length of their
waggon trains was prodigious.⟩ A wealthy democracy is
sure to care well for all its citizens.⟨ But the Southern
soldiers were called upon to endure great hardships.⟩We
find them left for days with no food but a little flour.
We find them ragged, barefooted, and without hats, fain
to bind old hats on their feet for shoes; we find them
without blankets, and piteous appeals are made by their
commanders for something to cover the defenders of the
country who were keeping guard amidst sleet and snow.
There must also have been terrible suffering in their ill-
provided hospitals, especially when the stern policy of war
refused to let medicines pass. Pay they had none. Few
of these men were slave-owners, and they were fighting
for what to them was their country. Lee, however, suffered much from straggling.⟩

To face the storm which threatened Washington
Sept.
1862. McClellan was replaced in command. On the Antietam
he met Lee with superior forces, and fought a bloody
battle which though indecisive was followed by the retreat
of Lee. Bloody the battle was, enough to satisfy all
critics of American valour. A visitor to the field saw the
bodies lying in swathes. In the length of five hundred
feet he counted two hundred dead. A lane was filled
with a battalion of them. The field where he stood was
black with corpses; he was told that the field beyond was
equally crowded, but he had supped as full of horrors as
he could bear.

Antietam, though a drawn battle, was for a momentous
purpose made to do duty as a victory. Lincoln had
at length decided to strike slavery, which by this time
must have been seen to be the great enemy, and against
which in fact Congress had entered the national verdict
by abolishing it in the District of Columbia. He had
hesitated long, fearing to outrun opinion, his constant
guide, his index of that "will of God," conformity to
which he always made his aim, and to estrange the
border States. Meantime he had been checking his
generals of both parties, enemies of slavery who set the
negroes free within their command, and friends of slavery
who gave back fugitive slaves to their owners. A shrewd
move had been made towards emancipation, and a cue had
been given to the President by Benjamin Butler, a sharp
lawyer turned soldier, who pronounced the negro, as he
helped the enemy on military works, contraband of war,
and confiscated him to freedom. But now the President
thought that the hour had come, and that something must
be done to put new life into the cause. He waited only

or a victory that his act might not seem one of despair.
Ie made a solemn vow before God that if General Lee
vere driven back from Maryland, he would set the slaves
ree. After Antietam he announced his intention of issu-
ng, and on the first of January, 1863, he issued, a memo-
able proclamation, setting free by his military authority
ill the slaves in rebel States. He still founded his action
)n policy and the constitution. Later on his moral feel-
ngs found free utterance. " If we shall suppose that
American slavery is one of those offences which, in the
)rovidence of God, must needs come, but which, having
:ontinued through His appointed time, He now wills to
·emove, and that He gives to both North and South this
:errible war, as the woe due to those by whom the offence
:ame, shall we discern therein any departure from those
livine attributes which the believers in a living God
iscribe to Him? Fondly do we hope, fervently do we
)ray, that this mighty scourge of war may speedily pass
iway. Yet if God wills that it continue until all the
wealth piled by the bondman's two hundred and fifty
years of unrequited toil shall be sunk, and until every
lrop of blood drawn with the lash shall be paid by another
lrawn with the sword, as was said three thousand years
igo, so still it must be said, 'the judgments of the Lord
ire true and righteous altogether.' "
There presently followed the enlistment of negroes as
soldiers, for which the country was more ready as its
industry was losing many hands, and the black 54th
Massachusetts, under its devoted white colonel, Shaw, May
marched out to glory through the streets of Boston amidst 1863.
great demonstrations of public sympathy. There was a
throb of race feeling by which the negro soldiers were at

first disrated.⟩ This was overcome ; yet it cannot be said that they were ever received by their white fellow soldiers, or have since been acknowledged, as brethren in arms. They fought not ill, being docile, though not dashing ; but the half of manhood which, Homer says, slavery takes from a man cannot be restored by merely putting on him the cap of liberty. ⟨ By the sight of negro soldiers the evil passion of the slave-owner was fearfully aroused. ⟩⟨At the

April 1864. taking of Fort Pillow by the Confederates, the negroes of the garrison were shot down after surrender, some were nailed to logs and burned, some were buried alive, and even whites taken with the negroes shared the same fate.⟩ The evidence for this seems conclusive. Why should we reject it when at this day negroes in the South are being burned alive ?

⟨The slaves never rose. They continued to till the soil, supplied their masters with food, and faithfully took care of the planter's wife and daughters. The slave-owners are entitled to the benefit of this fact. But the negroes were children of habit, and ill-informed of events. The proclamation of freedom would scarcely reach their ears. They welcomed the Northern armies, gave them all the information in their power, and, it was said, never deceived them.⟩

The tide, however, had not yet turned. McClellan received orders from Washington to follow Lee. He stood still, was removed from command, and replaced by Burnside, a brave and loyal but hapless officer, in the selection of whom Lincoln's judgment strangely failed him. Burnside sent his troops to storm a strong position

Dec. 1862. in which Lee had entrenched himself on the heights of Fredericksburg between Washington and Richmond.

The issue was a ruinous defeat followed by still more
ruinous demoralization. ⟨Irregularity of pay conspired
with the influence of defeat.⟩ More than 80,000 soldiers
and nearly 3000 officers were absent from the standards,
and more than one-half of them without regular leave. The
service of the outposts was neglected; the bonds of discipline were being loosened. "Gloom, home-sickness, and
a disposition to criticise," says the Comte de Paris, "were
becoming daily more prevalent among that large body of
troops, lying torpid amid the mire and rime in the clayish
slopes of Stafford County." Deserters were aided by their
relatives, who sent them citizens' clothes. The keener
the soldier's perception of the incompetence of his generals, the greater was his discouragement under defeat.
Burnside lost control over his lieutenants; he demanded a
holocaust of insubordinates; but the government preferred
.to remove him, and Hooker, called Fighting Joe, took his   Jan.
place. Hooker formed a dashing and, it appears, a good   1863.
plan for throwing himself across the Rappahannock, cutting off Lee from Richmond, and overwhelming him. But
in the execution his nerve or his head failed him. He
stopped short, and instead of attacking allowed himself
to be thrown on the defensive, and was out-generalled by
Lee, who daringly presumed on his irresolution. Stonewall Jackson, after prayer in his tent, made a bold movement through the woods, which brought him on Hooker's   May
flank, and by a sudden attack rolled up a division of the 1863.
Federal army. Hooker, who had proclaimed to his soldiers that they had got Lee where he must fly or be
destroyed, fell back across the Rappahannock, covering
his disgrace with a bombastic order of the day. This was
the nadir of Federal fortunes. The friends of the North

in Europe desponded, and Confederate bonds sold well. Yet the Confederates had bought their victory dear, since it cost them Stonewall Jackson, who was killed by the fire of his own men.

On the board between Washington and Richmond the eyes of the world were fixed, and by the turns of the balance on it the chances on it of the combatants were measured. But in the western and central zones fortune had been far more favourable to the North. There fought the western husbandmen, never so perfectly drilled as the army of the east, but strong, brave, hardy, and heartily loyal to the cause; for the notion that the West was hanging back and was being dragged on by the East, though prevalent in Europe, was wholly untrue; the same spirit pervaded all the States which had remained in the Union, extending without abatement even to far-distant California. In the West appeared Ulysses Grant, a sledge hammer of war, a man of unconquerable resolution, and unsparing of blood enough to fight on the principle that the North would gain by the sacrifice of two men for one.

Feb. 1862. The capture by Grant of Fort Donelson on the Cumberland River, the great bastion of Confederate defence in the west, with a large garrison, was the first bright gleam of Federal victory; it, at the same time, revealed the commander whose tenacity had snatched success out of the jaws of defeat. Another general, the most skilful of Northern strategists, Sherman, destined at last to deal the death blow, also showed himself on that scene. Again the Federal army of the West conquered, though after narrowly escaping destruction, at Pittsburgh Landing on April 1862. the Tennessee River, in a battle, perhaps the most desperate of the war, named from the old church of Shiloh, round which for two days it raged. Grant and Sherman, with part of the Federal army, lay carelessly encamped on the river bank waiting for the rest under Buell to come up. In the dusk of dawn a Confederate army, which had stolen upon them by forced marches, awakened their sleeping camp with the yells of Southern onset. A day of most murderous bush fighting ensued. The Federals were overpowered and swept out of their camps; the river bank was crowded with their flying soldiers. Nothing saved them from utter defeat but the rugged and wooded character of the ground, and the hunger which made thousands of the enemy break their lines to pillage the camp. (But the Confederates were exhausted; their leader fell) Buell having come up, they were overpowered by numbers and compelled to retire. An eye-witness of the retreat says that in a ride of twelve miles he saw more of human agony than he trusted he should ever again be called to witness. Along a narrow and almost impassable road wound a long line of waggons loaded with wounded, groaning and cursing, and piled in like bags of grain, while the mules plunged on in mud and water belly deep, the water sometimes coming into the waggons. Next came a straggling regiment of infantry, pressing on past the train. Then were seen soldiers with arms broken and hanging down, or other wounds. At night-fall a cold drizzling rain set in, which turned to pitiless hail, from which the wounded and dying had not a blanket to shield them. Three hundred men died in the retreat, and their bodies were thrown out to make room for others, who though wounded had struggled on, hoping to find shelter, rest, and medical care.

One after another the forts of the South on the Missis-

sippi fell, and the Confederacy thus lost its western territory, which though it sent not many men, sent large
supplies of cattle.✕ To complete the opening of the great
water-way, the capture of Vicksburg, the Confederate
Gibraltar, alone remained. ⟩ The work to that point was
done from above by flotillas in concert with the Federal
army of Grant and Sherman.   From below it was done by
Farragut, the Nelson, or rather as his chief exploits were
attacks of forts by ships, the Blake of the American navy.
A sailor of the old school, Farragut, fought in wooden
ships, and when desired to shift his flag to an ironclad,
▪replied that he did not want to go to hell in a tea-kettle.
With extraordinary daring he ran, with his wooden fleet,
the gauntlet of the forts of New Orleans amidst a "hell"
of fire-ships, and in the face of a formidable steam-ram,
still delivering his broadsides when the fire was high up

April
1862.

the mast of his ship, and captured the great commercial
city of the South together with the southern entrance to
the Mississippi.   The prize and the blow were immense.
Benjamin Butler, the lawyer soldier, became commandant.
He played the ædile also, gave the city a strong police,
cleansed it, and saved it for that season from yellow fever.
A coarse proclamation, which he put forth against women
who insulted his soldiers in the streets, being misread or
misrepresented, raised a storm of indignation on both sides
of the Atlantic.   But if the temper of the male slave-
owner was fiery, that of his help-mate was not less so, and
Butler's proclamation might have been necessary, though
its coarseness was not.   A worse charge was that of
connivance at illicit dealings, particularly in cotton, by
which, if the commandant himself did not gain, there was
reason to believe that those about him did.

In the central zone, where the Federals sought to reach the heart of the Confederate territory through middle and eastern Tennessee, there was hard fighting without decisive result. A typical battle was that fought at Christmas, 1862, in the cedar brakes of Murfreesborough between the Federals under Rosecrans and the Confederates under Bragg. The two armies were nearly balanced in numbers, equipment, discipline, and experience. The two generals had formed the same plan of attack each upon the other, and moved against each other at the same time. Each was foiled by the other's movement. The evergreen cedar thickets prevented a general's eye from ranging over the field. For three days, with breaks for rectification of position, reorganization, and refreshment of men and animals, the eighty thousand combatants struggled for the barren honours of a field in different parts of which each lost and won. The carnage was great. The killed and wounded were thirty per cent of the numbers engaged, and dreadful were the sufferings of the wounded through the cold winter nights. In the end the Confederate general withdrew to a better position. There followed a pause of eight months, after which the armies grappled on another indecisive field of slaughter, both generals being swept away by routed portions of their own forces.

In reading the history of this war, the tangled character of the country must always be borne in mind: it made the handling of troops difficult, disconcerted plans, and rendered battles indecisive, since the vanquished withdrew into the woods, and there could be no charges of cavalry to gather the fruits of victory. The horse were, in fact, as a rule, not cavalry, but mounted rifles. General Meade, who had gone through the whole war, said he had only twice seen a large mass of the enemy. Battles were vast bush-fights, and a large proportion of the wounds were in the head and shoulders, which in taking aim protruded from behind the tree.

On the coast, the Federals were successful in their operations. With marvellous energy and ingenuity in adaptation, they had improvised a navy sufficient to blockade three thousand miles of coast much indented and masked with islands. The Confederates had the ships taken with the Federal Navy Yard at Norfolk. One of these, the *Merrimack*, they turned into an ironclad. Sallying forth, she sank the unarmoured ships opposed to her, and seemed likely to sweep the waters and break the blockade. But in mid-career of devastation she was met by the *Mon-itor*, the turret-ship of Ericsson, who had with difficulty persuaded the government to make trial of his invention. The *Monitor* conquered. The ironclad monster limped back to her lair, and in a moment the navies of the world were disrated, and naval tactics were changed. Blockade-running went on with ships low-built and painted grey to elude the Federal cruisers. Some cotton, precious in the dearth, was run out, and some munitions of war were run in. But these were driblets of relief to the South. More effectual, though somewhat piratical, was the enterprise of a few cruisers, which the Confederates, partly by violations of British neutrality, had contrived to launch, and which cut up Federal commerce. Notable above all for her ravages was the *Alabama*, commanded by the daring Semmes, who displayed a collection of the chronometers of the Federal vessels which he had captured, and, having no port into which to take them for condemnation as prizes, had burned at sea, in contravention of the law of

March 1862.

nations as was loudly protested on the other side. Two steam rams were being built for the Confederates at Liverpool, but an embargo was laid on them by the British government.

The stress of calamity and danger in the West, the need of supplies, and the hope of producing a political effect, by shaking Federal resolution and impressing Europe, probably all combined in determining Lee, after his magnificent success at Chancellorsville, once more to assume the offensive. He entered Pennsylvania with his seventy-five thousand victorious veterans, but now with no Stonewall Jackson. Amid the rich farms he refreshed his hungry troops, while he threatened Baltimore, Philadelphia, and Washington. But no political effect was produced, unless it were at New York, where the Irish rose against the draft and the negro, maltreated and murdered negroes with their usual fury, wrecked property, and filled the city, then destitute of defenders, with riot and panic till the arrival of troops, when the insurrection was at once quenched in the blood of a thousand of the insurgents. Hooker, counter-manœuvring Lee, it seems with skill, was nevertheless removed from command, and replaced by Meade, a trustworthy, though not a great commander. With an army superior in numbers, but inferior in spirit and confidence, Meade approached his enemy. At Gettysburg, in a rolling district, the two moving hosts were brought into collision. During two days of detached encounters among the ridges, in one of which there was a charge of cavalry and the sabre was used, the advantage rested with the Confederates. On the third and decisive day, the Federal army was concentrated in a good defensive position on the Cemetery Hill of

July 1863.

Gettysburg, while the army of Lee confronted it in crescent shape along a semi-circle of wooded slopes. After a furious but ineffective cannonade, which exhausted the Confederate ammunition, Lee, against the advice of Longstreet, the most renowned of his lieutenants, launched his infantry in column across an open space of three-quarters of a mile against an army strongly posted, and with a powerful artillery, which after a deceptive lull again opened its full fire. The column, though its veteran valour carried it up to and into the Federal lines, was destroyed after a struggle more intense than that with the Old Guard at Waterloo, and when its remnants drifted back in disarray, Lee must have felt that the Confederate cause was lost. Defeated, but still terrible, he was allowed to fall back into Virginia unmolested, and to carry off the booty which he had swept from Pennsylvanian fields. He even in a defensive position again offered battle, which Meade was too prudent, the exulting North thought too timid, to accept.

⟨ On the day after Gettysburg, Vicksburg, the last and most redoubtable stronghold of the Confederates on the Mississippi, fell, after a long siege and much outpouring of Federal blood, before the indomitable energy of Grant, which afterwards turned the wavering balance decisively in favour of the Federals on the battle ground of middle Tennessee.⟩ When the next campaign opened the resources of the South were running low. She had begun to think of enlisting negroes, thus setting the house on fire to save it. Her conscription had drawn her last ablebodied man ; it had come to the old men and the boys, robbing, as Grant said, the cradle and the grave. Her railroads were worn out ; the sea was inexorably closed

to her; her paper money had lost all value. There
remained to her only the army of Lee, Lee himself, and
another army commanded by Joseph Johnston, which lay
between the invader's force, gathering for attack in Tennessee, and Atlanta in Georgia, the great Confederate
place of arms. Now, too, Federal operations, which
hitherto had lacked unity, the armies moving, as Grant
said, like a team of balky horses without reference to
each other, and had been marred by political interference,
were combined under Grant, who, placed in supreme com-   Mar.
mand with the title of Lieutenant-General, grasped the   1864.
whole war in his single hand, thrust political meddling
aside, formed his own plans, kept his own counsels, and
proceeded unsparingly to apply his principle of attrition,
wearing down by incessant battle what remained of the
Southern force.

The plan was that Grant should move on Richmond, or
rather on Lee who covered it, taking Richmond if he
could; at all events, holding Lee there and exhausting
him, while Sherman from Chattanooga moved on Atlanta,
piercing the Confederacy to the heart. Grant crossed the
Rappahannock with an army greatly superior in number
to that of his enemy, though reduced in quality by
the substitution of the draft for volunteering. In the
Wilderness, a gloomy tract covered with a dense growth
of scraggy pine, scrub oak, dwarf chestnut, and hazel, a
tract where the general could not see the length of a   May,
brigade, was fought during two days the first battle of   1864.
a series, all equally blind and bloody, which is stated to
have cost Grant on the whole 64,000 men, while the
loss of his opponent also was heavy and could not, like
Grant's, be repaired. If carnage can ennoble war, war was

ennobled here. From dawn to dusk, we are told, the roar
of the guns was ceaseless. A tempest of shells shrieked
through the forest and ploughed the fields. When night
came, in the angle of the works where the fire had been
hottest, men in hundreds killed and wounded were piled
in heaps, some bodies that had lain for hours under the
concentric fire being perforated with wounds, while the
masses of slaughter were at times moved by the writhing
of the wounded. At the battle of the Wilderness the
woods caught fire and the wounded were burned. Bullets came in such a stream that a tree eighteen inches
in diameter was cut in two by them. It is wonderful that
humanity should not be extinguished on such scenes;
that, on the contrary, brave soldiers should be generally
humane.

So dense was the wood that when abatis were being
made on both sides only two hundred yards apart, while
the ringing of the axe could be heard, neither side could
see a man of the other. In this war, fighting always in
woods, or broken ground, the men learned not only to seek
cover but to make it. Whenever they were in position
they threw up earthworks. With their wood-craft they
easily constructed abatis, and battles were fought with
the axe and trenching tool as well as with the musket.

Lee, while vastly outnumbered, had the advantages of
perfect knowledge of the country, of the defensive, and of
the interior line. With these, and his superior general-
ship, he held his own, presenting everywhere a front
strengthened by works to his pertinacious foe. At Cold
Harbour, where in the course of their wrestle the combatants were brought close to Richmond, Grant delivered a
desperate assault upon Lee's defences, which was repulsed

in half an hour with the loss of 7000 men. After the
battle of the Wilderness, he had proclaimed his intention
of "fighting it out on that line, if it took all summer."
But he found himself baffled everywhere by the moving
rampart. Trying to turn that which he was unable to
pierce, he worked round to Petersburg on the south of
Richmond, before which, after an unsuccessful assault, he
was set fast, and had to resign himself to a regular invest-
ment. By this movement he uncovered Washington, the
constant object of Lincoln's excessive solicitude, showing
thereby that the control of the war had really passed from
the White House to the camp. Upon Washington the
Confederate general, Early, swooped from the Shenandoah
Valley, filling the city with alarm. To close that sally-
port, and punish the zeal of the people of the Shenandoah,
the rich and smiling valley was ravaged by Sheridan "so
that a crow flying down it would have to carry his own
rations." Two thousand barns filled with wheat and hay
and farming implements, and seventy mills filled with
flour and wheat, were among the things destroyed.
Sheridan, the hardest of hitters, having run a swift career
of victory, had nobler achievements to record.

When it is asked, of what use was all this slaughter in
the Wilderness, the answer sometimes given is, that public
opinion called for action. Grant, however, had applied
with effect his strategy of attrition. Lee's army had been
worn down. It had also been held fast while the other part
of the plan of campaign was being executed by Sherman.
Advancing from Chattanooga, Sherman pushed before
him, by manœuvres, the Confederate army under Johnston, a first-rate strategist, who, with far inferior forces,
played the game of chess with stubbornness and skill,

maintaining himself in successive positions, and when he was attacked in one of them, gaining a victory. In the campaign of Sherman were most fully displayed the military mechanics in which this war, made by the most mechanical of nations, and by armies fuller than other armies ever were of skilled workmen, transcended every other war. Sherman bears his testimony to the management of the railroads. "No matter when or where a breach has been made, the repair train seemed on the spot, and the damage was repaired generally before I knew of the break. Bridges have been built with surprising rapidity, and the locomotive whistle was heard in an advanced camp almost before the echoes of the skirmish-fire had ceased. Some of the bridges, those of the Oostanaula, the Etowah, and Chattahoochee, are fine, substantial structures, and were built in an inconceivably short time, almost out of material improvised on the spot." The trestle bridge across the Chattahoochee River near Atlanta was 780 feet in length, and 90 feet in height, and was reconstructed in four and a half days. The Potomac Creek bridge, 414 feet long and 82 feet high, was repaired in forty hours. The Aquia Creek Railroad on the Potomac, thirteen miles in length, was opened in five days after the order to begin the work was given. The Federal hosts were acting in a country where war would not support war, and could not have moved without railroads to supply them. The telegraph marched everywhere with the armies, and must, on the whole, have greatly aided operations, though it might sometimes have been the instrument of unwise interference with commanders. In the waggon trains, and in every mechanical department, American ingenuity introduced improvements which the skilled mechanics in the ranks

:new how to use and repair. Wonderful feats of transportation were performed. An army corps was transported
ourteen hundred miles, equally divided between land and
vater, in eleven days along rivers obstructed by snow and
ce and over mountains amidst violent snow storms without the least loss. A division, including a brigade of
artillery, and comprising 17,314 men, 1038 horses, 2371
mules, 351 waggons, and 83 ambulances, was embarked on
he Tennessee and sent to New Orleans, 1330 miles in
hirteen days. Thus it was that Sherman's movement
vas rendered possible.

When Johnston, retreating, and Sherman, following,
approached Atlanta, the Confederate President, never,
ike Lincoln, master of himself, lost patience, and from
he wary Johnston transferred the command to the impetuous Hood. Hood at once fought a battle in which Nov. 1864.
he was defeated. Atlanta fell and was made desolate,
all its store-houses, dépôt-buildings, and factories of
arms going up together in a vast flame. Sherman, now
disembarrassed, could venture to leave his base, and with
afe temerity march through Georgia, foraging on the
ountry, and destroying as he went everything that
ould serve the purposes of war. The rich city of Dec. 1864.
Savannah, with its forts and stores and its facilities for
blockade-running, surrendered to him. The defences of
Mobile, the military port of the Confederates, had been Aug. 1864.
orced and the flotilla, which they protected, had been
destroyed by the valour of Farragut. Charleston surren- Feb. 1865.
lered without a blow, fired, in destroying the stores, by the
etreating army of the Confederates, and Garrison stood triumphant beside the great marble slab of Calhoun. Mean-
ime, Hood, with what remained of his army, attempting to

Dec. strike northwards, had been annihilated at Nashville by
1864. Thomas. ⟨The Confederacy, now become a hollow shell,
collapsed on every side.⟩

⟨Lee at last, overwhelming forces gathering round him,
was compelled to fly.⟩ One Sunday the Confederate
President, sitting in church, where he was a regular
attendant, received a dispatch which caused him to turn
pale, rise, and depart. It was from Lee, saying that
April, Richmond must be evacuated. The evacuation was a scene
1865. of the widest disorder and woe, fire being set to the
military stores and spreading to the city. Lee was soon
overtaken in his retreat, overpowered, and compelled to
April surrender to Grant. At Appomattox Court House was
9, enacted the closing scene. The victor behaved with
1865. generosity to the vanquished, paroled their army, and
bade the privates of the cavalry as well as the officers
take away their horses, saying that they might need them
for the spring ploughing and other farm work. His good
nature was the earnest of a reconciliation, which after a
conflict so desperate seemed to the world to be hopeless.
"Men! we have fought through this war together; I
have done the best I could for you," was Lee's parting
address to his army; it might have served for Hannibal,
as well as for Lee.

⟨The last victim was Lincoln. He had been re-elected
President, and by an overwhelming majority.⟩ General
McClellan was the Democratic, and the only other candidate, for Fremont who had been nominated by the radicals
was withdrawn. A plank in the Democratic platform
denounced the war as a failure, but was belied by victory,
and repudiated by McClellan. Greater effect was prob-

ably produced by the denunciation of arbitrary arrests, and other strong measures, to which the government had deemed it necessary to resort, and which offended the American sense of personal liberty. Party, as an organized interest and force, was not extinct, and the Irish vote was always Democratic. But the nation agreed with Lincoln that it was dangerous "to swap horses when crossing a stream," and few would desire another interregnum like the last days of Buchanan. Lincoln was now digesting his plan of reconstruction, which was sure to be inspired by good sense and mercy. This tyrant, as his enemies styled him, had always neglected to surround himself with guards, though threats of assassination were in the air. ⟨He was relieving his over- April wrought brain in the theatre, when he was shot in his 14, 1865. box by Wilkes Booth, a Southerner, and a ranting actor of melodrama, who then vaulted upon the stage, and brandishing a bloody dagger with which he had struck one of Lincoln's suite, shouted *sic semper tyrannis*, the motto of the tyrannicide republicanism of the Virginian slave-owner. Booth was hunted down and slain by his pursuers⟩ happily, since evil passions might have been awakened by his trial. ⟨Lincoln was borne to the grave amidst an immense outburst of public sorrow, admiration, and gratitude⟩ Admiration has risen to worship, and Lincoln has, in the minds of some of his eulogists, become the greatest statesman and the master spirit of his age. He has even become a great strategist, though it seems almost certain that he did harm by interfering, or allowing his military counsellors at Washington to interfere, with the conduct of the war. He said himself that he had not controlled events, but had been guided by them. To know how to be guided by events, however, if it is not imperial genius, is practical wisdom. ⟨Lincoln's goodness of heart, his sense of duty, his unselfishness, his freedom from vanity, his longsuffering, his simplicity, were never disturbed either by power or by opposition.⟩ The habit which he retained through all the dark days of his Presidency, of throwing his thoughts into the form of pithy stories and apologues, caused him to be charged with levity. To the charge of levity no man could be less open. Though he trusted in Providence, care for the public and sorrow for the public calamities filled his heart and sat visibly upon his brow. His State papers are excellent, not only as political documents, but as compositions, and are distinguished by their depth of human feeling and tenderness from those of other statesmen. ⟨He spoke always from his own heart to the heart of the people.⟩ His brief funeral oration over the graves of those who had fallen in the war is one of the gems of the language. ⟨The death of Lincoln on the eve of reconstruction was an irreparable loss, especially to the vanquished.⟩With good reason General Sherman, when he received the news, told a Confederate general that the worst of all disasters had befallen the Confederate cause⟩

That the war had really been international, not civil, was felt by the victors, though not recognized. To the official theory that secession had been rebellion and treason, a nominal deference was paid by the imprisonment and indictment of Jefferson Davis, who, when Lincoln would have desired his escape, had been caught rather farcically disguised in woman's clothes. ⟨But no blood was shed on the scaffold, nor, saving the abolition of slavery, was there any confiscation⟩ ⟨The abolition of slavery in itself was a heavy punishment to the slave-owning authors of secession; it stripped them at once of their property and of their social grandeur. Of the planter aristocracy and of the "first families of Virginia" this was the grave. They had staked all, and all was lost. It is due, however, to the people of the North to say that among them generally there never had been any thought of vengeance, not even while the conflict was still raging, though the feelings excited were not much less intense than those excited by a really civil war. All but the fiercest fanatics said that the object sought was the restoration of the Union, and that the South would find mercy if it would only submit to the law. Good-nature and humanity not only survived, but reigned. Care was taken of Confederate as well as of Federal wounded. Confederate prisoners were well fed, and in the prison camps seemed to suffer no hardships but those which were inseparable from their lot; if many of them died, it was because the caged eagle dies. Prisoners in hospital were well tended, and in a prison hospital the table of the inmates was seen on Thanksgiving Day spread with the good things of the season. This was the more notable, because the accounts which reached the North of the sufferings of its soldiers in Southern prisons were heartrending, and were too true; they were, in fact, attested by the arrival of living skeletons, who had been exchanged. For scantily feeding their prisoners the Southerners might plead the excuse that they had little bread themselves; but such atrocities as those of the prison camp at Andersonville nothing could excuse, nothing except the temper bred of slave-owning could explain. Of that camp even the Confederate Inspector-General spoke as a place of horrors beyond description. There, in a stockaded field, 1540 feet long by 750 feet wide, were confined at last 31,693 prisoners of war. There was no protection from the sun or rain; the rations were of the worst quality, sometimes uncooked, and were barely enough to support life, while if one of a squad of prisoners was missing the rest were deprived of rations for the day. Into the brook, from which all drank, flowed the filth and excrements from the whole camp; its banks were covered with ordure and alive with maggots. When the rain set in the ground was covered with slush a foot deep, and the whole surface was like a cesspool, which when the heat came bred pestilence. In it wandered about, pushing each other, the crowd of shoeless, hatless, famished captives, many of them with scarcely a tatter to cover them. In August and September there were more than 3000 sick, lying on the ground, partially naked; some with broken limbs, some suffering from gangrene, scurvy, or diarrhœa, coated with vermin, and tortured by mosquitoes. The death rate reached eight and a half per hour. The dead were dragged to the outlet and hauled away by waggon loads. The stench we are told reached two miles. Hundreds went mad, and added moral to physical horrors. Whoever even put a hand over "the dead line" was shot: not a few courted that fate in despair. Bloodhounds were kept to run down fugitives. Out of 44,882 prisoners in the course of thirteen months 12,462 died. Wirz, the gaoler of Andersonville, a foreign mercenary, was hanged by the North, not for rebellion, but for murder, a doom which the heads of the department, if they knew what was going on, deserved to share. Such was the exit of slavery from the civilized world.

A noble and consoling part of this most tragic drama
was the Sanitary Commission of the Federals. This was
the creation of spontaneous effort and voluntary contribution, being merely recognized by the government. At
its head was a clergyman, Dr. Bellows. It received
contributions to the amount of three millions of dollars
in money, and nine millions of dollars in supplies. Its
organization extended over the whole scene of conflict,
and shed a ray of mercy on every field of carnage.
Its arrangements for removing the wounded from the
field to field hospitals and for transfer to permanent hospitals, as well as its improvements in the construction
of hospitals themselves, which were planned on the principle of isolation, formed a beneficent epoch in the history
of military medicine. The Mower Hospital at Philadelphia held four thousand patients. Great is the contrast which this picture presents to the practices of the
armies of the European monarchies such as Austria in
the last century. Anaesthetics, too, the most merciful of
inventions, were now lending the surgeon their blessed
aid.

Democracy might fairly say that in this case she had
been justified of her children. The patriotic effort of
a free community had shown well beside the force of the
Southern oligarchy or despotism. The Republic had
received a large measure of free-will offering and sacrifice.
There had been a good deal of volunteering at the outset,
and the army, though not volunteer, was in the main
native to the last. Of the head boards on the graves of
thirteen thousand soldiers of the Union at Washington,
almost all bore the name of the dead man, although
here and there was a board marked " unknown soldier."

That the men had homes for which to fight was proved by the constant return of corpses to those homes, and the activity of the embalmers' trade at Washington. The rich who, as a class, had least reason to be well affected to Democracy, and who in the United States had been too much shut out, or stood aloof from public life, showed themselves generally not wanting in attachment to the Republic, while some of them displayed the most devoted loyalty, pouring out freely not their wealth only, but their blood. Mr. Wadsworth, a wealthy landowner, left his mansion when he was past middle age to fight and fall in the Wilderness. He was the moral heir of the Sussex landowner, who also left his mansion in middle age to become the first Governor of Massachusetts. Not only was the war taxation, though heavy, grinding, and inquisitorial, cheerfully borne, but voluntary contributions were large, nor did the fountains of ordinary charity and munificence in the meantime cease to flow.

To the surprise of the world the constitution, barring State right, came out of the ordeal unscathed. The idea of national union had definitively triumphed over that of a federal league or compact. The nation had been consolidated, and its spirit had been raised by community of effort and peril. Southern oligarchy, with its influence on the politics of the Union, was extinct. The negro had been emancipated, and his admission to citizenship was at hand. Otherwise there was no political change. The exceptional power with which the government had been practically invested for the conduct of the war was resigned, or ceased as soon as the war was over. Of temporary interference with personal liberty there had probably been not much more than the exigencies of the

struggle required, considering that the South had many
allies and the government many enemies at the North,
while in the border States not only disaffection, but active
hostility was rife.   Habeas corpus was suspended, and a
number of arbitrary arrests were made.   Yet few, as it
appeared, which were not warranted by the necessities of
the war.   A limit was sure to be imposed by the constitutional sensitiveness of the nation, nor could anything be
more remote from the character of the President than
arbitrary violence.   The press appeared to enjoy reasonable freedom, and it criticised the acts of the government with little restraint, though it was necessary to
forbid the preaching of sympathy with the enemy, or
denunciation of the draft.   A stranger, visiting the
Republic at that time, saw nothing like a reign of terror.
At the second election of Lincoln, though passions were
fiercely inflamed, the minority was allowed freely to exercise its political rights, and not only to put up its candidate, frame a platform denouncing the war as a failure,
and vote with perfect freedom, but to hold its public
meetings, array its processions, and hang out its party
banners in the street.   Nor was any serious act of violence
committed, or even apprehended, unless it were on the
part of the foreign mob of New York. The current of
life at the North flowed calmly on. A stranger would
not have suspected that he was in a country engaged in
a civil war.   Engaged in a civil war indeed the country,
properly speaking, was not.   The war was one of invasion,
and had the visitor been transported to the invaded
country, to Georgia after the desolating march of Sherman, or to the Shenandoah Valley when it had been
ravaged by Sheridan, a different scene would have met

his eye. Still it was remarkable how small the visible signs of disturbance at the North were, considering the perils of the times, and the number of citizens who were in the camp.

ᴄNor did the military force show any tendency to get the upper hand of civil government.〉 When General Sherman, after his career of victory, encroached, probably without intention, on the sphere of civil authority, in offering terms to the vanquished, he was with ease recalled to his proper functions. Europe, judging from historical precedents, had believed that the army would be left master of the nation and would not suffer itself to be disbanded, but would raise its chief to supreme power.ᴄ At the close of the war the army was a million strong, as well as flushed with victory. Yet it was disbanded with perfect ease, at once returned to the trade and callings of peace, and mingled with the community at large. Not the slightest tendency to usurpation or sabre sway was shown by any of its chiefs.〉 General Grant himself was not only guiltless of any such disposition, but was averse from military pomp and parade, disliking, it was said, the very sound of the drum. His camp equipment, his dress, and his habits were as simple as his character, more simple they could not be, and he showed, what an aspirant to dictatorship and empire could hardly afford to show, remarkable justice and generosity in his conduct towards his colleagues. The story was current that his most formidable rival having formally protested in writing at a council of war against Grant's plan of attack, and the attack having succeeded, Grant, instead of keeping the protest, or forwarding it to headquarters, handed it back to the author.ᴄNor was the nation infected with military

fever. There was no sign of it, saving a multiplication
for the time of military titles as harmless as it was common.   In one respect the military character, at least that
of the professional soldier, enhanced its claim to public
confidence, for amidst all the charges and suspicions, true
or false, of corruption, with which in that season of temp-
tation the air was laden, none adhered to the honour of a
graduate of West Point.

One who, at the end of the war, predicted in European
company, that the Americans would pay their debt, and
redeem their paper currency, was apt to be met with
derision.   But, if he knew the American people, he
replied with confidence, that, setting morality aside, they
well understood the value of their credit, and were too
wise to destroy it.   The result is well known.   Some
demagogues there were who breathed repudiation into the
national ear, but their evil promptings took no effect;
the national faith was strictly kept; specie payments
were resumed, and the debt was reduced with a rapidity
that astonished the world.   Nor, looking to the amount of
war taxation which had been borne, and that of the free
contributions, could it be said that the generation which
made the war had cast an excessive burden on posterity.
Confederate bonds, of course, could not be paid, though
they maintained, for some time, a spectral existence on the
stock exchange.   Their holders were thus fined for abet-
ting, or at least confiding in a slave power.

Industry, though it was for a time diverted from the
increase of wealth to the work of slaughter and destruction, lost nothing of its activity or thrift. Invention was
stimulated, especially in the making of farm implements
to supply the place of the labour withdrawn to the camp.

In this way as well as in the way of medical and surgical improvement peace made a little profit out of war. ‹When peace came American prosperity appeared to bound forward more vigorously than ever.› An exception to this at first, and for some years to come, was the South, which lay wrecked and ruined. Yet even for the South a better time was coming. ‹Emancipation was to prove an economical as well as a moral and social blessing.› The negro was to become a better producer; cotton crops, instead of ceasing to be raised, were to increase; the higher industries, no longer barred out, were to develop resources hitherto dormant, and from the blackened ruins of Atlanta was to rise a city far larger and wealthier than Atlanta had ever been.

Evils, economical and moral, attended this as they attend all wars. Profuse expenditure leads to a violent displacement of wealth, opens the door to frauds, especially in the dark region of contracts, and gives birth to fortunes of sudden growth, often ill made, and when ill made pretty sure to be ill spent. In this case the expenditure had been more than profuse, and, till the administration was organized, had been little controlled. Inconvertible paper had inevitably led to speculation in gold, and the Gold Room became a vast gambling hell, which left its trace on commercial character. Among the unhappy results of an economical kind freetraders will reckon the war tariff, imposed for the purpose of revenue, but continued when the war was over, at the instance of the industries which had profited by it, for the purpose of protection. Much the same thing had happened after 1812, when the protection which the war had given was renewed in the form of a tariff. The political party which had made and sustained the war, in fact, presently became the party of the tariff, and appeals to war memories and war feelings were made in the interest of protection. Resentment against England, which had been created by altercations with her government, and the escape of Confederate cruisers from her ports, aided the native manufacturer in what he was able to represent as the patriotic exclusion of British goods.

A literary man may, perhaps, feel some disappointment at the failure of this mighty stirring of the national spirit to produce much literary fruit, especially in the way of poetry. There were poems, not a few martial and patriotic. But they read more like the laboured tributes of Laureates to the nation than like the offspring of inspiration, and none of them can be called great. Perhaps "John Brown," which became a sort of Marseillaise, and "Maryland, My Maryland," which breathed the yearning of a border State for peace, were the two most genuine expressions of sentiment among the poetic products of the time. We are still without a worthy history of the war. The materials abound, and include a number of memoirs written by the chief actors. Never were there so many soldiers who could use the pen as well as the sword. Marlborough could not spell.

The cost of the war is incalculable. To a declared Federal debt of $2,757,000,000 are to be added five years of war taxation, the debts of the several States, and now a pension list of a hundred and forty millions of dollars a year, together with the loss of industry, the ruin of commerce, and the destruction of property, which at the South was immense, and fell ultimately on the restored Union. It is reckoned that between battle and disease a million of men lost their lives, or were crippled in the war. So much did it cost to abolish American slavery. In Russia the emancipation of the serfs was effected without the loss of life or money to the State. The slaves in the West Indies were emancipated peacefully at a cost of twenty millions sterling, or a hundred and fifty millions of dollars, little more than two-thirds of the amount of the pension list for one year. There are some things, though they may be few, which a supreme authority in good hands can do best.

There were questions yet to be settled with foreign powers. The French emperor, having failed to lure the British government into an intervention, his secret aim in which probably was the recovery of Louisiana, had set up a Latin Empire in Mexico, of which he made the Austrian Prince Maximilian emperor, placing a French marshal at his side, and, no doubt, intending to treat him as a satrap. At the end of the American war the French emperor received from the Washington government notice to quit. He gave ear and withdrew his army. Maximilian, remaining behind out of chivalrous regard for his partisans in Mexico, was overpowered by the patriots, to whom American generals are believed privately to have supplied arms, taken prisoner, and shot. Of British neutrality both the contending parties, as was to be expected, had complained: the South denouncing it as a veiled alliance with the North, because recognition was refused to the Confederacy, Confederate envoys were not received, and neutrality laws were enforced; the North denouncing it as a veiled alliance with the South because the neutrality laws were, in a few instances, successfully evaded by the Confederates. From the shipyards and harbours of a nation, which, besides her own ports, has those of maritime dependencies all over the world, in the course of more than four years' war three Confederate privateers escaped. In one case, that of the *Alabama*, the British government was open to the charge of culpable delay, the evidence of the vessel's character, furnished by the American ambassador, having been allowed to lie too long before the legal adviser of the Crown, who happened to be incapacitated by sickness. The vessel escaped from Liverpool when the order for her detention was on its way, under pretence of a trial trip, without a clearance and unarmed; she took her armament on board at the Azores. That the British government desired or connived at any breach of its neutrality is absolutely untrue. There was understood to be only one member of the Cabinet who even wished success to the South, for Lord Palmerston, though he might not be a friend of the American Republic, was a zealous opponent of slavery. Some colour was perhaps given to the imputation of unfriendliness by the habitual haughtiness, it may be discourtesy, of Lord Russell. The North availed itself of the British market for the purchase of arms and munitions of war, while its agents recruited along the Canadian frontier, and the number of Canadians enlisted in its armies was reckoned by the Canadian government at many thousands. Nor did the Canadian government afford the slightest ground for the imputation that it fostered or failed to repress the machinations of Southerners who had gathered on its territory, and could not, without breach of law and hospitality, be expelled. For a raid which some of them organized it was in no way to blame. The ground for complaint in the case of the *Alabama* was

not so strong as that in the case of the French privateers
fitted out from American ports under the Presidency
of Washington, whose honourable desire to preserve
neutrality is beyond doubt.⟩ The *Alabama*, not being
effectively pursued, did much damage to American commerce. As compensation for this, and for the damage
done by her two consorts, the *Florida* and *Shenandoah*,
Great Britain paid, under the treaty of Washington, the
sum of three million two hundred thousand pounds,
whereof a part has remained in the hands of the
American government for default of claims. Compensation was refused for the raid of the American-Irish
community, called the Fenian raid, on Canada, and Great
Britain was fain to pocket the refusal. She feared, and
always fears, for her North American dependencies as well
as for her trade. The principle of arbitration, however,
gained a step.

⟨ Now came the problem of reconstruction. There were
two questions to be settled, the emancipation of the negro,
and the re-annexation of the conquered States to the
Union.⟩⟨Lincoln's proclamation, issued in exercise of
his military power, had only set the slave free, and this
only in the States with which the North was at war; not
in Maryland, Kentucky, and Missouri, which had remained in the Union. It was his earnest desire, and he
made it the chief platform in his second campaign for the
Presidency, that there should be a constitutional amendment abolishing slavery everywhere and forever.⟩ What
his plan with regard to negro suffrage was, he seems not to
have made known. He had shown himself aware of the

inferiority of the race, while he recognized its human
rights. He could hardly be blind to the warning example
of negro self-government in Hayti, where it has been, and
still is, a disastrous failure, even when all due allowance
has been made for the evil training of slavery, and for the
storm of frenzied and murderous revolution amidst which
the Haytian Republic had been born. Garrison himself,
the preacher of emancipation immediate and unconditional, had seemed to halt on the verge of negro enfranchisement. Emancipation having been accomplished, he
questioned whether the President could safely or advan-
tageously enforce a rule touching the ballot which abolished distinctions of colour. Nothing, he thought, would
be gained by forcible enfranchisement without a general
preparation of sentiment, because as soon as the State was
left to manage its own affairs, the whites would surely
dominate, and would exclude the flat voters from the
poll. On the other hand, how was the personal freedom
of the blacks to be guarded, unless the whites were controlled by political power vested in the negro, or by
military force? In fact no sooner did the whites in some
of the Southern States recover a measure of self-government than they began to frame sharp vagrancy laws for
the purpose of compelling the freed negroes to work. It
was a problem, like emancipation itself, hardly capable of
solution, except by a power supreme over both races, and
able to hold the balance of policy and equity between
them. The difficulty of blending two forms of society,
radically antagonistic, into a single self-governing community, had survived Appomattox in a modified form.

The other question, taken by itself, was somewhat less
difficult, provided it could be seen in the true light and

disembarrassed of the metaphysical controversies respecting the relations of subjugated rebel States to the Union, in which, seen in a false light, it is involved. ↗The theory was that the North had put down a rebellion. The fact was that it had conquered, wrecked, and re-annexed a short-lived nation or group of communities, severed from it by a stroke of nature.↘ Of this the trophies preserved at the North are signs; for civil war or suppressed rebellion has not trophies any more than it has triumphs. Military occupation of the conquered States would have been simple and feasible. ‹Reconstruction on a republican footing could be effected only by the best men and the accepted leaders of the States themselves.↘ This was seen by General Sherman. "I perceived," he said, "that we had the unbounded respect of our armed enemies, and that by some simple measures we could enlist them in one cause. By their instrumentality we could not only restore our whole government according to its written fabric, but could have in every vicinage men used to subordination and government, who would employ their influence to create civil order. I am sure that my own army, now disbanded, makes the best of citizens; and I am also sure, that at the close of the civil war the Confederate army embraced the best governed, the best disposed, the most reliable men in the South; and I would have used them in reconstruction instead of driving them into a hopeless opposition." John A. Andrew also, the great war governor of Massachusetts, said in his valedictory of January the 4th, 1866, that the natural leaders of the South, who, by temporary policy and artificial rules, had been for a while disfranchised, would resume their influence and their sway; that they would challenge the validity of public acts done during their disfranchisement; that for the work of reconstruction their co-operation ought to be secured, and that without it reorganization would be delusive. (The politicians at the South, who had made the war, were discredited by defeat, and the leadership would have passed to the soldiers, in whose worth and honour confidence might have been placed.)(Lincoln seems to have been inclined, like Sherman and Andrew, to the liberal view. Indeed, he had adopted this policy, and had begun to carry it into effect, so far as the constitutional version of the case, teaching him that he was dealing with rebels and traitors, which necessarily had possession of his mind, would permit.)(In December, 1863, he had offered general amnesty to insurgents and disloyalists, special classes excepted, on condition of their taking and keeping an oath of allegiance to the Federal government. He also offered to recognize and protect any loyal government, in an insurgent State, set up by those who should take the amnesty oath, if they had been legal voters before the secession of their State and amounted in number to one-tenth of the votes cast in the Presidential election of 1860.)(He was further willing to aid in any other mode of reconstruction that might be adopted in any other State.) (The admission of representatives to Congress he left to Congress itself.)(Under this plan loyal governments were created and recognized in Arkansas and Louisiana. The enunciation of this policy, however, caused a revolt of the radical party in Congress, which formed a plan of its own, providing for a military governor invested with all the powers of government, till the rebellion should be over and the people return to Federal allegiance, when a new government and constitution should be framed by a convention, elected by popular vote, with a sweeping exclusion of all who had held any kind of civil or military office under the "rebel usurpation," or had "voluntarily" borne arms against the Union. The plan also provided for the perpetual disfranchisement of all who held other than petty civil offices, or military grades above the rank of lieutenant-colonel, under rebel authority. This, as the result proved, was reconstruction by elimination of all that was most capable of governing or worthy to govern in each State.

Lincoln was gone. Into his place stepped the Vice-President, Andrew Johnson, of Tennessee, a strong man in his way, but a man of violent temper and coarse habits, who had been nominated for the Vice-Presidency in compliment to the Unionism of the South, with that want of foresight in regard to consequences, in case the Vice-President should become President, which had been displayed and punished by the event in the case of Tyler. As a radical leader of humble birth, Andrew Johnson had writhed beneath the social pride of the slave-owning aristocrats of Tennessee. He longed to have them at his feet as condemned traitors, suing for his mercy; and he seems to have been ignorant enough of human nature to fancy that for his mercy they would owe him gratitude. But the negroes he loved little more than the other Southern whites of his class, and his heart was on the side of State right. His political sentiments, in short, were those of the Unionist and war-Democrat, not those of the Republican party. On the subject of reconstruction, his policy was, in the main, that of Lincoln, and, before the meeting of Congress, he ventured to carry it into effect by reconstructing, under military authority, Republican governments in several States, and readmitting them, so far as was in his power, to the Union. But he had neither the influence nor the address of Lincoln. When Congress met with a strong Republican majority, it proceeded at once to take reconstruction, and, at length, so far as it could, government, out of his hands. A violent conflict between the executive and the legislature ensued. Under the Parliamentary system of Great Britain the struggle would at once have been brought to an end by the resignation of the minister who had not the confidence and support of Parliament. Under the American system there was no such mode of terminating the disagreement between the two powers. Congress, at length, by an Act deprived the President of his prerogative of dismissing officers of the government, except with the same consent of the Senate which was required for appointment. The President resisted, and brought the question to a decisive issue by the dismissal of Stanton, Lincoln's great Secretary of War. Being a man of violent temper, he vented his wrath in unmeasured vituperation against Congress. He thus lost his few remaining supporters. Congress then proceeded to impeach him. He had done nothing really worthy of impeachment, and the measure was, in truth, a rough mode of forcing the executive into unison with the legislature, like impeachments of unpopular ministers in England before constitutional government was settled on its present footing. This was felt by moderate Republicans, and President Johnson was acquitted by a narrow vote.

Reconstruction was now in the hands of the Republican party in Congress, which showed the usual temper of parties victorious after a desperate struggle by giving its principles a thorough-going application. By two amendments to the constitution, not only was slavery universally and forever abolished, but the negro was invested with the full rights and powers of a citizen. To guard him against vagrancy laws, and watch over his industrial liberty, a freedman's bureau was established. Political reconstruction was carried out according to the plan of Congress, with a sweeping disfranchisement of all who had taken an active part in the rebellion, which for some years excluded the Southern whites from political power, and handed over legislation and government to the enfranchised blacks, who were the clients of the Republican party. Ostensibly the negro was master of the States; but his utter ignorance, incapacity, and credulity made him the dupe and tool of white adventurers from the North, nicknamed Carpet-baggers, who, in alliance with some apostate Southern whites, nicknamed Scallywags, got the Southern governments into their hands. There ensued a reign of roguery, jobbery, and peculation under the military protection of the party dominating the North. States were loaded with debt, and the money was stolen by the Carpet-baggers. In the appointment of judges and the administration of justice the same corruption prevailed. This was not the way to reconcile races. To wreak vengeance for their wrongs and avenge their pride, thus wounded to the quick, the whites organized a secret society, called the Ku Klux Klan, parties from which were sent forth by night, and committed horrible atrocities on the negroes. Like secret societies in general, the Ku Klux Klan went beyond its original design, became the organ of private malice, and inaugurated a reign of terror. At last the scandal of the system grew insufferable, military protection was withdrawn from the carpet-bagging governments, which fell, and the whites were enabled to reinstate themselves in power. They did not fail practically to disfranchise the negro, either by driving him from the poll, or refusing to count his vote. So it is still. The negro at the South enjoys, as a rule, personal and industrial rights which the war won for him, but is excluded from political power. From social fusion and equality he is, if possible, further than ever, since concubinage has become rare, and there is an end of the kindly relations which sometimes subsisted between master and slave. Nor is there an entire equality even of personal right, since the negro is too often lynched where the white would have a fair trial.

The soldiers of Meade and Lee, the soldiers of the blue and the soldiers of the gray, have met as brethren on the field of Gettysburg; but the question between the races of the South still awaits solution.

INDEX.

Abolitionists, 232, 233.

Adams, John, 71, 72, 77, 93, 101, 113, 139, 141; elected president, 150; his principles, 151; his character, 151, 156.

Adams, John Quincy, 191, 192; his election to the Presidency, 191; his character, 192; his political principles, 192; attacks on, 194; his contest for a second term, 194, 195.

Adams, Quincy, 229.

Adams, Samuel, 75, 119.

Adultery, Puritan method of punishing, 21.

Adventurers, the early, in America, 2, 3,

Alabama secedes, 242.

Alabama, the, 272, 293, 294.

Albany Regency, 179.

Alien and Sedition Acts, 153.

Amendments to the Constitution, 126.

American Party, the, 216.

Ames, Fisher, 146.

Amnesty, 297.

Andersonville, prison camp at, 283, 284.

André, Major, 107, 108.

Andrew, John A., 296.

Andros, Sir Edmund, 33, 34, 55.

Anti-Mason Party, the, 207.

Anti-Slavery Party. See Liberty Party.

Antietam, battle on the, 264.

Appomattox, 280.

Aquia Creek Railroad, 278.

Arizona annexed, 212, 214.

Arkansas, 259, 297.

Army, the Southern, in the Civil War, 263.

Arnold, Benedict, 107, 108.

Atlanta, fall of, 279.

Aurora, the, 146, 148.

Bacon's, Nathaniel, junior, rebellion, 47, 48.

Baptists, 13.

Baltimore, Lords, 48, 49.

Battles of the Civil War, character of, 271, 272.

Bell, 238.

Belligerent rights exercised by Great Britain, 161; question of, 161, 162.

Bellows, Rev. Dr., 285.

Benton, Thomas Hart, 185; his character, 185; on the tariff of 1828, 188, 189.

Berkeley, Governor, 47.

Birney, J. G., 211.

Black Beard, 51.

Bladensburg, fight at, 171.

Blaine, J. G., 246.

"Blue Laws" of Connecticut, 23.

Blockade of the southern coast, the, 272.

Blockade running, 272.

Board of Trade, 58, 59.

Booth, Wilkes, 281.

Boston, Howe evacuates, 90.

Boston massacre, 82; "tea party," 82.

Bounties and bounty jumping, 256.

Bragg, General, 271.

Brandywine, battle of the, 95.

Breed's Hill, fight on, 89.

Brooke, Lord, 17.

Brooks, 236.
Brown, John, 237, 238.
Buchanan, President, 237; his manifesto on secession, 245.
" Bucktails," 179.
Buell, 269.
Bull Run, fight at stream of, 260.
Burgoyne's expedition, 98; his surrender, 99.
Burke, 68, 69, 81, 113.
Burns, Anthony, 233.
Burnside, General, 266.
Burr, Aaron, 155.
Butler, Benjamin, 264; at New Orleans, 270.

Calef, 34.
Calhoun, J. C., 168, 170, 179, 182, 183; his character, 183; his political principles, 183; his advocacy of slavery, 183, 184, 201, 213.
California annexed, 212, 214; stands by the Union, 248.
Callender, 154.
Camden, fight at, 108.
Canada and the Maine and Oregon boundary questions, 174, 175; in the war of 1812, 169, 170; invasion of, 93, 94.
Canadian rebellion of 1837, 174.
Canadians in the Civil War, 293.
Canals, 217.
Canning, 163, 169.
Carleton, Sir Guy, 94.
Carolinas, the, 50; constitution of, 50; division of, 50.
Caroline, the, 174.
Carpet-baggers, 300.
Cemetery Hill. See Gettysburg.
Chancellorsville, battle at, 273.
Channing, 230.
Charles II and Massachusetts, 31, 32.
Charleston, 51; taken by Clinton, 108; in the Civil War: surrenders, 275.
Chase, Chief Justice, 161.
Chatham, 68, 70, 79, 81, 93, 106, 116.
Chattahoochee, 278.
Chattanooga, 259.

Chesapeake, the, 163, 171.
Church establishments after the Revolutionary War, 118.
Church of England, in the colonies, 61.
Church, the, in Maryland, 49; in Virginia, 42.
Churches in Massachusetts, 9, 10, 27.
Clay, Henry, 168, 170, 172, 176, 179; his character, 179; his political principles, 180; his tariff policy, 185, 186, 187, 188; on American industry, 187, 190, 191, 199, 200, 201, 205, 206; a candidate for the presidency, 207; his unsuccessful compromise, 210, 211; his defeat, 211, 213.
Clergy, the Puritan, 10, 11.
Clinton, De Witt, 179.
Clinton, Sir Henry, 95; evacuates Philadelphia, 100; takes Charleston, 108.
Civil Service, the, under Jackson, 196.
Civil War, 204, et sq.; chief scene of, 260; cost of the, 291; histories of the, 291.
Code of New England, 21, 22.
Cold Harbour, 276.
College of William and Mary, 43.
Colonial relationships with Great Britain (1764), 68 et sq.
Colony, the Hellenic, compared with the British, 6, 7.
Columbia, District of, 264.
Columbus discovers America, 1; typical of his generation, 2; a devotee, 2; a type of the age, 2; his life and character, 2; his dealings with the natives, 2.
Confederacy, the Southern, 243, 244; its Constitution, 244; its Congress, 244, 252.
Congress, dealings of, with Burgoyne's troops, 99; first session of, 131; character of, 124, 125; powers of, in 1775, 86, 87, 104; weakness of, after the Civil War, 119; offers concessions to slavery, 245.
Connecticut, 7; constitution of, 19, 20; " blue laws " of, 23.

Conscription in the South, 274.

Constitution, the American, 123 *et sq.*

Constitutions of the States after the Revolutionary War, 117 *et sq.*

Convention, the (1787), 122 *et sq.*

Conway, 81.

Copperheads, 255.

Cornwallis at Yorktown, 109.

Cotton, John, 8; on an hereditary upper house, 18; on democracy, 19.

Courant, the New England, 62.

Cowpens, fight at, 109.

Craik, Sir James, 163.

Crawford, William H., 191.

Cromwell, policy of, towards the colonists, 30.

Cumberland Road, the, 190.

Currency, paper, wholesale issue of (1775), 104; results of this, 105.

Davis, Jefferson, 243, 244; captured and indicted, 282.

Death penalty in New England, 21, 22.

Declaration of Independence, 87 *et sq.*

De Grasse, 109.

Delaware, 55.

Delaware, Lord, 40.

Democracy, in Massachusetts, 18; political growth of, 219.

Democratic Party, 206, 207, 236, 237.

Democratic press, the, on secession, 246.

D'Estaing, 106, 116.

Development of the United States before the Civil War, 217 *et sq.*

Dighton Rock, 1.

Dix, General, 245.

Dixwell, 30.

Donelson, Fort, 268.

Douglas, Stephen, 234, 238, 250.

Duane, William, 147, 199.

Dudley, Joseph, 33, 34.

Dudley, Thomas, 9, 16.

Dustin, Hannah, 27.

Dutch, the, of New Netherlands, 55.

Early, General, 277.

Eaton, Mrs., 197.

Eliot, John, 26.

Ellsworth, Oliver, 122.

Emancipation discouraged, 222; effects of, 290.

Embargo on trade placed by Jefferson, 164; its effects, 164, 165.

Emerson, 229.

Emigrants to America, the first, 4 *et sq.*

Endicott, 9.

England's attitude during the Civil War, 257; towards the South, 258; her treatment of America after the separation, 140.

Ericsson, 272.

Erskine, British Minister at Washington, 169.

Etowah, 278.

Everett, 238.

Excise, Hamilton's, Pennsylvania revolts against, 143.

Expansion, provision for, 129.

Farragut, Admiral, 270, 279.

Federal bank, 155, 159.

Federal principle, the, 20.

Federalist Party, 150, 153, 154.

"Federalist, the," 128.

Federation (1774), 86.

Fenton, Captain, maltreatment of his wife and daughter, 99.

Fillmore becomes President, 213.

Finances in 1775, 104; during the Civil War, 257.

Financial crisis of 1837, 199, 206.

Florida, the, 294.

Force Bill, 201.

Fort Donelson. (See Donelson, Fort.)

Fort Pillow. (See Pillow, Fort.)

Fort Sumter. (See Sumter, Fort.)

Fox, 80, 113.

France aids America, 105, 106, 112; condition of in 1789, 115; preys on American commerce, 151.

Franchise, the, 220.

Franklin, Benjamin, 62, 63, 65, 67, 71, 79, 122.

Fredericksburg, 266.

Free Soil Party, 214, 235.
Free trade, internal, 126.
Fremont, 237.
French Canada, 64; compared with the English colonies, 65.
French Canadians in the War of 1812, 170.
French Revolution, American sympathy with, 143.
Freneau, Philip, 138.
Friends. (See Quakers.)
Fusion of the black and white races impossible, 221.

Gage, General, 89.
Gallatin, Albert, 166.
Garrison, William Lloyd, 230, 231, 232; and negro enfranchisement, 295.
George III's reception of John Adams, the first American Ambassador, 141.
Georgia, founding of, 52; secedes, 242.
Genet, 144, 145.
Geneva award, 293, 294.
Germaine, Lord George, 85, 89.
Germantown, battle of, 95.
Gerry, Elbridge, 122.
Gettysburg, battle of, 273, 274.
Ghent, treaty of, 172.
Goffe, 30.
Gold Room, the, 290.
Gold-seeking in Virginia, 3.
Gorges, Sir Ferdinando, 33.
Gorton, Samuel, 13.
Governors of colonies, 59, 60.
Grand Remonstrance, the, as a precedent, 88.
Grant, General Ulysses, 268 et sq.; put in command, 275; crosses the Rappahannock, 275; his simplicity, 288.
Greeley, Horace, 252.
Greene, General Nathaniel, 92, 107, 111.
Greenland, discovery of, 1.
Grenville, 67, 68, 73, 79, 81.
Guildford, fight at, 109.

Half-breeds, numerous, 224; their status, 224.
Hamilton, Alex., 112, 122, 131; his political character, 132; his principles, 132, 133, 134; his financial skill, 134; his purity and patriotism, 134, 149; death of, 155.
Hancock, 75.
Harper's Ferry, 237.
Harrison, Wm., his candidature, 208.
Harvard, University of, 11.
Hayti, 295.
Henry, John, 163.
Henry, Patrick, 75, 76; his associates, 76; his oratory, 76, 77, 128.
Hessians, 85.
Holland joins America against England (1780), 106.
Hood, General, 279, 280.
Hooker, General, 267, 273.
Hooker, Thomas, 19.
House of Representatives. (See Congress.)
Houston, Samuel, in Texas, 209.
Howe, General, 90, 94.
Huguenots in Florida, 3.
Hutchinson, Mrs. Ann, 13.
Hutchinson, Governor, 75, 79, 82.

Independence, colonial disavowals of, 71 et sq.
Independents, 7, 8.
Indians, early relations with, 25 et sq.
Indians, employment of, in the war (1775-76), 93; defeat of, by St. Clair, 142.
Imperial control, 59 et sq.
Impressment of seamen, 162.
Inter-marriages, 28.
Irish immigrants, 175; influx, character, and influence of, 216.
Iroquois, the, 26, 27.

Jackson, Andrew, 148, 172, 191, 193; his character, 193; his execution of Ambrister and Arbuthnot, 193; his democratic tendencies, 194; his inauguration, 195, 196; his treatment of the Senate, 198, 200; his influence on public life and character, 202, 203.

Jackson, "Stonewall," 262 et sq.

James II and Massachusetts, 33.

Jamestown, 3.

Jay, John, 112.

Jay's treaty, 146, 147.

Jefferson, Thomas, 71, 87, 131 et sq.; his character, 135; his political principles, 135; his theories, 135, 136, 137; as a political leader, 138; becomes President, 155; his simplicity as President, 156; his inaugural address, 157; his purchase of Louisiana, 158, 159; prosperity of his first term, 159, 160; his second term, 161; his jealousy of the judiciary, 160, 161; retires, 165.

Jesuits, 26; their utopia in Paraguay, 3.

Johnson, Andrew, 298; his character, 298; his political opinions, 298; his struggle with Congress, 299; his impeachment, 299.

Johnston, Joseph, General, 275.

Jones, Paul, 105.

Judges, United States, 126.

Kansas, struggle in, on the slavery question, 238.

Kansas-Nebraska Act, 234.

Kentucky admitted as a slave State, 127; character of its inhabitants, 167.

Kidd, Captain, 51.

King, Rufus, 122.

Knownothingism, 215, 216, 237.

Ku Klux Klan, the, 300.

Lafayette, 106, 116.

Land tenure in New England, 23.

Las Casas, 26.

Law, American, based on common law of England, 118.

Lecompton constitution, 236.

Lee, General Robert E., 262 et sq.; surrenders to Grant, 280.

Leisler, 55.

Leopard, the, 163.

Lexington, fight at, 89.

Liberator, The, 230, 231.

Liberty bills, 233.

Liberty Party, 211.

Life, manner of, in New England, 23 et sq.

Lincoln, Abraham, 238; his early life, 239; his appearance, 239; his character, 240; his abolitionism, 240; as a speaker, 241; elected President, 242; opinions on rebellion, 248; his position as President, 250; enters Washington, 250; his statesmanship, 250 et sq., 282; is murdered, 281.

Literature and the Civil War, 291.

Locke's constitution for the Carolinas, 50.

Long Island, fight on, 94.

Longstreet, 274.

Lopez attempts to seize Cuba, 215.

Louisbourg, capture of, 66.

Louisiana, 259, 297; secedes, 242.

Loyalists vacate Boston, 90; treatment of, after the war 91, 110, 111, 140; England's treatment of, 112.

Lundy, the lecturer, 230.

McClellan, General, 261 et sq.; a candidate for the Presidency, 280.

McDuffie, 189, 190.

"Machine," the, in politics, 179.

Madison, 122, 138, 139; elected President, 165; his character, 166.

Maine, 33; boundary question, 174; admitted into the Union, 178.

Manufactures, colonial, 57, 80; development of, 218.

Mansfield, 74.

Marcy, 195.

Marshall, Chief Justice, 92, 155.

Maryland, founding of, 48, 49; the church in, 49; puritanism in, 48, 49; slavery in, 49, 263.

Mason, the confederate envoy, 258.

Massachusetts, founding of, 7, 8, 9; the Puritan Commonwealth in, 9;

the Massachusetts Company, 8, 18;
churches in, 9, 10; education in, 11;
religious feeling in, 11, 12; policy
of, 16 *et sq.*; elections in, 17; federation with Plymouth, Connecticut,
and New Haven, 20; allegiance of,
to the British crown, 28; practical
independence of, 28; changes in religious and political feelings of, 31 *et
sq.*; charter annulled, 33; restored,
35; Shays' rebellion in, 121; and
the slave trade, 127.
Mather, Cotton, 36, 38.
Maximilian, Prince, 292.
Mayflower, the, 4, 8.
Meade, General, 271, 273, 274.
Mechanical skill shown in Sherman's
campaign, 278, 279.
Merrimack, the, 272.
Mexico, war with (1836), 209, 210,
211, 212; Latin Empire in, 292.
Michigan lost to the United States in
the War of 1812, 170.
Middle States, 53 *et sq.*; population of,
56; self-government in, 56; consti-
tution of, 56; education in, 56; the
church in, 56, 57; slavery in, 57.
Military influence, a factor in the
choice of presidents, 193.
Military obstacles to repression, 85.
Military strength of North and South
compared, 253 *et sq.*
Militia, the American (1774), 85.
Militia, Pennsylvanian, conduct of,
in the Revolutionary War, 103, 104.
Miller, Rev. Mr., 61.
Mineral resources, 218.
Ministers of State, 125.
Minute Men, 89, 90.
Missionary enterprise, 3.
Mississippi, the, 259, 270.
Mississippi secedes, 242.
Missouri and the Union, 177, 178, 259.
Mobile, 279.
Monitor, the, 272.
Monmouth Court House, fight at, 100.
Monroe doctrine, the, 175; object of,
175, 176.

Monroe, James, president, 175; char-
acter of the period of his presidency,
177.
Montgomery, General, 94.
Montreal taken, 94.
Morgan, William, 207.
Morris, Gouverneur, 122, 142.
Morris, Robert, 119, 122.
Mower Hospital, 285.
Murfreesborough, battle of, 271.

Napoleon's confiscation of American
shipping, 166; his Rambouillet de-
cree, 166.
Nashville, 280.
National Bank instituted by Hamil-
ton, 134; under Jackson's Presi-
dency, 198, 199; its fall, 199; vetoed
by Tyler, 209.
National Republican Party, 214.
Naturalization Act, 153, 154.
Negro, the, as a soldier, 266; status
of, after the Civil War, 301.
Negroes, enlistment of, by the North,
265.
New England, 4; climate and soil of,
38; material resources of, 38; growth
of, 38.
New England colonies, 7 *et sq.*; pop-
ulation of, 56.
New Hampshire, 7.
New Haven, 20.
New Jersey, 56.
New Mexico annexed, 212, 214.
New Netherlands, 55.
New Orleans, battle of (1815), 172,
173; taken by Farragut, 270.
New Plymouth, 4.
Newport, old mill at, 1.
Newspapers, 62.
New York, 54, 55; taken, 95; riots at,
273.
Norfolk Navy Yard, 255.
North Carolina (see also Carolinas,
the), immigration to, 50, 51; secedes,
242.
North, Lord, 74, 80, 81, 85, 106.
Northmen, discoveries of, 1.

Norumbega, 1.
Nullification, 153.

Oglethorpe, General, 52.
"Old Hickory." See Jackson, Andrew.
Oligarchy in the South, 220.
O'Neil, Peggy, 197.
Oostanaula, 278.
Oratory, 219.
Oregon boundary question, 174.
Ostend manifesto, the, 215.
Otis, 75.

Paine, Tom, 87, 105, 149.
Pakenham, General, 172.
Palmerston, Lord, 259, 293.
Pequod War, 27.
Paris, Comte de, 256, 267.
Parker, Theodore, 230.
Parliament and the colonies (1764), 68.
Parties, political, distinctly formed, 150.
Party Government unforeseen by the framers of the constitution, 126.
Penn, William, 53; his scheme of government, 53.
Pennsylvania, founding of, 53; religious toleration in, 54.
Pension list, the, 291.
Peters, Hugh, 8.
Petersburg, 277.
Philadelphia, 54.
Philip, King, 27; war with, 27.
Phillips, Wendell, 246, 247.
Pierce, President, 215.
Pillow, Fort, 266.
Pinckney, 122.
Pitt, 115, 142.
Pittsburgh Landing, 268. See also Shiloh, battle of.
Planters of Virginia, character and life of, 42, 43.
Plug-uglies, 250.
Plymouth pilgrims, 4 et sq.
Poems of the Civil War, 291.
Polk, J. K., 210.
Pope, General, 263.

Potomac, army of the, 275 et sq.
Potomac Creek Bridge, 278.
Presidency, contests for, heat of, and its consequences, 179.
President of the United States, powers of, 124, 125.
Press, the political, birth of, 62; early growth of, after Washington's reign, 154; during the Civil War, 256.
Princeton, fight at, 95.
Princeton University, 56.
Printing-press, the first in North America, 11.
Prisoners in the Civil War, treatment of, 283. (See also Andersonville.)
Protective tariff of 1828, 188, 189. (See also Clay, Henry, and Webster, Daniel.)
Public lands, 190.
Puritan legislation, 21.
Puritan theocracy, 9, 10.
Puritanism, its political character, 15, 16; in Maryland, 48, 49; in New England, changes in, and their causes, 36 et sq.
Puritans, 8.

Quakers, character of the, 14; in Rhode Island, 15; laws against, in Massachusetts, 14, 32, 33.
Quebec Act, 94.
Quebec, fall of, 67; taken by Wolfe, 94.

Race problem, the, 301.
Railways, 218.
Randolph, John, 162, 185.
Reconstruction, 281 et sq.; problem of, 294 et sq.
Repression, measures of (1774), 83, 84.
Republican Party, the, 214, 236, 246.
Restoration, the, accepted by New England, 30.
Revolutionary War, the, 88 et sq.; general character of, 110; events following, 110; consequences of, to England, 107, 114; to the colonies, 114 et sq.; to France, 115, 116.

Rhode Island, 7; liberty of conscience in, 12; Quakers in, 14.
Richmond, 244, 259, 260, 261, 262; evacuation of, 280.
Riedesel, Mme. de, 99.
Robinson, John, 10.
Rochambeau, 109.
Rockingham, 68, 81.
Rodney, 114.
Rosecrans, General, 271.
Ross, General, 171.
Russell, Lord, 293.

St. Clair, Arthur, 142.
Salem, 37, 38.
Sanitary commission, the, 285.
Savannah, surrender of, 279.
Say-and-Sele, Lord, 17.
Scallywags, 300.
Scott, Dred, 234.
Scott, General, 247.
Secession, 241 et sq.; possibilities of peaceful, 247; and State right, 248.
Sedition Act, 153.
Semmes, 272.
Senate, the United States, 124; the chief arena for slavery debates, 184; cause of this, 184, 185.
Sewall, Judge, 38.
Seward, 238, 246, 250.
Shannon, the, 171.
Shaw, Colonel, 265.
Shays, Daniel, 121.
Shelburne, 113, 142.
Shenandoah Valley, 277.
Shenandoah, the, 294.
Sheridan, General, 277.
Sherman, Mrs., case of, 19.
Sherman, General, 268, 277; his march through Georgia, 279, 288, 296.
Sherman, Roger, 122.
Shiloh, battle of, 268, 269.
Simcoe, Governor, 141.
Slave industry inferior, 225.
Slave laws of South Carolina, 51; Virginia, 43, 44.
Slave trade, Columbus and the, 2.

Slavery, in Georgia, 52; in the Middle States, 57; in New England, 25; in Pennsylvania, 53, 54; in South Carolina, 51; in Virginia, 41; clauses of the constitution relating to, 127; and the admission of Missouri, 178; Calhoun's advocacy of, 183, 184; the result of soil and climate, 221; American compared with ancient, 221; not elevating to the negro, 222; nor christianizing, 222; sinister aspects and influences of, 222, 223, 224; aggressive, 226; dominance of, 227, 228; denouncements of, 230; political protests against, 229; the cause of secession, 243; abolished, 300.
Slavery question, the, re-opened by the acquisition of Texas, 213; now dead, 221; possibility of a peaceful solution of, 226, 227.
Slidell, the Confederate envoy, 258.
Smith, Adam, 70.
Smith, John, 3, 4, 40.
South American Republics, the, 176.
South Carolina (see also Carolinas, the), 51; slave code of, 51; rises against a protectionist tariff, 201; secedes, 241.
Spain joins America against England (1779), 106.
Speaker of Congress, the, 125.
"Spoils system," 196.
Squatter sovereignty, 234.
Stamp Act, 68, 80, 81.
State right, 237; and the right of secession, 248.
States, rivalries of the, after the Revolutionary War, 120; general condition of, after the Revolutionary War, 120.
Steam transport, 217, 218.
Stephens, Alexander, 242.
Stowe, Mrs. Beecher, 230.
Suffrage, the, 220; and the negro, 294, 295.
Sumner, 236, 246.

Sumter, Fort, 253.
Supreme Court of the United States, the, 126; under Jefferson's Presidency, 161.

Talleyrand, 151.
Taney, Chief Justice, 234, 235.
Tarleton, 109.
Taxation (1764), 68, 69.
Taylor, Zachary, president, 212; his character, 213.
Tea-duty, 80.
Tennessee secedes, 242.
Texas, annexation of, 212; secedes, 242.
Thomas, General, 280.
"Tippecanoe." (See Harrison, William.)
Topeka Constitution, 236.
Tories, 82.
Townshend, 68, 74, 79, 80, 81.
Trade and Navigation Acts, 57.
Trade, colonial, 57 et sq., 80.
Treaty of Ghent, 172; of Washington, 294; Jay's, 146, 147.
Trenton, fight at, 95.
Tucker, Dean, 70.
Tyler, John, Vice-President, 208; becomes President, 209.

University of Virginia, 137. (See also Harvard, Yale.)

Valley Forge, 95 et sq. (See also Washington, George.)
Van Buren, Martin, 197; his ability, 206, 210.
Vane, Henry, 8, 13.
Vergennes, 113.
Vermont and the slave trade, 127.
Veto, the Presidential, 125.
Vicksburg, 270; fall of, 274.
Virginia, 3, 39 et sq.; society of, 41; settlement of, 40, 41; planters of, 42, 43; slave laws of, 43, 44; political development of, 45 et sq.; the church in, 46; education in, 46, 47; loyalty of, 47; secedes, 242.

Volunteering in the North in the Civil War, 256.

Wadsworth, Mr., 286.
Walker's invasion of Nicaragua, 215.
Waller, Sir William, 91.
War, the Revolutionary (1775–6), cruelties of the, 92, 93; War of 1812, motives of, 168, 169; votes on, 170; England's naval reverses in, 170, 171; close of, 172; alleged justification of, 173; consequences of, 173. (See also Civil War.)
War Democrats, 255, 256.
"War-hawks," 170, 171.
War tariffs, 290.
Ward, Nathaniel, 21.
Washington, 71, 72; appointed Commander-in-Chief of the Continental forces, 90; concentrates his forces at New York, 94; victories of, at Trenton and Princeton, 95; takes up position at Valley Forge, 95; hardships suffered by his troops, 96, 103; his importance to the confederacy, 96; his character, 96, 97; compared with Wellington, 97; jealousy against, 97; character of his troops, 100, 101, 102, 103; his descriptions of the times (1775), 100, 101, 106; President of the convention (1787), 121; first President, 130; his power and state as President, 130; his wisdom, 131; his second term, 143 et sq.; his farewell address, 147; his retirement, 147.
Washington (the city), 149; taken by General Ross (1814), 171; threatened by the South (1861), 260.
Washington, treaty of, 294.
Watertown, dykes at, 1.
Wayne, Anthony, 142.
Wealth, increase of, before the Civil War, 218.
Webster, Daniel, 176, 179, 180; his character, 181; as an orator, 181; his style, 182; his political principles, 182; his opposition to a pro-

312 INDEX.

tective tariff, 186, 187, 196, 200; speech on the vetoing of the National Bank charter, 203, 204, 205; his candidature for the Presidency, 213; his changes of opinion, 213.

Wedderburn, 73.
Wesley, John, 52.
Whalley, 30.
Whig Party, the, 206, 207; fades away, 214.
Whigs, 82.
Whitefield, 52.
Wilderness, battle of the, 275, 276.

Wilkes, Captain, 258.
William III and Massachusetts, 35.
Williams, Roger, 12.
Wilson, James, 122.
Winthrop, 9, 16; on liberty, 16, 17.
Wirz, Captain, 284.
Witchcraft, 37 et sq.
Wolfe, 65.
Wyoming, 93.

"X. Y. Z. Correspondence," 152.

Yale, University of, 11.
Yorktown, capitulation at, 109.

www.ingramcontent.com/pod-product-compliance
Lightning Source LLC
Chambersburg PA
CBHW021214270326
41929CB00010B/1123